DEMOCRAT

OLLY WYATT

AZIMUTH BOOKS

The Democrat
Olly Wyatt

Copyright 2012 by Olly Wyatt
Published by Azimuth Books

www.ollywyatt.co.uk
www.thedemocratbook.com
www.azimuthbooks.com
For film rights, see author's website.

A CIP catalogue record for this book
is available from the British Library.
ISBN 978-0-9573918-0-2

Cover Image:
Bust of Thomas Muir of Huntershill (1765-1799)
Alexander Stoddart, sculptor, 2003
Bishopbriggs Library,
(East Dunbartonshire Leisure and Culture Trust)
Photographer, James Higgins.

I have devoted myself to the cause of the people.

It is a good cause. It shall ultimately prevail.

It shall finally triumph.

Thomas Muir (1793)

THE
DEMOCRAT

55° 55' N
004° 10' W

As Thomas Muir returned to the opening page of Mozart's last piano sonata, the final notes lingered like echoes from the recent past. He then remembered his lift into Glasgow and, in the fusion of beginnings and endings, lamented that the composer had been lost to an unmarked grave.

Outside, the coach had gone.

Lapslie, their lodger had left without him.

A little resigned, his spirits resumed when sunlight briefly lit up a grove of blustered oaks to the east but just as he thought it not too bleak a day to walk to the city, rain began to tap against the window.

A few minutes later, he was pacing down the lane against a stiff westerly. Lapslie's coach was just visible but slowly shrinking into the distance. The rain then turned to stair rods and, between a flash of lightning and a clap of thunder, his client's case crept into his mind.

At Glasgow's half built Miller Street, the winds were tempestuous. A barricade, stating 'no entry', stopped him in his tracks. The court case was imminent. He had to ignore the warning. His usual short cut was required more than ever but the storm was sweeping away scaffolding. Whilst he ran along the abandoned street, masonry plummeted from a fourth floor tenement.

Deeper into the city, his chambers appeared to him through a wash of spray from the gust bitten river Clyde. He had made it just in time. As he changed into his advocate's gown, the clerk, Gathersby, knocked on the dressing room door and handed him a note. New evidence, he wondered. Well, in a sense, yes.

'June 1792. Dear Mr Muir, I'll not be attending court today. Those in power have already made up their mind over my fate. The courts are a farce. I appreciate you not charging.

Soon, thanks to yourself, I will be an American.'

It was signed J. Lambert; the woman he was supposed to be representing. He quickly dressed. A verdict of guilty would be passed in absentia, her home would be ransacked and ports would be informed of the attempted escape.

'I suspect she's long gone,' said Gathersby, 'it was a young lad who delivered the letter. Her son I suspect...'

'And who's going to look after him?'

'You can't help everyone. They'll go over later on.'

'Gathersby! If they can't afford legal fees, how on earth are they going to afford passage to America?'

Muir waited for an answer but none was forthcoming.

'The law should represent people not divide them.'

Marching back out along the banks of the Clyde with his gowns flapping in the wind, the anger he felt conveyed itself in the rigging. As it beat against the spars he watched a sailor up on the third yardarm trying to tie back canvas.

Scared of heights, he could barely watch and he spared a thought for the poor folk caught in it at sea, especially Mrs Lambert. He could do nothing for her now; she would have to battle the elements alone.

Scotland should be hers though, he thought; the air, the glens, the lochs, the rain, the people she loved.

Rereading the note, he realised that by 'thanks to you', she meant that what would have been spent on legal fees could pay for her Atlantic crossing. For a moment, he regretted shouting at Gathersby but he was still unsure they'd have enough money for them all to emigrate. She might have avoided transportation aboard a coffin ship for throwing one stone at a British soldier, but she hadn't avoided the loss of her entire family.

He prayed for her safety but her rejection of his profession intruded upon his meditation. The law had made him who he had now become. Was it really a farce? That it was being used merely to 'legitimise' the clearance of ordinary Scots outraged him.

He had not become an advocate to facilitate injustice. Imagining Lambert's face, he wondered how someone he'd never seen could cause him so much self doubt. Why was he thinking of her at all? They had never met nor were likely to. In a matter of weeks, the Atlantic Ocean would separate them.

His mind could wander.

With no court case, he was far too early for his next appointment. For some reason unbeknown to him, his friend Professor Anderson wanted to meet him at two in the morning. It was only just going dark so he stopped on Drygate Bridge. The rioters he'd witnessed there five years earlier appeared in his imaginings, swarming the occasional merchant that passed by before disappearing without a trace as they'd done all those years before.

With the rioting in Edinburgh, in recent weeks, they had surfaced in his mind and he wondered whether this was to be another summer of discontent like that of half a decade ago.

Then just an adolescent, he recalled breaching his curfew time at Hunters' Hill, the family home, to watch the gathering masses as they marched from Calton just outside Glasgow to the city's cathedral where, coincidentally, he was to meet Professor Anderson.

And it was on Drygate Bridge that they met resistance to their complaints against wage cuts. Newspapers had put their numbers at somewhere near ten thousand. He hadn't been able to get close on the night of the riot but had heard firing from afar.

Three days later he'd seen James Granger, the union leader, being whipped through the streets. Six protesters were shot dead. Scores more were injured. His friend, Skirving, had told him that the soldiers each received new shoes and socks for crushing the troubles.

Granger would still be serving his sentence of exile, now five years in with two to go. Along the stonework Muir noticed indents scored from musket shots, each a chalk mark on Granger's prison wall, he thought.

His experience of that half decade had been quite different. As undergraduates crossed the bridge returning from their evening lectures, he recalled the shame he'd felt telling his parents he'd been kicked out of Glasgow University.

Contemplating Mrs Lambert again, he was starting to wonder whether finishing his degree in Edinburgh was worth the bother. She shouldn't have thrown the stone but what other avenues of protest were available to her? It could hardly be compared with firing upon defenceless individuals.

If only people had a means of protest that was legal, he thought, they wouldn't have to resort to rioting and law breaking to make their views known. Then, the 'powers that be' would have to listen rather than cart the discontented off to some foreign land, emptying Scotland of its people.

He headed for Glasgow Cathedral. The storms had been relentless for the past fortnight and the professor was keen to test his latest invention indoors.

An unnatural blue flame lit up the altar.

At its base, Anderson lay on his back fiddling beneath his contraption before spotting his former student out of the corner of his eye.

'You're late. The air intake's giving me trouble again.'

'You're lying on the sacred stone of St. Ninian.'

'And?'

'This is a place of worship.'

Anderson rolled his eyes upwards.

'What good has that done us?'

He blew into the varnished paper balloon, aiding the gas gills, without the slightest intention of listening to a possible answer from Muir.

'Professor Millar and I told you to leave divinity behind. This will save more lives than a thousand prayers. Dare to think for yourself my lad and inventions you shall have!'

A bundle of leaflets poking out of a cage rubbed against Anderson's ear. 'It will carry newspapers and manifestos over encircling enemy troops. Have you read the message?'

'It's in German.'

The professor sighed.

'I will translate!'

'Over hills, dales and lines of hostile troops, I float majestic bearing the laws of God and Nature to oppressed men!'

As the echo returned down the nave, he reduced the gas output and lit a six inch fuse leading to the cage latch.

'Let it go then!'

Anderson stood up and towered over his former student.

'Not until you've put yourself in the shoes of French soldiers tired of the old regime, or enemies of the revolution, ready to defect.'

He rubbed his eyes. His tiredness was not imagined.

'Êtes-vous prêt?'

Muir nodded and the balloon ascended, lighting up the saints who until then had been sleeping. Those few hallowed seconds ended though as the scrape and clank of a lifted door latch ricocheted around the cathedral.

An almighty draft then sent the balloon towards some flags.

Their delighted faces contorted as they saw a squat man, who they quickly identified as the churchwarden, marching towards them as if carried in on the very same breeze.

'What are you doing? You'll set the bloody flags alight!'

Anderson turned the warden's accusation back where it had come from.

'If you hadn't let that blasted draft in, it'd be nowhere near the bloody flags.'

Leaflets rained down on them.

Once they'd settled, Anderson patted the churchwarden on the shoulder.

Reading one of them, the warden declared the entire operation, 'blasphemous'.

Anderson smiled. 'This is progress!'

He then insisted upon a nightcap at his house.

The warden choked pointing at the balloon.

'What about that monstrosity?'

Now at the opposite end of the cathedral, Anderson shouted past Muir who was pacing towards him, 'it'll be

5

down in the morning once the airs warmed and reduced the pressure difference.'

'You scientists think you know everything.'

'Good night.' Anderson closed the door before adding 'God bless,' on the other side.

Now alone, the churchwarden watched the balloon spontaneously ignite, briefly lighting up the face of Christ before plummeting downwards and smashing on the mosaic floor.

Having only just recovered from that, from above he was horrified to see light intensifying.

The heavens hadn't opened.

Far from it, flames were trickling up the union jacks.

Breakfast at Professor Anderson's was never dull but Muir was still in two minds whether to take up the offer of a trip to Culloden to see at first hand, in Anderson's words, the legacy of the rampage inflicted by British forces nearly half a century ago.

'I've made notes on The Lyon in Mourning.'

Muir stopped chewing a piece of bacon, 'the what?'

'It documents their suffering. I'll show you it sometime.'

Rather incapable of concentrating on complexities so soon after a pre-dawn session of heavy drinking, his concentration drifted to studying the chair he was sat on. The arms ended with eagle's heads and the legs, with eagle's claws. For a moment, he thought he was hallucinating until Anderson explained.

'It's an American import, now, what about Culloden?'

Muir strove to match Anderson's enthusiasm with what he thought was a good dose of common sense, 'is there really much point travelling all that way north to see an emptied glen?'

'Of course! Only then will you understand the madness of it all.'

If truth be told, Muir didn't want to be away from Elisabeth for an entire week but he concluded that such romantic reasoning would have gone down even more badly than advocating common sense.

Anderson stretched his arms upwards.

'I'd like to settle this dispute with a contest.'

'My breakfast's barely been introduced to my stomach.'

'I'll provide armour. If I win, you'll carry my bags to Culloden. If you win, you can choose whether to come or not.'

In the drawing room, Anderson opened a cabinet. Two suits of fencing armour fell out. Muir reluctantly removed a pair of pariser swords from the wall. As he turned around, the professor was trying desperately to pull on his fencing trousers but the alcohol of the early hours was getting the better of him. Hopping around trying to insert his other leg, he tripped and fell flat on his face, thankfully, onto the rug that would mark the boundary of their duel. Undeterred and with seams close to breaking point, the sixty seven year old got back on his feet and tapped the dead bluebottles out from his mesh visor.

'He who first strikes his opponents five times, wins.'

'What's that on my jacket?'

'Millar's blood. He survived don't worry. Ready? On guard!'

Anderson saluted his blade upwards and advanced.

At the last minute Muir stepped to one side.

His tutor went flying and as he passed, Muir struck him on the shoulder. They returned to their starting positions where ensued, the longest of duels interrupted by numerous changes of engagement. Eventually, the professor was forced on to his left side and his former student hit him two more times in the torso.

Back at their starting positions, this time Anderson didn't salute and whilst his opponent had his sword in the air, the professor stepped forward and struck Muir under the arm. Overwhelmed by the bad sportsmanship, Muir upped his game and locked blades forcing Anderson off the rug hitting him twice as he ploughed into the empty cabinet where the fencing suits had once hung. Closing the doors with Anderson still on the inside was tempting.

Instead, Muir offered a hand to his old friend.

Culloden was to be a choice not an obligation.

'Well done, but don't forget how I beat you in that boxing match. It was my sixtieth birthday party if I'm not mistaken. I knocked out a man half my age.'

'Those classes were a spectacle. I'll give you that. Waking up to a hall full of artisans all wondering whether you'd killed me was a defining moment of my first year.'

They both caught their breath.

'I fear those days are coming to an end, though. The universities are closing in on themselves, what with the threat from France. Some topics are not even up for discussion according to our current chancellor.'

'Is it time to learn from life, not these ivory towers?'

'Thomas, you do know Millar was Adam Smith's favourite student?'

'Apparently so...'

'And you were Millar's?'

Muir tried to look out at Glasgow from the Georgian window but saw only Anderson's reflection looking across at him.

Silence consumed the room.

Yet in his mind, an objection formed against being placed within the same lineage as Smith, a philosopher who, he thought, saw the wealth of nations only through the prism of ruthless individualism.

'Millar saw in you more than a Church of Scotland probationer! That's why we dragged you out of divinity and into law! He sees in you now, an advocate able to fight against the corrosive conservatism that plagues our country, someone with a fine mind but also a strong heart that'll counter the insensitivities of those in power. Only you and a few others were willing to fight the corruption in the Law department that I so objected to.'

'We all paid the price.'

'Was Edinburgh University that bad?'

Muir laughed briefly and then found focus in the cityscape.

'I'm not sure the legal system is working any more, professor.'

Anderson put his hand on his student's shoulder.

'You mentioned the stone thrower absconding. Don't let one case put you off. What are your plans?'

'A meeting with Reverend Palmer, then, another court case later on in the week.'

'Another stone thrower?'

Muir nodded.

'Perhaps his attendance will reinstate your faith in the law.'

'If he turns up, you're assuming. Even when they do, regardless of how articulate I am, the judges rule against us.'

Anderson frowned. 'They're in the pay of the government. That's why. But you can't give in to the tyranny.'

In Edinburgh, Muir and Reverend Palmer walked through Charlotte Square. Its renaming, they commented, was a shoddy attempt to disassociate the place from the King's unpopularity. The old name, George Square, was still legible in the stonework.

In the centre, officers were dismantling an effigy of Henry Dundas. Muir told Palmer the people had nicknamed Dundas, 'Harry the ninth, the uncrowned King of Scotland.' He was not a particularly enlightened individual, they agreed, given that he'd repeatedly blocked attempts to ban the slave trade.

On the outskirts, revolutionary slogans had been daubed along the walls.

'Damn the King.'

'Down with the government!'

Soldiers scrubbed at them, but half heartedly. Muir walked to where he'd stood during the riot. Amongst the foul language he recalled the more hard hitting protests demanding that individuals enter into contracts to produce governments. A woman next to him of considerable wit, he recalled, insisted that it was a pretty business indeed for a king to be allowed eight hundred thousand pounds a year for making wars and giving away places.

Leaving the memories of that eventful night, he pointed out to Palmer the sooty charred branches where the effigy of Henry Dundas had hung. The inferno had made a chimney through the heart of the oak tree, blackening branches and incinerating leaves all the way up to the canopy, as if winter had come early.

'One of the protesters shouted, there's more worth in one honest man to society, than all the crowned ruffians that ever lived. He said all hereditary government is in its nature tyrannical. Thousands rioted, Palmer, for three long days. I only caught the tail end of it. One of those accused of stone throwing is Alexander Lockie. As his barrister I'll do my best to reduce sentencing, but it could be fourteen years' transportation!'

Palmer grumbled. The late June sun slipped behind the only cloud in the sky. It was still far too hot though to be wearing vestments and gowns.

'The protesters were quoting this booklet.'

Muir pulled out a dog eared copy of Paine's Rights of Man. Sections had been underlined whilst waiting for Anderson the other day.

'What do you think of this direct quote...? The act called the Bill of Rights is but a bargain, which the parts of the government made with each other to divide powers, profits and privileges. You'll have so much and I'll have the rest, and with respect to the nation, it's said, for your share you'll have the right of petitioning.'

Whilst listening Palmer noticed a senior officer, who was overseeing the clean up operation, turn his attention to the booklet.

'You're being listened to.'

'What?' Peering upwards Muir slipped the booklet into his lapel pocket before making haste. 'I've memorised it anyway. Paine goes on to state, this being the case, the Bill of Rights is more proper, a Bill of Wrongs, and insult. Do you agree, Reverend?'

Palmer turned to see whether they were being followed before speaking.

'Parliament's been coalescing with aristocratic tyranny for years. The election of its members isn't free, fair or frequent but after this Paine and I part company. I'm no revolutionary. I am a man of God. Paine isn't.'

He had trod this ground with Palmer before.

'But Reverend, your good friend Mr Priestley has synthesised revolution and Christianity. He supports the French revolution.'

'I like Priestley but I don't agree with everything he says. The House of Commons is there to defend the people against the Lords and the King.'

Muir thought of Mrs Lambert's criticism.

'And what about the judiciary?'

'If they mistreat the people, yes them too. It's through petitioning that the Commons learns of the people's complaints. It's therefore our duty to petition parliament, to give it its purpose. Petitioning isn't a mockery of man's real political power, as Paine would have it. Burke understands it more than Paine. The question is whether our petitions and grievances are addressed after they're made.'

They walked into a dingy tavern off Charlotte Square.

'What of republicanism?'

Palmer wiped the sweat from his brow.

'I see nothing humane in killing a King.'

'Louis isn't dead yet.'

'That's just a matter of time though isn't it?'

'One of my clients absconded from trial yesterday because of the lack of representation in the courts. I found myself...'

'Agreeing?'

11

'Well, yes. There doesn't seem to be anywhere that offers justice for the people.'

'Perhaps if politics is a branch of morals as I believe it is, then changing that's our duty.'

Now with a seat, Palmer described how he saw things in his friend's country. 'You have to cross your own border to England to have any chance of petitioning the King. No Royal has visited Scotland in the last seventy years or so. Yet, you're compelled to be their subjects. It's not surprising the people are so angry with them. You are too young...'

Muir got up and left his friend, mid sentence.

Whilst he went to the bar, Palmer noticed whom Muir had spotted.

The senior officer was talking to two old men.

One had an amputated leg.

The officer checked their identities to see if they had the booklet.

Utterly ridiculous, Palmer thought; surely he had the wisdom to remember how many legs his suspect had.

It did, however, buy them a little more time.

'You've dispensed with Paine?' asked Palmer on Muir's return.

'Leave it to me. You were about to say something before?'

Palmer's concerns were replaced by an enthusiasm for the drink he was handed. Checking its quality, he couldn't help noticing the wrinkles on his hands, that were absent in Muir's.

'I was saying that you're too young to remember the American war. I was fifteen when it started. That old man with half a leg, I bet, went over there to fight. Particularly horrific, it was. First three years, nothing was offered to the Americans but slavery and death. Unconditional submission was the language avowed by the ministers of the British Crown. For three years, victory hung in suspense. The British Army possessed and abandoned Boston, New York and Philadelphia.'

12

Palmer sipped from his glass of Ferintosh; the whisky fired him up some more.

'German mercenaries were ransacked to dragoon America into unconditional submission. Domestic insurrections were excited among the slaves who were encouraged to kill their masters. Even the native Indians were brought into it, their known rule of warfare, the massacre of all ages, sexes and conditions. Women and children were shut up in their houses and set aflame. Cornfields ready for the sickle, were roasted. Horses and cattle had their tongues cut out and were left to long agonising deaths.'

Palmer's almost biblical descriptions were curbed as he watched the senior officer continuing his search in the darker corners of the tavern.

His suspicions were put on hold, though, as their friend arrived. Skirving stooped beneath the beams to order from the bar and spotted Palmer as his eyes adjusted to the drab light.

'We're talking about the American war. Was about to ask Muir whether he knew what stopped it? Our prime minister, before he was elected, recommended associations all over the country. Twenty nine counties petitioned parliament to procure redress and state their objections to the war. You know what happened?'

Now with a drink, Skirving imitated his friends' enthusiasm by sitting on the edge of his seat. He was about to hazard a guess when they were intruded upon. The senior officer took one look at Muir, grinned ominously and pulled him up by the jacket shoulder.

'What exactly are you looking for, officer?'

'Seditious material...'

'Search my jacket too, if you like.'

Every pocket was searched but he found nothing and left.

Another reassuring gulp of whisky seeped into Palmer's head space.

'Have you joined a magicians' club? Where's that booklet?'

'The Rights of Man's in safe hands.'

Muir tapped his nose in secrecy.

'You were saying... about the American War.'

'Go on, Skirving. You're itching to finish the story.'

Like Palmer, Skirving inspected the quality of his whisky inadvertently spotting Muir through the haze.

'In short, once the people petitioned, Britain stopped fighting the war. Two hundred thousand died but it would have been a lot more had we not started petitioning for peace. Talking of which, believe I may have befriended a collared dove, though, I'm not sure whether it's just a pigeon.'

He unbuttoned his jacket and revealed a chick peering out of his inside pocket.

Over in Fife, whilst Muir and Anderson had been drinking until the early hours, Skirving had been up before the sun tending to his orchard, picking the under ripened apples off the ground whilst enjoying the rhapsody of birdsong that triumphantly spoke louder than the past winds; the wood pigeon's coo, the blackbirds' territorial chatter, the swallows' swoop into the cider house thatch that had lain empty all winter.

Skirving recalled how they glided past his ears as he wheeled a half barrowful under the eaves.

What world they'd been to in his absence he knew nothing of, it was as much of a mystery as the storm's resting place, but every summer his swallows returned as predictably as the bursting of the hedgerows. Despite the storm, nothing seemed to have cooled in the night. It was, he sensed, going to be the hottest day of the year so far. As he circled the orchard boundary for more fallen apples, he chanced upon something struggling on the grass. Its wings were featherless, closer to limbs with hair as soft as eiderdown and a scrawny neck that leant backwards as it looked up at Skirving, the giant towering overhead.

'A pigeon or a dove chick, perhaps,' Skirving muttered, looking for plumage with his whisky hand just as he had done with the dawn sun coming up over his shoulder.

And it was that light that shone upon an upturned nest struggling in the waves of long grass, like a capsized boat on the ocean.

He described righting it with his other hand. In its shadow, two bird eggs lay smashed against each other whilst a bloody yoke had dribbled down the blades of grass, a wholesome breakfast for something nearby, he thought. Whilst preoccupied with the nest, the chick had tried to make distance away from him but it couldn't lift its wings over the apples and eventually gave up its flurry with independence as it found itself scooped up in a hand, placed back into its nest and taken into the kitchen to the delight of Skirving's wife and their eight children.

Now twelve hours later, at least one of Skirving's two companions found the chick intriguing as it sat content in the jacket pocket, for it was all medicine for Muir who'd hidden his fear of the senior officer as well as he'd hidden the booklet. Whilst he recreated Skirving's morning in his mind, he laughed at something he always associated with his friend; a lifelong insistence not to eat apples imported from England. Palmer, on the other hand, was more convinced by his own lengthy narrative that now seemed a world away, than either Skirving or the bird.

'How about...' Palmer waited for his friends' attention remembering his days at the pulpit.

'How about we set up a society to petition parliament?'

The chick looked at him as if it was also being asked.

Palmer requested that Skirving button up his jacket.

'That's what this city lacks; somewhere to meet that doesn't involve drinking yourself senseless, litigating or...'

'Praying?'

'Yes, oh very good, Muir. I'm not just a reverend you know. Get the next round in.'

Muir picked up their empty glasses.

'I'll go and rescue Paine.'

Palmer banged his glass on the table in disbelief.

'You left him with the barmaid? A drinker he might be, but to leave the rights of man in the hands of a woman. Whatever next?'

'It avoided wrongful arrest didn't it?'

'What about my idea?'

Muir ignored him. He thought it a good one but he hadn't given up on being an advocate just yet. That said Palmer's idea seemed to chime with Lambert's conviction. Perhaps he just didn't want to acknowledge it as Palmer's. Heading to the bar he noticed some legal colleagues standing around Francis Martin-Shore. What they will have thought of him being searched he did not know but he sensed that rumours would soon be spreading. That he, of all people a fellow advocate, was allegedly on the wrong side of the law. He tried to listen in on their conversation whilst catching the barmaid's eye.

Francis would represent the prosecution against him and Lockie, the stone thrower, later that week. Watching the barmaid, Francis noticed him ordering more than just three double whiskies.

'Good luck with the case, Mr Muir.'

'I'll need it more than you, Francis. It must be nearly impossible to lose a case with the British establishment and King George III on your side. The sentence was decided when the stone landed, I'm sorry to say. Argument will not play its part.'

Francis surveyed the barmaid's behind as she continued to search for something.

'It's strange how I win all my cases whilst…'

'Have you ever tried representing the underdog, the disenfranchised, the poor? I'll happily swap clients tomorrow.'

Francis finished his drink, 'I leave the representation of the poor to their poor advocates.'

'Good day, Francis. God forbid I interrupt your riveting debate on the intricacies of feudal land law.' What was supposed to be their Parthian shots didn't quite turn out that way, for when the barmaid returned, Francis smelt a rat.

'What's that?'

'Paine's Right's of Man.'

'That's illegal.'

'No it isn't.'

'Yes it is!'

From the periphery of the group appeared Henry Erskine who left a private conversation with an older advocate to provide advocacy for a younger one, thankfully, Muir.

'It isn't illegal!'

Francis cowered pathetically and prepared to leave.

'There's only a proclamation against it being read.'

'Thank you, Henry. And a proclamation is not a law.'

'Right. Learn laws properly, Francis.'

Francis turned to Muir at the door.

'See you tomorrow in court. How's Elisabeth, by the way?'

'Fine... far as I know.'

'I haven't seen you together for some time. But you must be in Glasgow a lot. Well, send her my love, won't you?'

As Francis left, Palmer walked over belatedly to defend his friend but law was not his forte. Instead, he saw it as an ideal opportunity to advocate his new venture. 'Mr Erskine, a new society for the people is being created. Will it have your support?'

Muir glared at Palmer.

Erskine thought a little. 'That would depend... in principle, perhaps. I'll have to give it more thought.'

It was a little darker outside but the night's stealing of day was a drawn out affair at this time of year in Edinburgh. Passing across fields beneath the castle, Skirving recalled from his childhood how the North Loch, just a few decades ago, submerged the fields and the reed fringed pathways they now walked along. It entertained Palmer, the Englander, who still had it on his mind as they passed up the steep ravine leading to the Royal Mile.

Muir, though, sensed they were being followed again.

They passed posters notifying folk of tax increases.

Some were scored through with blades.

They then turned into Writer's Court to enter Lucky Wilson's tavern. Having found a seat, Muir tilted back his head to down his drink and felt a hand on his shoulder.

Not another search, he feared. Welcomingly however, an eloquent voice started up in his right ear. 'What was it Adam Smith said; the use of a standing army in times of peace is to defend the liberty of the press? Clearly that soldier in the last pub wasn't as well versed on Smith as you or I. More is the pity.'

'You followed us, James?'

'You're quick walkers and hard of hearing too. I called you twice.'

The man sat down.

To Palmer, he looked like he hadn't eaten for days.

'Skirving, Reverend Palmer, this is my dear friend, James Tytler. Son of a minister...' Muir added the latter comment sensing Palmer's premature judgements forming.

'And you follow the teachings of God like your father?'

'I'm a writer, Reverend.'

'You're modest. He's a qualified surgeon.'

Tytler put them in the picture.

'I no longer practice. No profits can be made unless you've capital. I rent a pharmacy in Leith.'

Muir gave his glass to Tytler. 'Here. Have some. You undersell yourself. This man compiled the Seventeen seventy six edition of the *Encyclopaedia Britannica*!'

Tytler refused the generosity.

'And they paid me the wages of a labourer for doing so. Perhaps because I called on the British not to pay their taxes! I now write on electricity, believe it has a future.'

Palmer was intrigued, having abandoned the judgements he'd initially made. 'I should introduce you to Mr Priestley. You could work out how to store and use it at will. You'll have to converse by letter though, he has left these shores.'

'Why so?'

'Commemorating the fall of the Bastille, Priestley held a dinner party. That evening, the mob found out about it, marched to his house, destroyed his library, manuscripts, apparatus, the lot. England's no place for him. He sailed to America. I can give you his address though. He writes.'

Muir let Palmer finish and then inquired, 'Tytler, you still manufacturing magnesia?'

'No. My business partner seems to have made a fortune out of my chemical capabilities. Without me in the contract, I should add.'

'Oh well, your achievements in aeronautics will always be attached to your name. Tell my friends.'

'I constructed a contraption thirty foot in diameter and forty foot high, known as the Edinburgh Fire Balloon. Filled it with the best hydrogen I could source. Half the city joined me in the Sanctuary for the big day. My creditors feared I'd be off, escaping to the Americas like Mr Priestley. As it happened, the basket narrowly missed hitting the sanctuary wall. Within minutes, I'd landed on a dunghill a few hundred yards from the launch site, near enough to hear the crowds laughing and jeering at me. Lunardi might have won the ladies, but he didn't take the record like Balloon Tytler. I was the first balloonist in the known world, three weeks before Lunardi.'

When Tytler's drink arrived, they chinked glasses and Muir described his balloon antics in Glasgow cathedral with the professor.

Skirving then entered the conversation, 'what's your next enterprise?'

'I'm writing a System of Surgery. The doctor I'm writing for, wants the credits but there's not much I can do about that.'

'If you're writing it, surely you're the author?'

'When you've no money the world doesn't work like that... ...also starting a newspaper: The Edinburgh Monthly Intelligencer. These are exciting times.'

Reverend Palmer sat more upright.

'Mr Tytler, we intend to set up a society...'

Muir closed his eyes discouragingly but Palmer was not affected.

'...That makes no distinction between rich and poor, educated, uneducated. We'll welcome labourers, artisans, doctors, the classically educated, anyone wishing to improve society. Will your paper support us? Advertise meetings? Argue our case?'

Tytler laughed so much his hat nearly fell off. 'You'll have a hard time getting it. Parliament's made up of a vile junta of aristocrats, there's not a common man in the Commons!'

'Yes. Good point, Tytler. Hang on a moment, Palmer...' Muir was irritated. '...I haven't even agreed to the society yet!'

'What's your background?' enquired Tytler.

'Reverend Palmer went to Eton, then Cambridge,' Muir said, hoping Palmer's privilege might put Tytler off.

'And you want to better the commoner's lot? Only one from those places who does, I bet.'

'I'll put you in touch with Priestley. He's just discovered something in the air. They call it oxygen.'

Tytler beckoned the others towards him. 'Something in the air right here, revolution by the sounds of it.'

Skirving hadn't blinked for several minutes, so intrigued was he by the talk.

'No. No, I'm no revolutionary,' Palmer clarified.

'Palmer, all in good time remember I've my legal career to think about. Not all of us are practically retired like you.'

*

At his lodgings on Carrubber's Close a few days later Muir sat at his desk preparing the court case he'd deliver that afternoon, mere spadework, digging out arcane laws from dusty statute books.

As he sat there, the sun found its way between the high sided walls, down the close and into his study window. Like a sundial, the chimney opposite, by the shadow it cast, told him it was somewhere near midday.

That moment also coincided with Elisabeth entering the study. She hung over his shoulders to read the defence. Muir explained to whom it referred.

'Alexandra Lockie. Not that plebeian who threw stones at our troops?'

He shuddered at Elisabeth's disregard for those poorer than her, a considerable proportion of the population. She had inherited status into one of the wealthiest families of Edinburgh; the Andrews. Her father was a judge and his father a judge before that.

'Elisabeth, my clients may have no money but they're entitled to legal representation, whatever their class.'

'How's she paying you, by favour?'

He struggled to remind himself why he was involved with her and refused wholeheartedly to accept that it was to get a foothold into the legal establishment, but searching for other factors and not finding them he had to concede that this was the dominant reason.

His ego mitigated against his conscience but without much success. In the end, he was drained of the energy required to explain to her that the name she'd misheard as Alexandra was in fact, Alexander. His client was a man not a woman.

Now in the Edinburgh office, he watched the minute hand as it rotated from five past, to twenty five to three. It seemed symbiotic with his dwindling affection towards Elisabeth. Other cases would have been brought forward now pushing Lockie's to the back of the queue, no way to impress the judge, he thought.

It was then that Gathersby waltzed in with a smile from ear to ear. 'It appears your client's fled in Lambert's footsteps. This note was left yesterday. I've been in Glasgow, only just found it at the bottom of this pile of post. He thanks you for your assistance but considers that even with the best advocate in the world he'd not see Scotland again what with Lord Braxfield against him. Sorry you were the last to know, thought it prudent to inform the court and prosecution first. Francis Martin-Shore, that is.'

Muir handed over all of his hard work.

'Another easy win for Francis... Lockie's only charged with throwing a stone.'

Gathersby took the case file, bound it in string, scrawled 'Lockie' down the spine, kicked the wheeled stepladders to the other side of the bookshelf and filed the folder on the top shelf before looking down.

'Oh Muir, in summing up, the judge made it known that he wanted to see you about the case.'

'Was it Andrews?'

'Yes, now don't keep your future father-in-law waiting...'

'For my sake or the chambers?'

Gathersby was so preoccupied with getting down safely that he nearly missed Muir's quip, but descending the ladder he sent a case file flying after snagging it on a jacket button.

'Good catch. Who did I drop?'

'Henderson, the murder charge, my first ever case.'

'And your first win also don't forget. That doesn't happen every day. Your advocacy saved his life. It's not all a lost cause.'

Walking towards court, Muir wondered whether Gathersby had dropped Henderson's file on purpose to lift his spirits. The public gallows on the Grass-market that he walked passed had not wrung Henderson's neck thanks to him. However, success years ago, offering the darkest of souls a ray of light, did little to annul the frustration he felt with Alexander Lockie. He'd implied his guilt by disappearing and defying the legal process but in his private mitigation of the occurrence, Muir remembered Lambert's assertion that in effect, these were show trials and no one was ever given a proper hearing.

Sickened by the legal establishment's effective collusion with the government, he decided to bypass going into court to go straight home. He felt bad about his negative thoughts towards Elisabeth. She had been neglected due to his workload and he wanted to make it up to her. She might also have some tips on how best to approach her father.

As he past the court, though, Judge Andrews called to him from a first floor window. 'If you just sign these papers Thomas, it means it's all done and dusted. Either way, he's out of the country and the more of them out, the better. Breed like rabbits, have no grasp of monogamy, no hope of bettering themselves. Don't you agree?'

The water carriers, filling up at the public well, shook their heads but had no say.

Inside, he signed the papers.

'How's my daughter?'

'That's where I was going. To surprise her...'

'Why you work for no fee is beyond me. If you earned a little more you'd really be able to surprise her wouldn't you, and me, in the long run.'

Laughter from the top floor window welcomed him home. The curtains he'd drawn earlier had been pulled together and bellowed outwards. A water carrier at the front door had grown frustrated that he couldn't supply the building.

Turning the key, Muir found the door bolted from the inside. Annoyed at being denied access to his own home, he strode down the alleyway, around the back and scaled the pan tiles over a first floor kitchen.

Lifting the lower window, something he'd done countless times returning from the tavern having forgotten his keys, he tumbled into the communal hallway.

The laughs from his bedroom stopped abruptly.

As every floorboard creaked under the weight of his hastening steps, so too did his mattress that he and Elisabeth had bought three months earlier to consecrate their union.

He opened the bedroom door.

The culprits were half under the sheets.

Who was her accomplice, he wondered.

Francis Martin-Shore turned and looked straight at him, still embroiled in his guilty intimacy with Elisabeth, like a key stuck in a lock. Elisabeth pitched a sympathetic smile Muir's way but he was numb to the world. She lashed out. 'If you'd earned enough money, you might have stood a better chance of keeping me. You're perpetually poor. It won't do.'

Muir turned to Francis, 'we'll settle this in court.'

After a stiff drink in the tavern on Carrubber's Close, Muir walked up around the back of Salisbury crags. Peering over the cliff edge, he watched a wine laden horse and cart pass along the track. From above, in his alcoholic stupor, the cart seemed shaped almost like a coffin.

The drink had annulled the vertigo he normally felt.

From the tavern, he'd brought with him a half full bottle of whisky. In the subsequent haze, it had plummeted the hundreds of feet down to the track below. He now hoped the horse wouldn't stand on the shards and looked for blood in its tracks as it passed.

Edinburgh seemed indifferent to his woes.

Perhaps he had helped others before helping Elisabeth.

Maybe he had driven her to betray him by insisting that the poor receive as much legal representation as the rich.

Did he only have himself to blame, he wondered.

His legs and feet hung over the precipice. One action would change everything utterly. The falling would then quicken until the ground crashed through him. The man directing the horse and cart was now probably too far away to hear his body hit the track.

Thankfully, though, Muir awoke to find that he'd fallen backwards not forwards. The chill of an easterly breeze and a sun that had just set sobered him up a little. It was time to return to Carrubber's Close, not to his place but to the tavern.

A few hours later, six emptied glasses of whisky had stacked themselves around him like the turrets of a castle under siege. Apart from Palmer, there was only one other man inside. The Balblair had long since passed Muir's lips and the remaining dregs had hardened, defying gravity in the upturned ones.

At least in the tavern he couldn't do himself any permanent damage, Palmer thought. The Reverend had listened to the unholy allegory and now sought to urge him on.

'Look to the future! In half an hour's time our first meeting will be under way.'

'What first meeting?'

'The one Tytler advertised in his newspaper, yesterday.'

Muir struggled to focus on a minuscule advert in the Intelligencer.

'The Society for the Friends of the People...'

'Who'll answer that? This rag has no readership but us.'

'They've really got to you haven't they? And these whiskies are handing you over to the advocates of gloom.'

'Leave me be.'

A few minutes later, he left. No sooner had the door settled on its hinges than it was swung to one side again. Palmer darted out to look for him, first left down to the gardens and then right into the old town.

The Reverend's sight had diminished in recent years and it took some time to distinguish his friend's silhouette down the close, lit up by the cloudy oil lamps from a neighbouring tavern.

The auburn shoulder length hair was unmistakeably Muir's but what he failed to see was that the only other man in the pub had also come outside and was watching the spectacle from a distance, with the copy of Tytler's Intelligencer in his hand.

As Palmer approached Muir, the sobs and splutters confirmed that it was, indeed, his friend.

Streetwalkers were drawn to his vulnerability.

Darker souls might have taken their anger out on them but not his, and before long, Palmer had freed him from them.

'Are you going to let two half baked aristocrats halt the people's progress, Mr Muir? For that's what I think of Elisabeth and Francis. And that's what you're doing by letting them get to you.'

Water cascaded above them from a cracked drain.

Palmer studied the blackened sandstone as he worked out how to get Muir back on his side.

'That's what's been going on since time immemorial, the frivolities of the rich debasing the needs of our fellow men. Leave the cause now, and you're just helping them.'

A light kindled in Muir's eye. Palmer suspected it was a prelude to his friend's second volte face of the evening. Over the next few minutes, he watched him regain his composure, as did the man who stood outside the tavern.

Muir thought through the ramifications of Elisabeth's affair. His position at the chambers would become untenable with her father's influence. Judge Andrews would certainly side with his daughter despite the finger of blame pointing directly at her.

The legal system had no concern for objective truths.

There were only partnerships, between clients and advocates, parents and offspring.

Perhaps other avenues of employment were not just desirable but necessary. Whilst he considered his options, Palmer thumbed through a few replies he'd received concerning the meeting. Muir then noticed a press gang drag four young men out of Mathews Tavern further down the lane.

'These letters are from a joiner, a tobacconist and two weavers. You can always rely on the weavers.'

As Palmer spoke, Muir watched the men being dragged down the street out of their past lives and into ones of uncertainty and brutality. The letters could have been from them for all he knew.

Something had to be done to stop this slavery.

He remembered Granger and the weavers' protests.

Palmer looked up when he got to the end of the last letter. Muir had gone.

The Reverend walked out of the close to find his friend marching towards the Berean Meeting House.

The space where Palmer once stood was now occupied by the man from the tavern. Curious to the details of their discussion, he began to question the streetwalkers who were still loitering close by and keen to do business.

Inside, a hive of activity met Palmer and Muir. Fears they'd entered the wrong meeting room faded when they spotted copies of Tytler's paper. The Leith man then embraced them in either arm, before spilling much of his tankard down Muir's gown. To compensate, Muir finished the ale and made his way to the lectern, spotting the Member of Parliament for Inverness in the crowd. He couldn't quite decide whether the MP's attendance was a good thing or not. But that he had travelled overnight gave the society a degree of status and potential.

The last few hours had brought into focus the injustice he had felt over the years. Now more than ever it felt personal. At the lectern, he waited for the conversations to end remembering again Lambert's scepticism in those few seconds.

'The danger to the success of reforms is in attempting them before the principles are laid out. The advantages resulting from reform must be,' he hesitated, 'sufficiently seen and understood. I welcome you all to establish those principles and goals.'

A man started clapping, a little earlier than Muir expected, he then recognised him as Dr Martins, his friend from school.

'As for our methods, I insist that they are moderate, legal, peaceable and constitutional...'

Palmer interrupted Muir.

'Perhaps it is wise for those who support militancy to leave our society now, for violence has no place here.'

Muir looked at the crowd of forty or so people imagining what lives they led. The bearded man that afternoon was perhaps repairing a loom, loose threads still on his clothes. By him, the tobacconist who'd closed his shop early to get to the meeting. Next along, a watchmaker, keeping pace of proceedings. Considering Palmer's guidance, the MP for Inverness seemed to take a couple of steps to the door. But after deliberating, he stayed. And as time passed, Muir was encouraged by the fact that nobody left.

Tytler's readers were decent folk.

Palmer then set the scene for the direction of his narrative. 'A few decades ago the government fought against a people struggling for their liberty. Those people were the Americans. As my good friend, Gerrald told me, the Americans tasted the sweets of independence and refused to accept that freedom as a boon, which they'd firmly established as a right. Nearly all people now think the British government were wrong to fight this once popular war. Once the fighting stopped, Mr Burke obtained a reform to diminish the Crown's influence and to deal with a corrupt legislature. For, it was only a corrupt legislature that would support the war without the support of the nation. The work of reform is not over but we're in good company. Our own prime minister, Mr Pitt, was an advocate of reform until power brought an end to that. Before the revolution in France, no man would speak ill of reform. When the Bastille fell, it was vilified as if it were revolutionary. We're not a revolutionary movement, nor will we have anything to do with those factions, frauds and villainies that have succeeded the revolution and steered it off course into anarchy.'

Catching his breath, Palmer stopped for a moment. Muir though wanted to keep the momentum going, 'gentlemen, law knows no distinction of persons. A beggar is as entitled to pursue reform as much as Mr Burke or Mr Pitt. The question is whether it's done legally. A reform of Parliament by petition will be our only method for it was the Bill of Rights that intended to banish despotism. One of its most sacred clauses is the inalienable claim of the citizens to petition Parliament. When that claim is removed the state is reduced to despotism. We will, therefore, exercise this long lost right. But first we must agree what our complaints are.'

The man whom they recognised as a weaver raised his hand. 'My pay has been going down month on month whilst the taxes I pay are constantly rising. I see no benefits from these taxes. They pay for wars in which my fellow men are slaughtered. I see no share of the lands acquired in these expeditions. These lands go to the Lords.'

The crowds groaned in agreement. Muir made notes on the lectern and agreed, adding, 'you're constantly taxed without being represented, as were the Americans. They did something about it. So shall we. The war swelled our national debt to two hundred and seventy nine million pounds, so Reverend Palmer tells me. It is us, the people that are left to pay it off. We're constantly compelled to obey laws to which we never gave assent. Aren't these the very definitions of slavery?'

The crowds raised their spirits and cheered whilst the cabinetmaker cleared his throat. When things had quietened he began, 'I work a skilled trade, I'm good at my job too, yet I've no vote as I've no property.'

The old man next to him let no silence prevail. 'Even if we had the vote there's only an election every seven years. I'll probably be dead by the next one. They need to be more regular. We need to do away with the Septennial Act. Seven years wait for a new government! That's too long. It's strangling any possibility of democracy.'

Then, an old woman leant forwards on her walking stick. After much delay, she spoke in broken mutterings. 'What of the numerous deaths your protests will cause... when sailors start mutinying... and naval officers start hanging them? You thought that through?'

Muir thought of the four men who he'd just seen press ganged that evening but he hadn't prepared for dissenters and was lost for words. This was hidden, however, by a man in the crowds, who was still holding onto Palmer's copy of the Intelligencer.

'Madame, I'm sure you've sons serving in the Royal Navy, not by choice I hasten to speculate, but you can't blame this society for the wrongful methods of another now can you?'

After the debate, Muir spoke personally to a number of people but cut the last conversation short to catch the man who had helped him.

'Thank you for your defence.'

'Sorry? You'll have to speak up.'

Muir repeated himself.

'I'm Robert Watt, a wine merchant by trade.'

'Welcome to the Society.'

They shook hands. Watt seemed a little nervous.

'Thank you but I must rest; it has been a busy week.'

Whilst talking they made their way outside but eventually Watt lost Muir's attention to a little fellow; it was the churchwarden. He wondered whether it was Tytler's rag or Professor Anderson's propaganda that had converted the least likely of conscripts to the cause.

Returning to his lodgings directly opposite, Watt sat at the writing desk by the window. Below, barrel runners were restocking the cellar hatch and crowds of workers gathered in the street, circling Muir and Palmer who spoke enthusiastically to them whilst locking the meetinghouse doors.

From his window, Watt listened.

Those on the street talked of how they might achieve equal representation and then moved onto demanding fairer taxes. He guessed that the others were weavers but couldn't be sure.

The society, Watt believed, was enamouring the weak in understanding and he resented the fact that he'd had to learn from private study whilst these folk could learn publicly en masse. He despised too, the sense that his independent thought would be lost to a general consensus.

As he wrote a letter, he heard Muir shout up at him.

Returning the greeting, he gestured that he was tired and wanted to be left alone.

Distantly, he watched the old woman berate Muir again.

This time Watt would not intervene.

Far from it, correspondences had to be written.

The nature of his letter could not warrant the use of his own name. He looked for something to mask his identity. In the same instant, a beer barrel rolled off the wagon and into Muir. It would have knocked him to the ground had it not been for the weavers who half steadied it.

As it was secured again, Watt read J.B. on one end.

With a dip of the quill, he signed off his note with those letters. When the ink had dried, he reread what he'd written.

'To the Home Secretary, Robert Dundas, I offer to put my wide knowledge of the reform societies at the disposal of the Home Office. I insist upon confidentiality of all future correspondence. Your diligent spy, J. B.'

He knew that 'wide knowledge' was something of an exaggeration but it wouldn't be in a few months, he thought, now that he'd made friends with the Society's leader.

Outside, Muir waved goodnight, then jaywalked the city's streets before deviating to climb Arthur's Seat.

On the other side of town, having arrived at the Lord Advocate's residence, Watt passed his letter to Dundas' secretary and twenty five minutes later received his first payment of two guineas, enough to appease his wife who had fretted about the lack of earnings he'd made as a wine merchant. He thought the spy trade a much better earner than traipsing across Edinburgh with his horse and cart, full of fine wine nobody had the money to buy. Information would be his new stock and judging by the advance he'd just received, it was in high demand.

The extinct volcano now beneath Muir's sore feet and burning calves dwarfed the fooleries he'd contemplated earlier that day on Salisbury Crag. He thought of the wine merchant who had passed him on the track below and hoped he could help people like him, ordinary people who were not privileged with connections to the establishment.

Arthur's Seat transcended him to a time when kingship was dutiful. His friend, Gerrald, had found democratic precedents in that old system of government. Muir looked over to Edinburgh castle. Unbeknown to him, where he looked, Watt was returning to his lodgings.

A street walker offered her services. He pushed her away before realising it was in fact one of those who'd refused to tell him what had been discussed between the Reverend and the advocate.

'Still interested in what I overheard them saying, are ye?'

'If you're willing to tell me...'

The streetwalker asked whether he'd had some recently, hearing from the clatter in his pocket that he clearly had the money to pay.

Watt prevaricated.

With her foot in the door, she followed him up to his room.

As Muir walked down through the grass thickets, gorse and crag, to his lodgings, he hoped something had started that night that would activate the people to have their say, and although the smell of Elisabeth's perfume would still pervade the pillows and lure him into some unwanted nightmare, he could at least remedy it with the imaginings that Mrs Lambert was aboard a ship destined for the free world.

As he descended, sunlight whispered above the water swept horizon in the east and he knew in his mind that what was upon him was that unforeseeable moment of enlightenment he had waited so long for.

He hoped it would last.

II
55° 55' N
004° 10' W

As the nights drew in and summer faded, the weeks passed by with Palmer's engagements in Dundee and Cambridge. However, no time was wasted for throughout October Muir had turned down several well paid requests for his advocacy to put all his energies into his society: The Associated Friends of the Constitution and the People, as they had become known. That included correspondence with some Irish politicians. Expectation of receiving their post led him to the door of his parent's house where he was residing away from the memory of Elisabeth.

He was surprised, however, to find not the postman but Reverend Palmer, travel wearied and a touch worried. Cambridge had clearly troubled him.

After making tea they went through to the family library.

Waiting for his drink to cool, Palmer browsed the heaving bookshelves. 'At Queens' College, they're using mathematics to solve social problems, Mr Muir. I spoke of the revolution and the folk in the tavern shrank away from me. Later, a poet explained the landlords were servicing the state on the lookout for revolutionaries attempting to convert the common folk. He said Oxford is even worse.'

'What's worse than denying freedom of speech?'

'They've been burning effigies of Paine and assaulting non-conformist ministers. French sympathies have evaporated in recent months. The poet and I left the tavern outside Jesus College to walk a stretch of the Cam. I recalled my time there in the sixties, explained how progressive it was with its agenda of reform. It made him disillusioned towards these days of...'

'English reactionary conservatism? That's what Anderson calls them...'

'Yes, I suppose, this chap was a man of principle, believed in the revolution almost as much as his poetry.'

Bowing to Palmer's pessimism, Muir lowered his head and noticed a silver medal from the University of Glasgow, on the floor. On its reverse side was a glass paste cameo of Professor Anderson looking rather more classical than he'd ever done face to face. It amused Muir how it had appeared just as he'd talked of his tutor.

The professor had given the medal to him, illicitly, for the degree he'd been denied. Anderson had drawers full of them and had talked of melting them down if tough times warranted. On several occasions he'd also confided in Muir that he was sick of the sight of them.

Remembering Palmer was in the room, he drew himself from the recollection. 'The Scottish universities are much more liberal than Oxbridge. You should have been at Professor Millar's lectures on law and politics. It was standing room only if you were late. Did you offer this poet membership of the Society?'

'I'd lost the enthusiasm.'

'Well you must find it again.'

Palmer cheered up a little bit on Muir's instruction.

'He was intrigued by my meeting with Dr Johnson.'

Muir had no time for the doctor.

'That poet, Burns... Robert Burns, he has joined the Dumfries branch. In secrecy, of course. Excise men, as you know, can't engage in political activity.'

'I've not heard of him.'

Muir finished his tea. 'We joked that even children lisp The Rights of Man. He's working it into a poem as we speak. He's a friend of Tytler's. It was he who introduced us.'

Hearing Tytler's name cheered Palmer up some more.

'And I should tell you, I've been made Vice President of the Association of the Friends of the Constitution and the People.'

'That's wonderful news.'

'It wouldn't have happened without your vision, you know before the first meeting. Law's a distant memory. Based on how things are currently going, if everyone had the vote I believe I might become Member of Parliament for Cadder.'

Palmer joked. 'If MPs were paid at all there'd be none but honest men to keep the Constitution clear. How was the last meeting?'

'At the Star Hotel, on Ingram Street? We focused on equal representation, shorter parliaments and the active diffusion of useful political information to the public.'

'And you clarified you were friends of the poor?'

'Yes, although there is a six pence subscription.'

Palmer nearly choked on the last of his tea when to his surprise a servant girl appeared from behind a bookshelf, duster and book in hand.

'Mr Muir!'

'Don't curtsy Ann, please, we don't do that in this house.'

Palmer then apologised. 'We hadn't seen you... Ann.'

'Fisher. Ann Fisher. Sirs. I didn't want to disturb your conversation, this book was on the floor, the?'

'Dialogue between the Governors and the Governed.'

'Yes, I've been making notes.' There was silence in the room as he meditated on the fact that the time he normally spent with Elisabeth, was now spent reading Verneux.

Ann stood up and balanced the cleaning equipment in one hand, the crockery in the other. 'I didn't know whether you wanted it putting back on the shelf or not.'

'Leave it with me, Ann.'

With only the pair of them in the room, he leant across to Palmer. 'Even these walls have ears. My parents don't need her really, but she was orphaned.'

Barely had he explained Ann's past when she was back in the room with the newspapers.

An awkward silence again prevailed until she left.

'Anything of note in the Glasgow Mercury?' asked Palmer.

'Rewards have been issued for handing in hidden crew. Crew that were press ganged in the first place. Where have our rights gone to? On my travels I found the people very aggrieved. Did you know, Palmer, there's only one MP for all of Glasgow, Rutherglen, Renfrew and Dumbarton?'

'I didn't.'

Muir turned the page. 'Another convict ship has sunk on its way to Botany Bay, thousands drowned for throwing stones.'

'Thank God your clients jumped ship when they could!'

'Lambert and Lockie you mean? Yes, poor souls, and if they don't drown, they die of dysentery or typhoid.'

Palmer exchanged newspapers as his friend stared through the library window onto what had, to him, become a depressing world. Tired of what he saw, Muir returned to the Caledonian Mercury. On one of the back pages he pointed out to Palmer an advert from the Lord Provost, the Magistrates and the Council of Glasgow. 'How did you miss this?' He read it out loud, '...they behold with abhorrence, the attempts which have of late been made to sew sedition in the minds of the people and intend to counteract the mischievous tendency of the said meetings and publications... That explains why the Caledonian Mercury wouldn't support us; they too are working for the government.'

A coach had pulled up outside. Muir hoped it was his parent's. Unfortunately, Lapslie stepped out onto his family's lands again. His perpetual presence around their home was becoming tiring.

'We must go, Palmer.'

Muir marched him through the house to the kitchen door.

'I called for a convention of the society in December whilst you were away. I also toured Stirlingshire, Dunbartonshire, Renfrewshire, and established new societies in Kirkintilloch, Lennoxtown, Campsie and Paisley.'

They sidestepped Ann who was knelt down cleaning out a cupboard in the corridor.

'Sorry, Ann... I kept on bumping into that chap, Robert Watt. You remember him, Palmer?'

The Reverend didn't answer.

'He's very keen, likes a glass too. But very hard of hearing.'

As Lapslie let himself in, Muir closed the kitchen door and winked at Ann through the glass pane, hoping she would cover their backs for them.

In the last of the sunlight, along the lane they watched the wind tease the leaves off the branches, making visible the local village across the way.

'In Kirkintilloch, I advocated lower taxes,' said Muir, 'the entire country is now engaged and not only do we have support from Tytler's paper, the Caledonian Chronicle vouch to support us too. Stuff the Mercury!'

Palmer was rejuvenated. His black vestment brushed through the dry autumn leaves as he lengthened his stride. Muir introduced him to the falconer walking the other way who handed them two gutted rabbits, delighting Muir. For, taking them to Skirving's they wouldn't become Lapslie's dinner that evening. Braised rabbits reminded Muir of his childhood and he'd only just renewed the order after it had been cancelled when he left for university.

After paying the falconer they walked through the night to Skirving's farm in the east where they would arrive after dawn. With the convicts' fates out of their minds, the world seemed a more pleasant place. Muir briefed Palmer on the declaration every Society member had to sign stating faithfulness to the British Constitution, lawfulness and the suppression of seditious, riotous or disorderly behaviour.

Palmer later paraphrased some ideas on nationhood he had heard from the poet in Cambridge. They laughed at the Mercury's unsubstantiated accusations and looked forward to an update from Skirving in around five hours time on work he'd undertaken since joining the Society.

The ground had hardened. Winter loomed. Autumn was nearly over. Back at Anderson's residence Muir paced up the garden path alone, slipping occasionally on the first of November's hoarfrost.

Reflecting on the meeting at Skirving's farm, a date for the first convention had been agreed but he hadn't found the moment to tell them about his correspondence with the United Irishmen. In part he didn't want to rupture their association and he also enjoyed his unique affiliation with those across the water.

Anderson answered as if he'd been expecting someone else.

'Millar! Come on in, I hope you're prepared for this sparring match.'

'Professor, it's Thomas.'

'Muir?'

The professor led him inside and quickly returned the pariser swords to their mounts. This was the last person he wanted to spar against and he was a little annoyed that it was not old Professor Millar, someone he knew he could easily beat. Anderson spoke first to steer the conversation away from fencing.

'Muir, my legal associates haven't seen you in months.'

'The society has taken up all my time.'

'I've read about it in the Mercury...and this too.'

Anderson unrolled a poster. A tear ran from one of the corners to the middle. 'It's still legible. I made a mess removing it from the faculty notice board.'

In bold capitals the poster's title read: 'The Association for Preserving Liberty and Property against Republicans and Levellers.'

Muir coiled it back up.

'I've no problem preserving liberty and property.'

Anderson unrolled it again and pointed to the smaller print.

'Thomas, you and your society must be careful. It's warning against French ideas, denouncing reformers as incendiaries!'

'Who's their leader?'

'John Reeves, a historian of English law. He and Burke are quite a duo.'

'It's ridiculous of him to tarnish us as French revolutionaries. Reform pre-dates the revolution. These accusations that we hate monarchy, despise religion, are intent on militancy in Britain... They're absurd.'

With the poster coiled up, Anderson prodded Muir with it as if it were a dagger.

'Absurd to us but not to everyone. The government could direct these fears towards you and your society.'

Muir creased the poster in two at its midpoint.

'I'm an elder of the Church of Scotland. My organisation supports reform and monarchy. Our method of protest is petitioning. I take it on board though, Professor, even if it hurts a little. We'll prepare ourselves.'

On the writing desk by the reading chair were two books. Muir recognised one as Paine's Rights of Man, the other as Burke's Reflections on the Revolution in France.

Anderson appeared a little embarrassed. 'Millar and I had each planned to argue the cases for Burke and Paine whilst fencing, to find higher truths by exercising both body and mind. It's what we of these ivory towers do in our spare time.'

'You chose to moot for Mr Paine, I hope.'

'Millar can't stand Burke's conservatism. But he's in my house and I get to decide who advocates whom. I've the advantage of representing someone I believe in. Not so, unfortunately for Millar!'

'Must be torture for him. He's fought against conservatism all his life. What's your argument?'

Anderson paused before commencing, 'once upon a time, the object of government was the welfare of the governing. Soon it will be the sovereignty of the people. Feudalism's all but disappeared between the King and nobility but it still haunts the peasantry. Why should they live chained to the nobility when the nobles have shed their feudal attachment to the King? That's double standards.'

Muir thought about it for a minute before Anderson concluded, 'the revolution recognises individual liberty. Serfdom will come to an end that's for certain.'

He agreed in principle to Anderson's championing of Paine. But he wanted to know the practicalities of acting on such beliefs.

'What of our government's reactions to it all?'

Anderson thought he had spoken enough of that already and he was searching for something else to say when in walked Professor Millar.

'Ah, ha! Millar! What'll the British government's reaction be to it all?'

No sooner had he sat down, when Anderson had handed him a glass and a bottle of Glen Garioch. 'Decide for yourself how much you dare to drink. But don't forget the duel, professor. So what's your answer to Mr Muir's question?'

'...Their reaction to the revolution? Well, the British Government have initially welcomed it with open arms.'

'Provided it stays in France.'

Millar welcomed Anderson's correction. 'Yes, for its paralysed England's greatest and most formidable rival and not one Englishman has had to cross the channel. The Government thought the Fall of the Bastille the best thing that had ever happened in the history of mankind. Fox was one of them. He's still holding to his convictions but now most have been persuaded by Burke's scaremongering.'

Anderson prodded the end of his pariser sword into Millar's lapel and with it also made an intellectual jab.

'What Burke here doesn't realise is that feudalism is doomed. The ancient regime's rotten to the core and needs replacing. Mr Burke would have it that nothing but evil will come from revolution. Time will tell, but already much good has been born, simply by relieving us of the ancient regime.'

Millar, reasserting his presence in the room, steered things away from their planned duel, conscious of Muir's presence.

'Returning to your question, in terms of what the British Government will do…'

'Reverend Palmer says every landlord in Cambridge is spying for the government.'

Millar withdrew the tumbler from under his nose.

'That's possibly true. What the government doesn't realise is that the factors that produced the inferno in France are absent in England. The national debt's protected us from state bankruptcy. They could have done with one in France. The government needs to understand its concerns and needs to look at them rationally. Whether they will is another matter. My worry's they'll use it as a pretext for war and land grabbing.'

Handing his sword to Millar, Anderson plucked out 'Truth v. Ashurst' from the bookshelf. Such a clear thinker as Bentham, Anderson hoped, might cast some light on the darkness Millar had cast.

'Bentham hit the nail on the head when he declared; whatever harm the French have done to one another they've done no harm to England.'

Millar took down second half of his whisky and before it stopped burning in his throat, returned to the debate.

'But Bentham is on about what has happened. Isn't it more pressing to predict what will happen? In this respect I do trust Burke's judgement. The revolution will not bring about political stability. Power will pass to the most violent. Burke's a conservative to his detriment, but probably the greatest. To use his expression, he ranks it among the public misfortunes that the House of Commons should be wholly untouched by the opinions and feelings of the people out of doors. That must interest you, Muir? From a bloody Tory too. Who would have thought it…?'

His mind still wasn't made up over concerns he had surrounding the correspondences with the United Irishmen but he feared discussing it with his mentors would only do more damage.

Anderson perused the bookcase and pulled out a copy of Mackintosh's Vindiciae Gallicae. He had just finished reading it for the third time since its publication the year before.

'Now here's a man who understands that what's happened in France is the revolt of a nation. I knew Mackintosh when he studied medicine at Edinburgh, a very able individual. Here. Look. See what he says about nationality, that it's the product of this idea of 'the sovereignty of the people'. Nationality is then, inseparable from the principles of the French Revolution.'

The United Irishmen's nationalist cause came to the forefront of Muir's mind and he found it increasingly difficult to keep the concern secret.

'What of Ireland? Should it have its nationality respected?'

Anderson calculated something in his mind.

'If the people desire its sovereignty then of course Ireland should have its own representation but saying such things might land you in trouble. You'd be undermining what Britain considers itself to be.'

The professors looked at Muir's troubled face.

'The question you must ask yourself,' Millar digressed, 'is how do you want to be remembered in all this, a Conservative with no sense of progress, or a champion of what'll eventually come our way?'

Anderson interrupted. 'But you must make up your own mind. Remember the slogan of the enlightenment?'

'To dare to think for ones self.'

The words drifted from Muir's mouth, effortlessly.

He bid farewell and walked out into the street, alone.

The skeletal trees hung over him like the gallows he'd seen in the Grass-market days before. Beneath him the once clearly formed frozen leaves had been mulched by the footsteps of passers by.

He set off home.

Turning down the street, though, he heard a bang from Anderson's house. He looked up. The Professor was slipping down the Georgian window. After a minute or two Muir gestured to Millar whether he should come back in and help but Millar insisted everything was okay. Mr Burke seemed to be enjoying having the upper hand over Mr Paine.

*

Staring into the fire, Muir realised he'd been toiling for several hours over last month's meeting with his mentors.

Snapping out of the trance he put down the toasting fork, donned his long coat and hat, collected his papers, left his fire warm lodgings in Carrubber's Close and trudged his way through the snow.

The Royal Mile was busier than normal, bustling with accents foreign to Edinburgh. Like Shakespeare's Henry the Fifth, he hoped to overhear the quality of allegiance amongst them prior to battle but as he walked towards the castle, the blizzard intensified preventing any chance of eavesdropping.

Along the way he recalled the latest letter he'd received from Wolf Tone, one of his Irish friends, describing how some years ago Wolf had written a paper on British foreign policy. After delivering it in person to Ten Downing Street, Prime Minister Pitt had ignored him. Wolf wrote that if ever the opportunity arose he would remind Mr Pitt of that arrogance.

Perhaps that might be fulfilled this evening, Muir thought.

Skirving, Palmer and Tytler met him at Lawrie's Room in James Court; they seemed disgruntled by something.

'The United Irishmen are here,' wheezed Palmer.

'I know. I met with Wolf Tone, earlier. He and his men were at my lodgings to deliver their Address of Fraternity.'

An awkward silence unsettled Muir.

'I've been in correspondence with them for months.'

'And not told us?'

'It was additional business I didn't think would interest you.'

Muir had more copies of the Irishmen's Address under his coat. Skirving and Palmer read one. When they finished, they looked up to find him handing copies to newly arrived delegates. They began retrieving the copies as fast as they were handed out.

'The United Irishmen urge the Edinburgh convention to openly, actively and urgently demand parliamentary reform. Is that not consistent with what we've been doing, the last seven months?'

Palmer thought not. 'An alliance between Scotland and Ireland will be seen as threatening to the King's authority.'

He remembered what his mentors had said about the importance of nationality for a people's freedom. 'But Ireland needs our support. It's in danger of losing its parliament like we have. Everything in this Irish Address is constitutional. Nothing's treasonable. Their people want their own sovereignty. Do you think I'd take risks?'

Skirving shouted, 'if we're seen to be reforming beyond this land, they'll consider us sympathisers with potential enemies of the state.'

Muir continued to hand copies out, welcoming Lord Daer, Colonel William Dalrymple and Richard Fowler, with one each.

After they had left, Palmer was almost volcanic in his anger. 'What are you playing at? You've just handed a secessionist pamphlet to three Unionists and powerful Unionists at that. Have you lost your mind?'

'If this society's to stand for something it's going to stand for the rights of all people, including the Irish.'

On his way to the lectern, his sleeve was pulled by one of the seated delegates.

'Good evening, Lord Daer.'

'Mr Muir, this Address contains treason against the union with England. I don't think it should be read or distributed at the convention.'

He was still rattled by his friends' complaints.

'We'll let the people decide if the views of the Irish Address are to be accepted or rejected, not the authority of a Lord or those clinging to his coattails.'

At the lectern, following prayer, Muir began.

'Welcome to the first convention of The Society for the Friends of the People in Scotland.'

All but three of the hundred and fifty or so delegates cheered.

'What follows is the Address of Fraternity from the United Irishmen.'

Wolf's animated eyes seemed bright with expectation and for some seconds he remained the last man clapping, something noted by Watt in the row behind.

'Let all,' Muir paused, 'unite for all, or each man suffer for all. In each country let the people assemble in peaceful and constitutional convention.'

Wolf's pockmarked complexion was graced by a smile as he listened.

'Let delegates from each country digest a plan of reform best adapted to the situation and circumstances of their respective nations. Let the Legislature be petitioned at once by the urgent and unanimous voice of Scotland, England and Ireland...'

Lord Daer interrupted.

'Mr Speaker, by supporting that Address, you're declaring yourselves enemies to the union with England.'

Mr Fowler stood up next to him.

'Scotland and England are but one people!'

Muir raised his voice some more. 'We do not, we cannot, consider ourselves as mowed and melted down into another country. Have we not distinct courts, judges, juries, laws etcetera?'

Skirving and Palmer cringed by the side of the stage, out of sight of the delegates believing themselves doomed. However, a second applause was instigated by Wolf and seconded by Watt.

Eventually, it gained widespread consensus.

As he left the lectern, he noticed Wolf handing Watt his original of the Address. Perhaps Watt had missed some of the detail due to his poor hearing and wanted to understand it in more detail. But as he passed down the steps, he lost himself to the crowds.

*

The second day of the New Year, 1793, brought with it some bad news. The Edinburgh Gazetteer reported that Thomas Paine had just been made an outlaw.

At the chambers Gathersby had informed him that Paine was to be represented in absentia by the great radical lawyer, Thomas Erskine, Henry's brother.

Another concern had arisen closer to home.

Tytler's circumstances had also drastically deteriorated.

He had been charged with sedition.

Muir's colleagues had not yet forgiven him for representing the Irishmen. So representing Tytler meant company, that he'd also found from Robert Watt over the festive season, sampling French wines and discussing the future of the Society.

He believed Watt to be a man he could trust as much as Palmer or Skirving, in the present climate perhaps more so, someone keen to understand every detail of the society, from the Irish Address to activities in the New Year.

Approaching Leith a ship sat in the calm as if in an oil painting, reminding him again of Paine, who he imagined had fled England by ship for France to join their National Convention.

Attacks by the Royal Navy flashed before him until he refocused on Tytler's indictment. He was on his way to the pharmacy to discuss the court case. It was to commence at midday.

Descending from Edinburgh to the port town, he read what had put Tytler in trouble with the law. His incriminating article had scorned those who had advised the people to petition The House of Commons.

The Commons, according to him, should be considered the people's enemy; they claimed to be a democratic part of the constitution but they weren't. They were, to use his favourite phrase, a vile junta of oppressive and enslaving aristocrats. Tytler had warned the people not to let the minister or his spies deceive them with promises of a reform because it would lead to a worse situation than at present.

The majority of those in the Commons were landholders, and every landholder, according to Tytler, was a despot on the grounds that he could directly or indirectly extort from the country what he pleased. He could raise the price of provisions. He could turn people out of their possessions and drive them to the utmost ends of the earth and in short turn the country, at least that part of which he possessed, into a wilderness.

It was this monstrous power of the landholders, according to Tytler, that had to be combated and it was the want of something to balance this power that was the true foundation of all the grievances laboured under.

In the article, Tytler then brought into question the whole method of petitioning, arguing that it was absurd to petition members of parliament who as representatives of the people should be the servants of the people.

The people, according to him, shouldn't petition parliament but the King. The members of parliament had in reality become servants to him and as such, he held the remedy as he could dissolve parliament and call it together as he pleased.

To gain representation, those not represented should petition the King to allow them to choose representatives for themselves, of good understanding and character.

No money, or land, or houses, should be thought to make a man fit for being an elector or representative. An honest and upright behaviour should be the only qualification. Wealth has too long usurped the place and rights of virtue. Virtue should now resume its own power and dignity, to the exclusion of everything else.

Tytler reminded his readers that it was by an unwarrantable stretch of power that the Commons extended the duration of their own sitting. If they had this power sanctified by a petition from the National Convention, they would have precisely what they want, and instead of obtaining reform, the chains of the nation would be riveted.

Muir spoke Tytler's publication in parts with frosted breath for Tytler was criticising men like himself who encouraged petitioning. But different points of view wouldn't stop him representing his friend.

Could he argue that Tytler was, in part, only quoting the ancient principles of Magna Carta Libertatum? He reminded himself what constituted sedition: vilifying the King and constitution. No vilification of the King existed in the Magna Carta. It had constitutional precedents stretching back nearly six centuries, prescribing the constitution with the monarchy at its head. None of the other sections of Tytler's article vilified the King, either.

Would the judiciary stomach such truths, he wondered. Or, would he have to state falsely Tytler's guilt with the intention of reducing his sentence on the basis of their cooperative approach to the court case and his contribution to surgery, hot air ballooning, magnesia production, historical registry and the running of a local newspaper?

Time was pressing and he had to decide on his methodology. Despite Tytler's unwise description of combating the land holders it wasn't clear that he had vilified the constitution either. He had in many ways only described those practising within the constitution, and the problems associated with petitioning. Even there he'd advised petitioning the King not abandoning it altogether.

Tytler's pharmacy was closed when he arrived.

He banged on the door. No one answered.

Shivering whilst he waited for a response, eventually an assistant arrived. After freeing the lock of ice, she opened up the shop.

Whilst she attended to those waiting outside he slipped behind the curtain separating the shop from Tytler's dwelling, assuming that his client had feigned illness to avoid a court appearance. Upstairs however, he found a bed without sheets, a shelf devoid of books and the drawers of a bureau strewn across the floor.

On the desk were a few rusty scalpels and a patch absent of dust where a microscope had once stood. On his last visit Tytler had recalled his trip to the Arctic seas as a surgeon on a whaling ship. Muir sensed he'd got his sea legs back, though this time with his own health in mind. By the wall, a burette was leaking acid onto the desk. Burning through the varnish, the drips syncopated between the ticks from the clock above the fireplace.

Under the desk was a cardboard box labelled 'hand'. He opened it expecting to see fingers pointing at him but there were just oily marks on the cardboard where the fingertips, palm and wrist had rested after being dismembered from a victim of the gallows.

Marks on the floorboards showed where the bed had been pulled away from the wall. By the skirting, floorboards had been removed. Through a crack in the shop's ceiling he could see the assistant mixing some concoction.

The compartment was empty. Around the edges oval crescents, marked by soot, suggested it had once stored coins. He sat on the bed and studied the fire hearth. It was black with ash. Up the chimney, layers of soot had been scraped away. Fire bricks were part exposed; something had been removed with haste from the chimney ledge higher up. The stains of smoke up the wall suggested this had been done whilst the fire was still lit for half burnt coals had burned the floorboards and still lay there, though now as cold as the rest of the room.

Over by the window an anatomical skeleton had fallen from its stand onto the windowpane. The skull had frozen to the ice on the inside of the glass. He hoped it no forewarning of Tytler's fate. For a moment Muir and the skeleton looked down into the back yard. Through an opened door a printing press could be seen inside a dilapidated old shed.

He prised the skull free. In doing so, the jaw broke away, sounding a hollow crack. Back on its stand he looked into its eye sockets. At the back of the cranial cavity light shone in through a musket ball wound the size of a shilling piece.

With the warmth of his hand, he melted the ice and freed the jaw from the window taking care not to pull the glass out of the rotten sill. Snaked in fracture lines, he imagined the shrapnel, shot or musket ball that had caused the damage. Whalebone glue spilt out of these tributaries. One led to the word, 'mandible'.

Studying the facial area he worked out where it fitted and slotted the two diverging columns at the top of the jaw, on the inside of what Tytler had labelled the 'zygomatic bone'. After feeling for a piece of fine thread, tied to hook around the two tiny incisions sawn into the bone tips, Muir let go of the jaw.

It dropped down a little way, as if to thank him.

Stepping back he wondered whether this was the skeleton of a Jacobite or a Hanoverian, imagining his final battle, perhaps during the Forty-five, at Prestonpans, Falkirk or Culloden.

The madness of the assailant's aim, its ability to steal souls from bodies, the present conflict with France, the killings, the rekindling of conflict as with the Hanoverians and in America. It all saddened him.

But perhaps as Palmer had reminded him with the American war, their forthcoming petition could stop the violence. If Palmer and Skirving would speak to him, that was.

Muir faced the skeleton and wondered what words it had last been party to, what beliefs it had last realised, and what thoughts it had once encased. He remembered Mozart's short life and how his music had continued after him. He imagined the additional living that the possessor of this skeleton might have had, had the injury not been fatal. Would the possessor still be living peacefully into old age or had that time passed? The distinction seemed resonant.

He wondered whether the soul could rest whilst life should still have been there for the living and he was disappointed to reflect that he had not learned Mozart's sonata by the summer's end as he had hoped. Perhaps that was a good thing. Rote learning someone else's ingenuity was nothing compared to searching for ones' own.

Occasional harangues from customers complaining about their ailments pocketed his meditations until the ringing of bells signified the last customer's departure. Then silence once again coupled with the cold to force him out of the room.

Trying to close the door quietly he found it had warped through the seasons and wouldn't shut fully without a concerted effort. The result was a jolting of possibly the entire room. Just as he was negotiating the keyhole he heard a clatter… and a bang.

He opened the door. The jaw had fallen as it had on the battlefield. The last moment of this man's life relived. This time the pain was Muir's for causing it but he told himself the soul had left the body. It helped but he shouldn't have imagined so much. In his hypersensitive state, he toyed with the idea that it was a warning from the other side, from the grave, a prophecy that he should try and remember should it guide him at some future time.

Clenching his own jaw, pushing the tips of his lower teeth against the undulations of his uppers, he sensed the ossification of his entire self. Despite losing Tytler, a dear friend, he still had flesh around his bones and thoughts in his head. He shut and locked the door more carefully this time.

Slipping the key into his pocket, he guessed that the longer the shop assistant thought Tytler was asleep, the later she would raise the alarm, the greater his chance of escape.

Down in the street he caught sight of the ship still in the estuary but a little further out to sea. Now with more sails hoisted and a little darker water along its hull, he wondered whether Tytler and the prized contents of his room were aboard and imagined him looking back at Leith from the transom waving farewell.

Muir returned the wave.

The street folk mistook him for a lunatic.

Back in the Old Town he handed the case file to Gathersby who reminded him to inform the court of his client's changed status, from accused to fugitive.

Up the steps to the court a shepherd accosted him then made for one of the tunnelled closes running off the Royal mile.

Muir looked around.

No one had seen the exchange so he followed.

In the darkness the shepherd was unused to speaking and drawled in whispers.

'Tytler sent me to find you.'

'Yes?'

'He's at my cottage to the east of St. Anthony's Chapel.'

'He must move fast.'

'Plans are being made to get him over to Ireland.'

'And then America?'

'Aye, he considers you a good friend and would like to see you one last time for reasons he wouldn't say.'

'I'm bound to report his fugitive status to the court.'

'Do so, master Muir, but send them on a wild goose chase with these letters. Then under cover of dark, come visit. My place has the dogs outside. Carry a lantern so I can see you.'

'I'll be there at midnight. Is he in need of anything?'

'Just your confidence.'

'Aye, of course.'

'I believe he wants you to have something of his; the printing press. It's too big to take with him but come see him all the same.'

'I will.'

'I've seen many soldiers on the Mile whilst I've waited, down at Carrubber's, also. Thought I should warn you...'

The prosecution was seated. The judge looked exceedingly annoyed. The jury seemed too friendly to have been picked anonymously though it was something Muir had grown used to.

After taking his place at the bar he said, 'I visited my client's property this morning. He was nowhere to be seen. I found these letters addressed to his pharmacy and his sweetheart. They're from London and tell of his intention to leave for France. I believe they may be of use to future criminal enquiries.'

The judge was angry that Tytler wasn't to be punished with the pains of law to deter others from committing like crimes.

In his absence he found him guilty of sedition.

After the judge had brought down the gavel, the clattering of soldiers outside encroached upon the silence.

As Muir left court he considered how he would make sure he was not followed on his way to Salisbury Crag that evening and thought it prudent not to return to Carrubber's Close, fearing spies in the vicinity.

Instead, he would make his way to The Sheep's Heid in Duddingston, eat and drink there, then at closing time, walk under the shadow of Arthur's Seat to the shepherd's cottage.

But as he walked the route in his mind and left the court, he was accosted by soldiers.

'We've a warrant for your arrest.'

The words were like hornet stings piercing his heavy mind. One moment, he was attending to his client. The next, he was preparing himself to be interrogated on the very same charge.

III
55° 55' N
003° 10' W

Shackled to a bench in the Tollbooth prison, with Saint Giles' Church just yards away, Muir looked his captors in the eyes.

'I decline answering any questions in this place. I consider a declaration of this kind, obtained in these circumstances to be utterly inconsistent with the constitutional rights of a British subject.'

Defiance of that ilk in this place was met with a fist.

Blood flooded his mouth. He lost consciousness.

Waking what seemed like only moments later and hearing an intruder, he braced himself for another beating but was relieved when he saw his old friend, Anderson, leaning on a pair of crutches.

'Burke and Millar got the better of me. Anyway, I'm more concerned with what's happened to you. I've requested bail on your behalf. I told them I was your lawyer.'

'Where will I find the bail money?'

'I'll be your bondsman. I wouldn't have held onto my university post had it not been for you.'

'McIndoe and Humphreys helped too.'

Anderson thought back to those days as he lowered himself onto the bench.

'You all paid the price. A debt I'm happy to repay now.'

The professor handed him a handkerchief and a hip flask.

'You know it was Henry Dundas who was the rector of the university at the time. It was he who refused to minute my allegations.'

'Concerning the mismanagement of college funds?'

'Aye.'

The dried blood on his face felt tight as he expressed his disbelief. Swigging some of the spirit, he poured a little onto the handkerchief and wiped his face clean inadvertently stinging his bust lip.

'Aye. And it's his son, Robert Dundas, we're up against now. My worry is that expulsion this time won't be to another university but to some distant shore.'

They looked out at the city folk entering Saint Giles' for the evening service.

'Those thoughts have crossed my mind, too.'

'As long as they don't hang you.'

'I'm told a charge of treason hasn't been ruled out.'

Anderson cringed.

The bells rang out and for a moment he regretted drawing Muir from divinity into law. The church goers seemed so content.

'Good God...' The professor then calculated, 'there hasn't been a judgement over an accused, charged with High Treason at the Edinburgh High Court, for a generation.'

'At least I'll be remembered for something.'

'Who turned against you, Thomas?'

'I don't know.'

'That man... The Reverend, Palmer was his name?'

Muir deliberated.

'No.'

'The farmer... Skirving?'

'We fell out over uniting with the Irish. But they wouldn't have turned on me for that. At least I don't think they would. There isn't any incriminating evidence anyway.'

Anderson stood up to leave.

'Thomas, I'll visit you tomorrow. In the mean time I'll finalise the case for bail. I'd intended to go to France had Millar not been so careless. Louis' fate is not quite inevitable and I'd hoped to sway the Directory towards exile rather than execution. Pending bail I think you should go as my envoy. What do you think?'

'I was supposed to see Tytler, but he'll be long gone now.'

'Did he flee from the sedition charge?'

'Yes. He wanted to give me his printing press, so the shepherd said.'

'I'll see to that. We must get you out of the country for a little while. There is a minor trade role you must also carry out; an exchange of Balblair whisky for Vieux Cognac with a dealer I met there on my last visit. But we can organise that later. I meant to stay with Talleyrand, in Surrey, on the way but I'm sure he'll welcome you instead.'

*

The darkness of the Northumberland tavern was akin to the prison cell. As Muir closed his eyes some more he retrenched back into confinement. Half sorrowfully, half in preparation for what longer imprisonments might lie ahead.

Part of him wondered whether hanging from the sentence of treason had its advantages. Two weeks in the Tollbooth had felt like a lifetime.

Setting out on the second day of their week long journey to the south coast of England, he couldn't acclimatise to the dank coach so opened the shutter to draw in some fresh air.

Unfortunately this meant speaking to the coachman, Mr Vear. In a moment of much needed light heartedness, Muir thought it an unfortunate name for someone whose main task was to stay on the straight and narrow.

Conversation did, however, take his mind off the leather suspension which was beginning to make him feel sick again. Though only eight in the morning, it was still dark. Their vision was restricted to what the coach lamp shone upon, the horses and a small patch of the road ahead. Occasional leafless bowers cascaded down, brushing the coach roof as they passed.

It didn't take long before the coachman's tales began as they had yesterday at around the same time. He claimed to have had 'that poet, Wordsworth' in his coach a few months back, 'over Cumbria way. He was going to Paris like you...' said Mr Vear.

'And what did he have to say about the matter?'

'Like you he thought the French King should be executed.'

'I thought I'd explained. I'm going there to try and stop it.'

The coachman strained his memory.

'I thought you said you supported the French revolution?'

'Its principles, yes... But nobody deserves death.'

'Really!'

'Besides it'll do untold damage to the reform movement.'

'You and your Society!'

'What is left of it.'

'Personally, I think they all should be executed.'

'Really?'

'They've the machinery for it, the French.'

'And you'd include yourself in that?'

'What do you mean?'

'Well, Vear... De Vere. You've French ancestry.'

'Mr Muir!'

The horses slowed.

'Would you care to walk to Dover?'

'No.'

'Well then.'

He set the horses back into a trot.

'I've never understood you liberals.'

He closed the shutter and tried to get some rest.

An hour or so later, however, the dawn brought a stop to that. Out of a semi slumber he woke fully when the cask of Balblair, Anderson had wanted him to trade, rolled along the backboard and crashed against his head.

Furious, he opened the shutter to see what was happening.

Mr Vear was standing up for the first time.

Muir did the same. From the elevated position a coach could be seen in the distance. It was stationary.

As they neared, it was clear it had been ransacked.

'Stay inside.'

Mr Vear pushed the shutter without looking and broke the scar that had momentarily sealed Muir's bust lip. Watching now through a gap in the panelling, a figure could be seen lying inanimately across the riding seat of the redundant coach.

As they ghosted past the figure rose up, pulling out a blunderbuss from inside his cloak. In almost the same moment Muir opened the shutter again and raised his arms.

The protest was too little too late.

Shot smashed away flesh from the coachman's shoulder. Muir was almost sick when he saw bone within the wound. He looked into the assailant's eyes, the only bit of him not hidden by a muffler.

Having trundled to a halt Mr Vear tried to bind his shoulder but couldn't fathom why the highwayman was reticent to disarm his passenger and plunder what they had, particularly the Balblair cask which was worth a fortune.

Muir, though, suspected a possible explanation.

'Are you a friend of the people?'

No reply came, only wreaths of breath, as the robber's trigger finger procrastinated.

Muir again broke the deadlock.

'Our society's been gagged. What's there left when people cannot meet to talk of progress? You aren't the only one on the other side of the law. The authorities will hang me if it's treason.'

He looked at Mr Vear and then back at the robber.

'Let us pass and I'll fight the handful of rogues that made it come to this, that drove you to this, that drove our countrymen into poverty, disease and starvation. Take our lives now and you'll be taking away from yourself a better life in the future, that much I can be sure of.'

Still the subject of the pistol's chamber, he dragged Mr Vear inside the carriage. Clambering onto the coachman's seat, he pulled on the reins hoping all the time that his words were shield enough. As they receded into safety he tried to work out which society member had turned to criminality with such vigour.

The enquiry was enough to stop his hands shaking.

The rest of the journey south paled into insignificance after the second day. By the sixth, they had made it to Surrey where he thought it wise to drop in on Talleyrand now exiled from France. He knocked on the door of the country house. The Frenchman had been expecting them, having received Anderson's letter.

As Talleyrand walked with elephantine grace around the gardens, Muir slowed himself to make little of his host's club foot.

'I can take you to Paris,' offered Muir.

'I'm still outlawed, my friend. Your mission, I fear will not yield the desired outcome. America will be my next salvation when England begins to alienate French subjects. It's only a matter of time.'

'You have a friend in Scotland when I return.'

'Do you need somewhere to stay tonight?'

'No. I'll leave for Dover this evening. Would you make sure Mr Vear is treated?'

They walked across the grounds to the gatehouse, opened the coach door and looked at him again whilst he rested.

'He was shot by one of his own countrymen. Would you believe it, Talleyrand?'

'The French are as divided.'

'Well, Mr Vear loves all things French. He supports the French revolution and like us thinks the execution of the King utter madness. Don't you, Monsieur de Vere?'

Muir enjoyed teasing the little fellow.

Vear dissembled a nod.

Talleyrand examined the wound. 'Monsieur Muir, you should stay a day or two for his sake. Doctors here pay little attention to a Frenchman like me, whereas they will you. His shoulder...'

Muir found it curious that empathy for Vear was coming from a Frenchman, someone whom the coachman had spoken so inhumanely about. He knew Talleyrand was right but he itched to get to France.

Having negotiated with a local doctor Muir dropped off the mainland towards the south coast, now on foot. Two days later than originally planned he broke into a run as he watched the approaching coastal town spill out into a sea of countless naval ships.

The nearer he got, the more the sea became merely a rumour shrouded in sails, blanketed by traffic. Eventually, past the chaos of chained convicts and press ganged recruits he found a ship sailing for Le Havre.

*

Citizen Joubert, his coachman in France, despite smallpox scarring was in far better health than his English counterpart yet no less talkative and eccentric in manner.

So it was with relief that Muir saw the ten foot wall surrounding Paris and with it the end of their tiresome conversation. Elongated by perpetual misunderstandings the only fact he'd discerned was that the city could only be entered through one of the tax houses they were now approaching. As the horses were reined to a halt, the building's classical pillars, domed roofs and imposing clock faces spoke of a regime that had recently past into history.

Citizen Joubert stopped his customer searching for money.

'Before the revolution we had to pay, not now though. You know Louis was a merde.'

'Was? Have they killed him? That is the purpose of my visit, to stop them killing the King.'

Joubert nearly rolled off his seat and down between the horses in front all the time murmuring something in French that was partially inaudible and entirely unintelligible to the

Scotsman. He then turned to Muir shedding his joviality as his breathlessness made his complexion even more cobble poxed.

'You don't have a clue what a bastard Louis was. You know he expected us all to pay tax whilst he and the aristocracy paid nothing. They lived off us!'

He offered his hand to Joubert, flattering him as most people stayed well away.

'But killing Louis will give Liberty a bad name.'

'Louis built a road around Paris to avoid having to go in and pay taxes! No doubt he paid for it with our taxes! He was a scoundrel, an utter scoundrel. He, more than anyone, deserves the guillotine. He attempted to escape from his duties. He was brought back to Paris, and we gave him one million, two hundred and fifty thousand francs. What did he do with it? He wasted it on pomp and administration. Then, would you believe it he's found to be acting against the French people, funding foreign troops to use against us. And what makes it even worse? He's paying for these troops with our money! Unbelievable! Case closed. He deserves to die.'

Muir reassessed the challenge ahead of him and gave up convincing Joubert to save his energy for more influential individuals he intended to meet later.

'You should've been here when we stormed the Bastille. It was the best day of my life. I carried out some of the invalided prisoners in this coach. They lay where you're sitting. Blood still stains the fabric.'

Muir stood up. 'I'll walk from here, Monsieur.'

Joubert grabbed Muir's throat with his scarred hand.

'Don't use that word you fool. You'll lose your head. Address everyone as citizen or brother from now on. You hear?'

With the coachman's advice, he first observed the peculiarities of Paris, the narrow filthy medieval streets, the dyers, gunsmiths, the hatters and the incubating smells previously unimaginable but now all pervasive in this sun drained abyss.

He took note of his location; the Rue Mouffetard.

Parisians weaved around each other careful not to collide their leather umbrellas together. Muir found these perplexing for it wasn't raining.

As the tanneries of the Mouffetard began to intoxicate his breath, he recalled Tytler's description of the process. To take the matted hair from the leather, the hides would be soaked in hydrated lime which would give off copious amounts of ammonia. To soften the leather they'd be sunk into bating, bird and canine excrement mixed with human urine and heated up to breed bacteria.

Everyone drank wine as the bating entered the water supply and the fumes permeated every mouth, nose, throat and lung.

Parisians covered their faces with handkerchiefs and walked frantically as if a foreign invasion was imminent.

He soon felt his tongue swelling and ulcers developing in the back of his throat. Then something unpleasant splattered off an umbrella and landed in his hair. He looked up. From a second floor window he noticed citizens throwing out bucket loads of excrement. A leather umbrella now seemed a very sensible purchase.

Staff at the Palais Royale Hotel took his bags whilst he walked the short distance to the Salle de Manege.

Inside the hall, pews skirted a debating floor. He looked up at the arched ceiling and the upper gallery. Wolf Tone, Napper Tandy and O'Conner watched a man addressing the crowds.

It was Robespierre. He flung his head of grey hair around as if confirming its connectedness to his body, whilst consolidating the case for Louis Capet's beheading.

When Robespierre returned to his delegation, Wolf delivered a speech from the United Irishmen.

He recognised his Scottish friend on the way to the debating floor and welcomed him to his own delegation pointing out the way to the upper gallery, before addressing the Directory.

'We, the United Irishmen, are here to inform the French government that Ireland is awaiting the landing of French troops in order to rise with them against the British...'

When Wolf returned to his seat, Muir enquired, 'is it too late to save the King? I hear Tom Paine thinks the King's exile to America, a possibility.'

'You're two days too late. They voted with a majority of seventy in favour of beheading.'

Wolf's words angered Muir.

He cursed Mr Vear, the highwayman and Talleyrand for stealing the time he needed to save the King's life.

*

A week later, before dawn, Muir's bags were in the hotel lobby and he was handing over his room key when he browsed the day's newspaper.

'Citizen, I may need that key back.'

'You want to stay now? Are you coming or going?'

Reading the headlines, the hotelier understood Muir's predicament. Britain and France were now at war.

Back up in his room he wrote to Robert Dundas warning of his delayed return. He then wrote to the Edinburgh Gazetteer publicly explaining his changed circumstances and intention to return to Edinburgh as soon as possible.

His notes and annotations from reading the newly written Declaration of the Rights of Man and Citizen had provided some comfort from not being able to sleep.

He now felt it safe to wander Paris. The low sun cast a memorable light on everything it awoke and for that matter those things it couldn't. For, half an hour into his walk he'd chanced upon one of the city's open mass graves. Death had become as normal a part of life as commerce and the arts but to him it was still a monstrosity.

Anderson's suggestion that Skirving or Palmer might have had something to do with his arrest revisited his mind. It made them the most distant of suspects. They'd hardly had time to visit him in the Tollbooth but that they hadn't was significant.

Long shadows lay over the piles of decapitated bodies. Severed heads swelling in their rancid heat defied the season and time of day. Pools of stagnant blood had crystallised at the shores, whilst further in, barrow after barrow of lime powder buried the horror in patches of an almost wintry beauty only for the illusion to be shattered with a protruding hand or foot.

Muir had to seek refuge in theorising on the declaration, as he sensed many had done in this newly resurrected country to mask the harsh realities.

The declaration heralded political liberty as the power of doing what does not injure another. It promoted government as a trust from the people and not a trade for the governing.

From article nine he read that the law ought to protect public and personal liberty against the oppression of those who govern. From article thirty five, he read that when the government violates the rights of the people, insurrection is the most sacred of rights and the most indispensable of duties. Both articles captured what was missing in British politics.

But not article twenty seven: 'Let any person who may usurp the sovereignty be instantly put to death by free men.'

This repelled him from the French way, jarring irreconcilably with his Christian upbringing. Anyone of those corpses could be Louis Capet but it was the sheer loss of life that astounded him.

The French hadn't just killed the King. They were killing a generation who said Monsieur rather than brother, Madame rather than citizen. Whatever happened in Scotland he did not want it to end this way.

Anderson had gone to Paris to celebrate the anniversary of the revolution and had joined the Altar of Liberty with the Bishop of Paris. But what would he have made of this? What kind of liberty laid humanity in the swamps of the dead? He turned to make his way back to the hotel but found a figure watching him.

The man's face was recognisable from the sketch in the Edinburgh Gazetteer; the curly hair, the thick eyebrows, the deep set eyes. He'd considered many of his ideas but had never met him face to face. The man shared the sight with a cognac in his hand before putting the hotel's crystal glass in his pocket to return Muir's handshake.

'I was too late, Mr Paine.'

'I was on time but lacked the persuasion of an advocate. My French could have been better too. I read about your arrest. I followed you, thought you might come up against more trouble.'

'I've a copy of the Declaration to make clear my allegiance.'

'Know your way back? I'm going that way. Join me.'

Warming up in front of one of the hotel's open fires, Paine emptied the rest of his bottle of 1788 Vieux Cognac into their glasses and demanded another from the bar as they opened for breakfast. As Muir hung his coat by the fireplace to dry, the cognac reminded him of the business he had to do for Anderson.

Paine initiated the clinking of glasses.

'So are you going to return for your trial?'

'That depends if the charge is high treason or sedition.'

'Until then you'll live with us in France!'

As Paine leant back in the leather arm chair he realised he'd toasted his friend's future a little too enthusiastically, for, having lost coordination to the cold the collision had forced a crack to run down between the regal cut patterning. Initially, he was concerned but that turned to glee as he absorbed what could be read from the occurrence.

'And later you'll join me in America. If it is treason, that is?'

Paine sipped the cognac and let it pass over his palate.

'I may represent myself if the charge is treason.'

Overwhelmed by Muir's sense of self sacrifice, Paine choked spraying cognac towards the fire.

A flame raced back towards his mouth but only reached as far as Muir's jacket.

'You're mad.' Paine's words lacked credibility and Muir knew it as he patted his jacket free of flames.

'If you'd represented yourself in London every well thinking Englishman would have been glad of it.'

'Erskine will do as good a job as the infamous Mr Paine!'

'His brother, Henry, wants to represent me. I've declined.'

'Muir, is he not the sedition expert I read of in the papers?'

'Supposedly…'

'And you're turning him down? You are crazy.'

'His brief is mitigation. Mine is representing the people.'

'What about representing your own interests? I've read Hume's work on suicide but you love life too much to…'

'It's not suicidal. What exactly would Erskine be mitigating? I've committed no crime. It's the charge that's illegal. Already Lord Cockburn has said as much.'

Paine leant back in his seat. 'The cause of the people is stronger in you than it is in me. But sometimes you have to look after yourself. You won't be much use dead. You must have learnt something from today's monstrosities. Is it always virtuous to endure?'

'You should live so that you live forever and dare to think for yourself.'

Paine reached for a pen and paper.

'You should have contingency plans, too. I know a hideout a few miles north of Paris where you'd be safe if ever you need it. Here, I'll write the address. It's in a little place called Chantilly.'

Muir slipped it into his jacket pocket before turning its damp side to the fire.

Postage hadn't been drastically affected by the war but it was still early days. Muir wondered whether the hotel's regal status deterred the English authorities from blocking the post in their keenness to reinstate royal authority in France.

That said it had been weeks since he'd written to Dundas and the Edinburgh Gazetteer. The hotel however seemed to have everyone's post but his own.

Checking the hotel deliveries had become a neurotic routine but on the eighth of February that came to an end. A bundle of letters arrived. Thankfully the Lord Advocate, Robert Dundas, had failed despite all his efforts to extend the charge to treason.

The charge would be sedition.

With that knowledge he realised he could represent himself without fear of hanging. Unlike Lambert he could see his family again and continue his solidarity with the Society.

But despite his heroic assertions in front of Paine, he knew Anderson's incentive behind getting him out of the country. The news of sedition, however, extinguished the pretext of self preservation that would have seen him seek asylum in America had the charge been treason. The pains of transportation and the life of a convict where a death worse than hanging was commonly experienced now marred his horizon.

He turned the page. The date of the trial would be the eleventh of February. He had three days to get back to Edinburgh.

Impossible, he thought, whilst the two countries were at war.

Dundas, in a moment of generosity, warned that failure to arrive on that day would make him an outlaw on the basis that he'd fled Scotland and exceeded the grounds of his bail. From there on in he would be treated as a common criminal.

They clearly had little sympathy for the problem of acquiring a passport. It rattled Muir for his inevitable late return would be the result of the very same war that had been agitated by none other than Dundas and his associates in Westminster. He had read in the newspapers that the channel was now a war zone.

French Republican forces had also become increasingly factionalised. Entrenched in their frustrations they blamed the government who were passing the buck onto foreign agents; people that looked like Muir. Being caught in the crossfire or being suspected as a British spy were two things he really wanted to avoid.

He remembered Paine drinking cognac opposite him a few weeks ago. Finding Anderson's dealer later that weekend and the spirit tasting that had followed provided respite from the inferno that had become his existence.

Perhaps Paine's suggestion that he should head to the Americas with him was the best possible plan. He asked room service to request his company at lunch but the news was not good. Paine had checked out the night before.

Muir's destination would, after all, be Scotland with Anderson's cognac in tow. He wondered whether returning was worth it doubting his friendships with Palmer and Skirving.

Then he remembered the United Irishmen.

They must still be in Paris, he thought. Wolf had stayed in the Palais Royale much to the dismay of his compatriots, who scorned any regal association.

He checked with the hotelier but they too had left that day for Le Havre. Scotland via Ireland would be safer and buy time to decide whether to head to Philadelphia and win the protection of George Washington or fight to clear his name at the Edinburgh High Court. A plan was in motion but he needed to get to Le Havre before Wolf set sail.

As Muir ran to the coach rank with his bags bulging with unopened post and the cognac cask under his right arm, he turned his attention to a man waving a bloodstained handkerchief by the entrance of the tax house.

'Tomas! Citizen Muir! I knew you wouldn't save the King. Look, I have some of his blood! My nephew crawled over the crowds. Wonderful days! You were naïve and now our nations are at war! I should shoot you now but first, perhaps, a little business?'

The coach's rhythmic jolting sent him off to sleep numbing Joubert's diatribe on kingship that, for two hours, made his horses trot faster than normal as if even they were sickened by his blood lust.

In his mind Muir revisited the Place de la Revolution where he'd watched the silver guillotine blade loom over Louis' head whilst tens of thousands of other heads stared in expectation at the half moon collar being fitted to secure the blow.

The horses' pounding strides triggered in his mind, the crescendo drum roll that the authorities hoped would drown out the rasping sound of the falling blade whilst the jolts of the carriage banged Muir's spinal notch against the backboard as he dreamt of the blade hitting the King's neck.

The King's head, now plucked out of the commoner's wheelbarrow, was held up high for everyone to see. Still conscious, the eyes focused at times on the detached body puking blood yards away.

It haunted him as did the fact that Britain was once again at war. He pictured the amputee in the Charlotte Square tavern that Palmer reckoned was a casualty of the American war.

As they approached a checkpoint, Joubert banged on the coach top.

'Passport, Citizen Muir!'

Minutes later, he fed papers through the shutter sensing they were at a border between conflicting factions.

The guard read the papers out loud.

'Thomas Muir, five foot three, auburn hair, blue eyes, aquiline nose, medium mouth, round chin, high forehead, longish full face.'

Comparing the description to Muir who had by now poked his head out, the guard gestured to let them through. As he handed the passport back, however, something caught his eye.

'British. Saint Christ! British!'

He made Muir step down from the coach.

'Why have you been in Paris?'

'To assist the revolutionary government.'

'With?'

'The trial and execution of the King...'

'You are...'

'An advocate and Vice President of the Society for the Friends of the People... I'm committed to freeing Scotland from British oppression.'

The guard raised an eyebrow.

'So the ancienne alliance is still with us?'

'C'est vrai.'

Inspecting the condition of Joubert's coach, the guard requested that Muir look into the woods.

'What do you see?'

An answer came reluctantly.

'A man hanging from a branch.'

'We do not have the luxuries of the guillotine here. He's not the only one. Deeper in the woods you'll see more.'

'What was his crime?'

'He was a spy leaving Paris.'

'English?'

'British, like you. Wait here, Mister Muir.'

The guard compared the passport details to papers an officer brought out from inside the wooden hut. The hanging body turned in the breeze revealing wounds to the torso.

Rule of law and due process did not count in these parts. Law was an extinct ideal in this crucible where foreign forces had converged; the armies of Austria and Prussia from the east, the Netherlands from the north east and Spain from the south; all driven by the rule of war. As Muir brooded on this present danger, tangled in thickets and crushed by snows that had been and gone, he noticed a punctured balloon and lines to a wire box.

Someone else had had Anderson's idea.

But Muir wished these oppressed men hadn't the freedoms they now had for his sake at least, and he thought it equitable to drink from Anderson's cask.

Citizen Joubert, Muir's coffin bearer, was sweating beads so he offered him some cognac too.

The horses seemed to sense something in the wind.

Anxiety bore into all minds present.

He was getting cold so searched for his jacket but realised he'd left it in the hotel hanging up by the fire.

Fortunately most of his documents were on his person.

Frantically, he tore open more of the post he'd collected from the Palais Royale.

A letter from Gerrald stated that rumours had begun to spread in Scotland that he had joined the French guard. If those scaremongers could see him now a noose away from death at the hands of French forces they would not be so sure of their idle thoughts.

He read on. Not only that, Gerrald had written to warn him that some suspected he'd joined Angus Cameron who had claimed the ability to raise an army of fifty thousand highlanders and fifteen thousand lowland troops for the purposes of insurrection.

He closed his eyes for a second amazed at what ignorance could muster. They were heavy to open again burdened with the accusation that he could be militant like Angus.

Ordered back to the checkpoint, subordinate soldiers began to bind his hands.

Then, he realised the value of the letter.

'Before you hang me please read this. I have just opened it. The balance of your judgement may be swayed.'

The guard disappeared with the letter into the hut to talk to another officer. The underlings continued to bind Muir's hands thirsty for more destruction.

Eventually, the guard returned.

'So they think you have joined the revolution? Who is this man, Gerrald?'

'He is French and a good friend.'

'That writes in English?'

'Scots, I think you'll find. In the coach there are letters from the great Thomas Paine. We're all advocates of the revolution.'

As Scotland's west coast and Portpatrick came into view Muir tended to the rope burns he'd suffered at the checkpoint.

They had healed during his days with the United Irishmen.

Facing the choice of going west to America or east to Scotland and the cause for the people, he maintained in Belfast a determination to fight for what he believed. He held no grudge against the United Irishmen in relation to his arrest. After all, he'd chosen to represent them at the Edinburgh convention.

They hadn't forced him.

The first customs officer he met on Portpatrick's harbour wall was his good friend, Robert Burns. Muir pretended ignorance of their prior acquaintance but Robert was agitated enough to warn him that Customs had been on the lookout for him and suggested that he hide in the belly of the ship or row ashore down into one of the lee coves around the headland.

Mr Cunningham, in particular, sought the reward for his capture so Robert insisted that hiding on the ship until Cunningham's shift ended might secure freedom for a few days longer.

Robert's concerns warmed him but he accepted what was inevitable, his imprisonment prior to the trial. So, it was without a fight that he was driven under armed guard to Edinburgh.

In the same cell as he'd spoken with Professor Anderson eight months earlier, he was visited by someone slightly less welcome. Henry Erskine had Muir's case notes and he hoped, Muir as a client.

The accused, though, had other ideas.

'Henry, I've told you I'll represent myself.'

'You'll represent the Society and end up forfeiting your life. Let me half your sentence and make a mockery of Francis.'

'Is he representing the prosecution?'

Muir stared out past Saint Giles' Church to Carrubber's Close where Francis had betrayed his affections for Elisabeth.

'I said we'd settle our differences in court. I didn't expect it to be like this.'

With his shackled hand outstretched he leaned over to the window to gain a view of Parliament Hall, beyond Saint Giles', where the trial would take place.

Erskine put his hand on Muir's shoulder.

'I'm an expert on sedition. Dundas knows that. You know that. But you're too stubborn to take a good offer when you see one. You could have fled to America but you seem intent on injury. You should be more pragmatic, Thomas.'

He stepped back down. 'I've won many cases in my time. I took on the capitalists against my church. I'll take on the government for the people. You should've joined the Friends of the People that day in the pub when Palmer invited you. Instead, you remained a friend of the establishment.'

Erskine passed the case notes over and leaving, turned to Muir at the door. 'The people won't be spending fourteen years in Botany Bay. You will. Put yourself first man, for once. The offer will still stand in court, Thomas. I'll be in the public gallery ready to fight your case should you come to your senses.'

IV
55° 55' N
003° 10' W

Muir was led into Old Parliament Hall, once, a debating chamber where opposing political views were heard, now since 1707 a workplace for advocates.

Along one wall three large fires roared beneath four towering stain glassed windows.

On the opposite side, within an alcove sat Robert Dundas.

He was only twenty two years old.

Nearest to him sat Lord Braxfield, a strongly built man with a dark complexion, Dundas' attack dog should he need him.

He stared with disdain at the public gallery.

Judges sat in crimson and white robes with cravats and ruffles of cambric around their throats and cuffs. Wall mounted candles strove to shed light on this darker side of the room, where further down a statue of Duncan Forbes of Culloden stood.

Forbes had lost popularity for suggesting leniency following the battle of Culloden and the so called pacification of the highlands. Muir sensed that the lack of leniency in his own case would again be based upon political not legal or moral precedents.

The Lord's Prayer and The Ten Commandments decorated the wall panels next to the statue. As he sought direction he realised the gold thread had faded.

'Thy shall not lie', was barely legible.

The public gallery heaved with members of the Society and some of its opponents. He recognised Elisabeth but made no eye contact. Instead, he nodded at Professors Anderson and Millar, his parents and Robert Watt.

Skirving and Palmer's attendance was proof, he hoped, that they had only ever meant well. As he reflected on his earlier doubts a man looked up from a pile of notes. It was Robert Burns.

The prosecution led by Francis Martin-Shore, said that it was 'humbly meant and complained to us by our right trusty Robert Dundas, esquire, that the defendant, Thomas Muir, wickedly and feloniously excited by means of seditious speeches and harangues, a spirit of disloyalty and disaffection to the King and the established government and produced in the minds of the people a spirit of insurrection and of opposition to the established government. His crimes are of a heinous nature, dangerous to the public peace, and severely punishable.'

Muir waited patiently for the first piece of evidence to support the charge. He had always thought that passionate language had no place in a court where fates were decided. Perhaps on this occasion he might excuse himself of this rule given that he was both client and advocate. For Francis there really was no excuse; he had nothing to lose but his pride.

The prosecution read word for word and rather inelegantly more details of the charge. 'You did advise Thomas Wilson, a barber in Glasgow, to read Paine's Rights of Man and to purchase the same. Furthermore, the said Thomas Muir failed to appear on the twenty fifth of February last, fugitate by a sentence of the said High Court and having lately in a private and clandestine manner, come into this country, he was discovered at Portpatrick.'

From the public gallery Erskine watched the defence preparations. In stark contrast to Francis' reading with his head down, Muir spoke the thoughts of his mind and didn't even open Erskine's legal notes on sedition.

'The criminal libel is false and injurious. Far from exciting the people to rioting and insurrection upon every occasion, the panel exhorted them to pursue measures moderate, legal, peaceable and constitutional. The charge of distributing seditious publications is false. On the great national question, concerning an equal representation of the people in the House of Commons, I have exerted every effort to procure in that House a full, fair and equal representation of the people as I consider it to be in the interest of the country. I advise you to read every publication upon either side, which the important question of parliamentary reform has occasioned.'

He looked up at the ordinary people in the public gallery.

Burns took a break from note taking. Their eyes met.

'The truth of every word in this defence I shall strongly prove before I leave the bar. Knowledge must always precede reformation and who shall dare to say that the people should be debarred from information where it concerns them so materially?'

Millar and Anderson seemed to be sharing a word and Millar's nod to Muir filled him with confidence, as did imagining the taste of the Vieux Cognac they were both helping themselves to, thanks to him. A little bit of French defiance that the authorities assumed was Scottish whisky.

'I am accused of sedition and yet I can prove by thousands of witnesses that I warned the people of the danger of that crime, exhorted them to adopt none but measures which were constitutional, and entreated them to connect liberty with knowledge and both with morality. This is what I, Thomas Muir, can prove. If these are crimes I am guilty.'

Apart from Elisabeth everyone in the public gallery rose to their feet. For Erskine, a seasoned advocate in this hall, he knew the clapping would only antagonise the high court judges.

They may have well have been slaps to their faces.

As everyone else sat back down it was only Elisabeth that stood up and clapped pathetically when Francis returned to the bar. Her support irritated him more than anything else. 'Gentlemen of the jury, either his guilt must be fixed or extinguished.'

His use of the word 'fixed' hung in Muir's mind like a disappointment as he looked at the jury. As Erskine had forewarned him they were all placemen, members of the Goldsmith's Hall, militant anti-reformers.

Before their argument Erskine had told him of assertions amongst legal circles that, the previous evening, Lord Braxfield had visited the house of James Rochhead. Over tea, he'd declared that the members of the British Convention deserved transportation for fourteen years and even public whipping stating that the mob would be better after a little blood letting. As Rochhead agreed, Braxfield thought him just the kind of man he needed on the jury. And there was Rochhead, one of the Lord's jurors, ready to seal Muir's fate.

Francis befriended them. 'Gentlemen, we all know the pernicious effects of the many instances of seditious writings and practices which have lately appeared in this country. All those persons who have had the courage to come and stand trial at this bar have met with the same fate. They have all been found guilty.'

Muir was amazed that the prosecution weren't even trying to respect due process thinking it respectable to consider cases generally rather than on a case-by-case basis.

'Mr Muir has been found making seditious speeches and harangues among knots of ignorant labourers and herds of poor manufacturers.'

Francis pointed to the public gallery whilst addressing the Lords. 'Why did he talk to them of the burden of taxes if he did not mean to light up the flame of discontent in the country? The lessening of taxes and payment of the national debt are subjects that always engage the attention of the lower ranks of men. And you'll judge the propriety of haranguing them on such popular topics. The evidence I chiefly rest upon here is Johnstone's, and no evidence can be more distinct, connected and clear. He and Freeland both agree that the panel spoke of the success of French arms. What could be his motive for discoursing on this subject to such low, ignorant and illiterate people?'

For a moment Muir was lost for words. He shuddered at the utter disrespect shown by Francis for his fellow man. A fine bedfellow he would make for Elisabeth. But suddenly there was a disturbance from the public gallery.

'A man's a man for all that!' echoed around the hall in an accent Muir had come to respect. He looked up. A court officer had Burns by the scruff of the neck and was pulling him past Anderson and Millar, out of Parliament Hall.

Francis looked again at his notes. 'He told them that if they were more equally represented they would not be so heavily taxed and that the burden of taxes prevented them from bringing their goods to market upon equal terms with the people of France. Could any measure be devised more calculated to produce discontent and sedition than this?'

Looking up again at the public gallery, Francis pointed his finger at Muir's parents. 'In his father's shop he harangued all the poor ignorant country people. He persuaded them to lay out their miserable sixpence to purchase The Rights of Man. If you're loyal to your King, if you love your country, you'll return a verdict against this man, Thomas Muir, who has dared to recommend that wretched outcast, Thomas Paine, and his writings.'

Spittle and gob rained down on Francis from the public gallery, and more of the public were removed arbitrarily. Such retaliation was not the mark of his parents but he sensed they enjoyed their widespread support. When things had settled Muir was pleased that they had survived the clearing.

Francis then walked around him as he faced the public but Muir remained disinterested in such tactics of intimidation. He was still in communiqué with the people and his parents.

'Thomas Muir's actions in some instances appear tinctured with madness and were it not that we find him everywhere a determined enemy and ringleader in a horrid scheme of sedition against our happy constitution it would be impossible to tell whether his conduct was marked more with wickedness or insanity. He fled from this country under the impression of guilt and now he is returned to be again the pest of Scotland with the same diabolical intention as before. Skirving told us the panel was sent to France to save the life of the French King but why were these people so much interested in averting this event? It was thought such an event would hurt their common cause. What cause? The design of overthrowing the Government of this country.'

Erskine looked for permission to intervene but it was not forthcoming, whilst Millar held Anderson back from confronting Francis face to face.

'By his father's letter we then find him in Ireland and who knows how he was employed there? We know nothing of him all this time except what we may discover from the diploma of...' Francis raised his fingers as quotation marks, '...the 'respectable Society of United Irishmen'. Gentlemen, you may know a man by the company he keeps. I conjure you to do justice to your country and honour to yourselves by returning such a verdict as shall stop this man in his mad career, who has been sowing sedition in every corner with so liberal a hand!'

Closing his file, Muir drank a glassful of water and turned to face those who'd decide his fate. 'Gentlemen of the jury, I've long looked forward with joyful expectation to this day. All that malice could devise, all that slander could circulate has been directed against me. After an inquisition perhaps unexampled in the history of this country, my moral character stands secure and not impeached. I regard that inquisition with scorn but in silence. With the paid and anonymous assassins of public reputation with such mean and worthless adversaries, I disdain to enter the lists, I've reserved my vindication to this day when before you in the face of Scotland I could manifest my innocence.'

He looked at his father who seemed to be guiding his eyes to the witnesses for the prosecution. At first he did not understand his father's point. Then, he noticed Lapslie, who after a lifetime of support from Muir's parents had now joined those who intended to take their son from them.

No doubt one day he would find out why.

Irritated by Muir's confidence, Dundas adjusted his wig but Muir did not wait. 'Gentlemen, I supplicate no favour. I demand justice. You are bound to grant it.'

The jury denied him any eye contact. 'This is not the time to temporise. The eyes of the country are fixed upon us. The record of this trial will pass down to posterity. And when our ashes shall be scattered by the winds of heaven, the impartial voice of future times will re-judge your verdict.'

His pacing steps echoed around Parliament Hall. It had succumbed to expectant silence until he spoke again. 'Do the circumstances attending my departure bear any resemblance to a flight? Did I not publicly announce it the preceding evening in numerous meetings of citizens?'

He held up an issue of the Edinburgh Gazetteer and turned to one of the back pages.

'Did I not cause it to be published in a newspaper?'

He then looked at the gowns of the prosecution and judiciary, needlessly sartorial compared to his tailored suit.

'Did I affect the garb of concealment? Did I not appear in a distinguished society - the Society of the Friends of the People? And did not that society afterwards publish a resolution announcing my appearance amongst them?'

Members of the public began rapping their hands against the pews. 'It's boldly argued that I went as a missionary from that body, the Society for the Friends of the People. Nothing can be more injurious: I'm accused of a species of 'High Treason' in being a missionary to a foreign power without any legal authority from this country. I challenge the Prosecutor to adduce the smallest vestige of evidence in support of this.'

The Prosecutor thumbed his notes. Patiently, Muir continued. 'I saw in the execution of the late French King a specious pretext for plunging the country into a war and for extending the effusion of human blood to every corner of the world introducing years of sorrow! I may have acted from enthusiasm but it was an enthusiasm for the cause of man. I went there in an attempt to stop his execution.'

Muir raised his voice a little. 'Gentlemen, the Public Prosecutor has boasted that he delayed the trial to give me an opportunity of returning, that he postponed it for some weeks and advertised it in the public papers which he supposed would find me 'roaming in some part of the world'. But was he ignorant hostilities were at that time commencing, and that it was tedious and difficult to procure passports? Of that difficulty surely every person here is convinced. In Ireland I did not conceal my name. I announced my situation and intentions. At Portpatrick I announced myself publicly and without disguise.'

Anderson and Millar, unblinking in their concentration, caught Muir's line of sight as he spoke. 'Those who dared to oppose arbitrary power, who ventured to stem the tide of corruption, or came forward in the hour of danger to save their country, have been branded with this epithet, sedition. Tell me where the smallest vestige of sedition has appeared? Has property been invaded? Has the murderer walked your streets? Has the blood of the citizens flowed? Oh no! But it is said that although the effects of sedition have not taken place, the attempt was mediated!'

In his mind Muir constructed a hypothetical whilst he got Anderson to fill his glass with Vieux cognac. 'Let it be supposed that an attempt was formed to overthrow the constitution, to kindle the torch of civil war, and to lead rapine through the land. Where I ask has the proof of this design been found? An inquisition unknown even in Spain has been carried on. I've addressed numerous societies. The doors were open. We disdained concealment for our intentions were pure.'

He turned his head from the bar to the gallery and found Watt's focus. He seemed out of place as if he somehow wasn't a member of the public, but Muir soon buried the thought concentrating his energies on the task in hand thinking it wise to draw matters back to what had actually happened.

'Let us advance upon fair and open ground. Let us throw away miserable pretexts. If standing forward for an equal representation of the people in the House of Commons is the impelling motive of this prosecution, let it be acknowledged. I will plead guilty to the charge. I openly, actively, and sincerely embarked in the cause of parliamentary reform in the vindication and in the restoration of the rights of the people. My motives are sanctioned by the great and venerable names of the living and of the dead. The stability of our boasted constitution consists in the just balance of the three great impelling powers of King, Lords and Commons. If one is absorbed by another the constitution is annihilated. Is it not known to you and acknowledged by all the world that the popular branch of our constitution has suffered the ravages of time and corruption?'

Lord Braxfield choked on what he had just heard and eyed Francis to initiate an objection but he dared not compete with Muir's oratory.

'The representation of the people is not what it once was and is not such, as I trust in God, what one day it shall be. If you find me guilty you implicate in my condemnation men who now enjoy the repose of eternity, and to whose memories a grateful posterity has erected statues.'

'Was not John Locke a friend of the British Constitution?' Muir asked. 'Yet he was an advocate for a Reform in Parliament for a more equal representation of the people. Will you brand him with the name of sedition? I have the greatest living characters on my side.'

Muir pointed to an oil painting of William Pitt by the fading Ten Commandments. 'The Prime Minister of this country, and the Duke of Richmond, have both been strenuous advocates of reform. Are they not then criminals as it is supposed I am? It can never be forgotten that, in the year 1782, Mr Pitt was tainted with sedition by proposing a reform in the House of Commons. Did he not advise the people to form themselves into societies?'

The public gallery beamed in Muir's faultless logical eloquence. 'Beware then how you condemn me, for at the same time you must condemn the confidential servant of His Majesty, who was in the year 1782, what I am in the year

1793 - a reformer. Shall the conduct that was deemed patriotic in 1782 be condemned as criminal in 1793?'

He studied the worn floorboards beneath him, smiled to himself and turned to the people. 'I have been honoured with the title of 'The Pest of Scotland' but if similar offences merit similar epithets, the same title must likewise be bestowed on the Chancellor of the Exchequer and the Commander of His Majesty's Forces.'

Laughter trickled from one side of the hall to the other. Having most of the time addressed the jury and the public gallery, Muir now turned to Dundas.

'And pray, my Lord, what term of super-eminent distinction will you, the Public Prosecutor, the Lord Advocate of Scotland, claim for yourself? You also were, not many months ago, a reformer. You contended for a more equal representation of the people in the House of Commons. Why, my Lord, in accusing me you charge yourself with sedition.'

Those in the public gallery burst into laughter at the prospect of trialling the prosecutor. Mr Ramsay, a short hand writer for a London newspaper, noted how even the clinical Henry Erskine enjoyed the defendant's majesty.

As the crowds settled again, Muir held his eyes and his wit on Dundas.

'If it was lawful for you and your friends to meet in societies and conventions for the purpose of obtaining reform, it cannot surely be illegal for me and my friends to meet, and to act on the same principle.'

'You claim I stated the imperfection of representation, that burghs were rotten, and other places had no vote. And do you call this sedition? Bribery at elections has for a long time been sapping the foundation of liberty, and ruining the morals of the people. Gentlemen, with regard to what was said about France, is it not notorious that the representation of the people in France is more equal and the taxes less, than in this country? Are incontrovertible truths to be construed into a libel? But who ever heard before that it was unlawful to compare the British Constitution with that of another country?'

He noticed Margarot and Gerrald, friends and radical reformers from England, on the edges of their seats.

What he said now mattered.

It would be remembered.

'We live and we act under the British Constitution, a constitution that has for ages consecrated freedom. We remember the Glorious Revolution of 1688 that banished despotism and placed the family of Hanover on the throne. We remember the Bill of Rights and one of its most sacred clauses - the inalienable claim of the citizen to petition Parliament. Our meetings were often composed of young weavers from eighteen to twenty one years of age.'

Muir looked at Francis, remembering his disdain for ordinary people and then turned to Dundas once again.

'Lord Advocate, instead of sneering at them, consider them the great mass of society who support the government by their industry and who fight the battles of their country.'

Having given Dundas time to absorb his point, he addressed more of the charges.

'As for Mr Paine's work, the witness does not say that I recommended it but that I recommended reading in general. The newspapers of the day are full of advertisements announcing where the works of Mr Paine are to be found. Every eye has turned to the situation in France. Is there a person on the bench, amongst the jury, or in this audience who has either not purchased or lent the treatise upon the 'Rights of Man'? Now, if one of you lent to a friend or relation a single pamphlet of Mr Paine's, you are just as guilty as I am. Was there a judgement of any court in England or Scotland against this book at that time? No. Therefore I had no cause for alarm. True,' he remembered being searched in Charlotte Square, 'some months before, a proclamation against seditious writings had been issued but a proclamation gentlemen, is not a law.'

Erskine smiled. He had at least been of some use.

'Your mighty charge of sedition,' Muir asserted, 'reduces itself to this simple fact that to gratify the natural curiosity of a person who lives in my neighbourhood and who is a distant relation, I lent a book which was in universal circulation, unnoticed by courts of justice and not condemned by law. Any writing that calls upon people to rise in arms, to resist the law, and subvert the constitution is something worse than seditious. It is treasonable. But do the writings of Mr Paine stand in that predicament? Can you point out a single sentence where he provokes insurrection? He investigates the first principles of society. He compares different forms of government.'

Muir paused to allow the court officers time to light candles as the daylight perspired.

'If the liberty of the press is extinguished, the constitution expires. Constitutions are the work of men. There are constitutions that have step by step without convulsion and without blood advanced their own reformation and avoided the calamities of a revolution. Writers like Paine impel us to rectify that which is wrong or more strongly confirm us in our love and in our attachment to that which is right. Mr Paine has composed no model of a perfect Commonwealth as Mr Hume has done, yet I dare say you have all read the political works of Mr Hume and even applauded them.'

Muir picked up a copy of Plato's Republic from within his own case notes.

'If gentlemen, to lend the works of Thomas Paine today be sedition, to lend a translation of the Republic of Plato tomorrow would be treason. Indeed, if the sad objects of reflection which present themselves to my mind, when I contemplate the state of my country, could permit me to indulge in a vein of ridicule, I would advise you to lay an axe to the root of the tree and bring an indictment against the alphabet itself, because it is the cause of the evil to be dreaded, its letters form the component elements of sentences and paragraphs which may contain the most dangerous sedition and the most horrible treason. But this is not the time for me to indulge in the sport of humour.'

'Gentlemen, I'll tell you the reason why I didn't recommend Mr Paine's books to the societies in Scotland and why I declare them foreign to their purpose. Mr Paine's a republican and the spirit of republicanism breathes through all his writings. This is his darling system but the object of our societies was, by constitutional means, to procure a reformation in the constitution and not a revolution, which implied its destruction. Gentlemen, I now close my observations on the subject of Mr Paine's works by calling you to remember that it was only a single copy which I lent.'

Ann Fisher walked over to the witness box, troubled in her demeanour, half committed to her prior statement, half persuaded by the defence and guilt ridden that she had gone against her adopted family. He let her finish before speaking remembering the day his parents had took pity on her as an orphan by providing her with a room.

Despite her betrayal he maintained his professionalism.

'Gentlemen, I am accused of making seditious harangues in public but this servant girl is adduced to swear to what she says she may have heard in private when she was probably instructed to take her watch and mark to destruction those who fed her. But what is the dreadful language she has heard me use, that, according to her statement:'

"If everybody had a vote, I would be member for Cadder, that members of Parliament would have thirty or forty shillings a day, and in that case there would be none but honest men to keep the Constitution clear."

'She proceeds to state that she has heard me say that France was the most flourishing nation in the world as they had abolished tyranny and got a free government, that the constitution of this country was very good but that many abuses had crept in which required a thorough reform. Therefore, gentlemen, even in my most unguarded hours this domestic spy cannot by her evidence support a tittle of the indictment where it charges me with vilifying the King and

Constitution. She states that I had sent her to employ an organist on the streets of Glasgow to play the French tune 'Ca Ira.' Was a tune like this to lighten up the flames of civil discord and be the forerunner of this most terrible revolution?'

'England has always cherished freedom, and shall it be deemed criminal in me to listen to the effusions of joy poured out by a neighbouring people, on obtaining that first of human blessings?'

Muir waited for an answer but none was forthcoming.

'If I had caused to have recited one of those noble choruses of the Republics of Athens or of Sparta my offence would have been deemed the same with that of amusing myself by hearing the national song of France. Vigilant has this family spy been in the course of her duty. She tells you what books she has seen on my table. Gentlemen, from this moment lock up your libraries. If they are extensive as you have heard mine is there is no crime in the whole Decalogue of which, by the testimony of your own servants, you may not be found guilty. The possession of Plato, of Harrington, or of Hume, a copy of the Ruins of Volney, will mark you down as a republican.'

Ann Fisher left the witness box.

The hairdresser took her place.

Muir asked whether he had tried to give him a copy of The Rights of Man.

The hairdresser said he hadn't.

Muir smiled, walked briefly over to Anderson and refilled his glass with cognac before hypothesising, 'could not some ruffians be procured who could at least give a manly testimony to our 'atrocious' purposes? But to adduce a girl and a hairdresser to prove a crime which required the cooperation of many thousands of bearded men?'

'Gentlemen, I now come to the last charge, that of having read in the Convention of Delegates, the Address from the Society of United Irishmen. The prosecutor has represented that society as a gang of mean conspirators and my admission into their number as an aggravation of my crime. The Lord Advocate has represented to you in general terms that their Address amounts almost to treason but he does not attempt to point out in his speech a single passage that could support the aspersion. I maintain that every line of that Address is strictly constitutional.'

'The first charge against me is that in public speeches I vilified the King and Constitution. My language was always respectful to the King. I always recommended the constitution. The second charge against me is that of advising the people to read seditious books and of distributing inflammatory publications. And you hear it proved by the almost unanimous voice of the witnesses for the Crown that I refused to recommend any books. I am accused of reading the Irish Address at the Convention, and of moving a solemn answer in return. That Address isn't seditious, wicked or inflammatory.'

'Gentlemen of the jury, this is perhaps the last time I shall address my country. I have explored the tenor of my past life. Nothing shall tear from me the record of my former days. The enemies of reform have scrutinised in a manner hitherto unexampled in Scotland, every action I may have performed, every word I may have uttered. Of crimes most foul and horrible have I been accused, of attempting to rear the standard of civil war, to plunge this land in blood and to cover it with desolation.'

'At every step as the evidence of the Crown advanced my innocence has brightened. So far from inflaming the minds of men to sedition and to outrage, all the witnesses have concurred that my only anxiety was to impress upon them the necessity of peace, good order, and good morals.'

'What then has been my crime? Not the lending to a relation, a copy of Mr Paine's works, not the giving away to another, a few numbers of an innocent and constitutional publication. But my crime is for having dared to be, according to the measure of my feeble abilities, a strenuous and active advocate for an equal representation of the people in the house of the people, for having dared to accomplish a measure, by legal means, which was to diminish the weight of their taxes and put an end to the profusion of their blood.'

'Gentlemen, the time will come when men must stand or fall by their actions, when all human pageantry shall cease, when the hearts of all shall be laid open.'

He faced his mother. 'From my infancy to this moment I have devoted myself to the cause of the people. It is a good cause, it shall ultimately prevail, it shall finally triumph.'

'If you condemn me which I presume you will not, say that it is for my attachment to this cause alone and not for the wretched pretexts stated in the indictment intended only to disguise the real motives of my accusation.'

'Weigh well the verdict you are about to pronounce. I can look death in the face for I am shielded by the consciousness of my own rectitude. I may be condemned to languish in the recesses of a dungeon, I may be doomed to ascend the scaffold but nothing can deprive me of the recollection of the past. Nothing can destroy my peace of mind, arising from the remembrance of having done my duty.'

V
55° 55' N
003° 10' W

It was one o'clock in the morning but the people were more awake than they'd ever been. A fabulous applause came from the public gallery, even the hairdresser. But not Ann. In her hands she cupped a tear soaked handkerchief. By her side, the London reporter was scribbling down the end of the speech in shorthand ready for publication that evening. Next to him, Robert Watt was reading the transcript, revisiting the spectacle for a second time.

Lord Braxfield cleared his throat in an attempt to cordon off Muir's popularity. 'The British Constitution is the best that ever was since the creation of the world. It's not possible to make it better. For isn't every man secure?' He ignored the shouts of 'no' from the public gallery. 'Does not every man reap the fruits of his own industry, and sit safely under his own fig tree?'

'Mr Muir had last winter gone about among ignorant country people, making them forget their work and told them a reform was absolutely necessary for preserving their liberty.'

He quaffed his wine.

'Running away from justice, that was a mark of guilt. And what could he do in France? Pretend to be an ambassador to a foreign country without lawful authority. That was rebellion. I never liked the French all these days but now I hate them.'

The court watched Lord Braxfield don his cloak. He hadn't listened to a word of the defence or the public discord. As he turned to leave he looked back briefly at the public.

'The government in this country is made up of the landed interest which alone,' he paused for effect, 'has a right to be represented. As for the rabble that have nothing but personal property… what hold has the nation on them? What security for the payment of their taxes? They may pack up all their property on their backs and leave the country in the twinkling of an eye. What right have they to representation? Mr Muir should've told them Parliament would never listen to their petition. A government should be like a corporation.'

He picked up his lantern and cudgel then walked into the adjacent chamber. The public still listened in disbelief. Down the corridor crept a voice, probably a court clerk's, 'remember my Lord, Jesus Christ was a reformer too.'

Braxfield growled a reply.

'Muckle he made of that. He was a hanget.'

Even the soldiers shackling Muir's hands shook their heads.

Lamps fuelled by fish oil lit the dungeon into which Muir was thrown. In the motionless air it lingered through the night. He escaped to recollections of the journey from Portpatrick, the Irish triggers selling linen on the roadside, their children flying kites in the westerly, their freedom and happiness that he wanted as his own.

The next day at noon the jury returned a verdict of guilty. Lord Braxfield decided that whipping was too severe and disgraceful, the more especially to a man who bore Muir's character and rank in life.

Imprisonment would be too temporary.

The criminal would be again let loose.

Transportation was to his mind the only alternative.

If he is somewhere else, Braxfield envisaged, he could do no harm. The sentence would be fourteen years.

The convict could not return within that period.

If he did, it would be under the pain of death.

'Sedition consists of many gradations,' claimed Braxfield, 'and might've run from a petty mob about wages even to high treason. If punishment adequate to the crime were to be sought for, there could be found no punishment in our law sufficient for the crime in the present case now that torture was abolished in 1708.'

Muir stood up, sickened by a figure of the establishment recommending torture. But he did not allow it to steer him from his own cause.

'Were I to be led this moment from the bar to the scaffold I'd feel the same calmness and serenity I now do. My mind tells me I've acted agreeably to my conscience, and I've engaged in a good, a just, and a glorious cause - a cause which, sooner or later, must and will prevail and by timely reform will save this country from destruction.'

Shackled to officers of the court, Muir left Old Parliament Square, past the front of Saint Giles' Church and into the old Tollbooth prison, surrounded by hundreds if not thousands of people disappointed with the verdict.

Mr Martins, the surgeon, reached out to him. Despite an altercation with the soldiers he managed to pass a small ointment bottle into Muir's hand.

The haar, a wet sea fog, had rolled in on the easterly wind making it unusually cool for the last day of August, the last day of summer for him in Scotland, he thought.

*

Robert Watt, of all people, surprised Muir on the first day of his sentence aboard the hulk ship in Leith dock. His company was welcomed. Muir had been staring out of the shutters for hours on the exact spot he had seen the ship on which he believed Tytler had escaped.

'I've written to Dundas to complain about the sentence. I think it's too severe.'

He raised his voice aware that Watt was slightly deaf. 'I doubt it'll do much good. We can't influence men as powerful as Dundas.'

Watt looked away.

'What is it, Robert?'

'I wish none of this had happened.'

'I share that sentiment.'

'No you don't. That's not what I mean. There's a...'

'A what?'

'...a guilt in me that I can't control.'

'You did your best for the Society.'

'I didn't, Mr Muir.'

'You were there from the beginning. I've fond memories when I returned from Kirkintilloch in the back of your wine cart, helping myself to a cup or two with your permission of course. I saw that cart before I ever saw you, you know, from Salisbury Crag on a day more dark than even today. You passed below whilst I was looking down.'

'Please Mr Muir, stop shouting. It's really not necessary.'

'I thought you were hard of hearing?'

'That was just...'

'Just a what?'

He tried to share the recollections of the Society's good times but Watt was debilitated by internal torment.

'This guilt, what do you mean by this?'

Watt hesitated. 'I've come to love this Society; I'm on the committee, where I must admit you should be, Thomas.'

'And you should help the cause where I no longer can. Shouldn't you?'

'You see it's not the first letter I've written...'

Muir applied some of the ointment to his aggravated wrists.

'You've... been passing information to Dundas? Have you been in his pay?'

'I told him about the Irish Address, the copies of Paine, Lapslie's assertions concerning the hairdresser, Ann Fisher and Mr Elder the bookseller. It haunts me everyday what I've done. I've become my unnatural self. I pretended not to hear you...'

'Can you hear me now, Robert? Stop this work. Do it for the others.'

'No one bought my wine. I had a family to support. I told them the Society sought to attack the British throne with more ease than even the French. I told Dundas to use his power to take vigorous, cautious and effectual measures to battle the wicked intentions of the Society's seditious body of men.'

Muir lunged out to strike him but the chains stopped his fist just inches before Watt's face. The flash of a skeleton's jaw passed before his eyes and for a moment he was glad his anger had been leashed except, that was, for the iron digging into his lacerated wrists.

'We were a constitutional, peaceful movement. Please, Robert, end your service now. They're all good men.'

As he listened to Muir's plea, he trembled, 'I'll try to draw my work to a close. Please forgive me.'

'Forgive you for plotting my imprisonment? On the first day of my confinement?'

'I've compiled resolutions for the benefit of the Society.'

Seeing no empathy, Watt slipped into attack mode.

'I'm more of a friend of the people than you. I'm on the committee.'

'And killing my Society from the inside like a disease!'

'I've written to Dundas advising him to move you to Woolwich. It'll calm the lower classes. I'm sorry I have betrayed you but Deacon Brodie haunts me and I don't know how this double life shall end.'

After the spectacle the other prisoners in the shadows had begun to talk amongst themselves. Now alone in the corner of the hulk Muir reflected on the frictions he could remember within the Society. He'd specifically told one member, the name escaped him, not to send threatening letters to anyone. But he expected his warnings to go unheard.

He vaguely recalled plans another member had to send something to the Justice Clerk, a veiled threat, in the hope of reducing his sentence. Again, he'd discouraged him.

A few others with revolutionary intent had dated letters to Robert Dundas, the first year of the French Republic and wrote of the downfall of monarchy.

He knew informers were being paid piece rate to put down gossip as fact and some had made a career of it but he never believed one of them to be Robert Watt. At times he had trusted him more than Skirving and Palmer.

A member of the Society working at the post office had told the Reverend that Mr J. Clarke, a delegate of the Society, had sent letters to Robert Dundas. One had been intercepted. It claimed that inside the Society, Clarke had been witness to a long series of laboured abuses against every department of the state. He'd also claimed that he'd seen Paine's Rights of Man distributed and heard of a poem describing Dundas as having a venal phalanx head.

Though Muir had nothing to do with such puerile nonsense, he could not have censured such behaviour. The people had been silenced enough. It would have gone against the whole ethos of the Society. That said the stupid few who'd talked of converting the kingdom into a republic had a lot to answer for.

A week passed when finally Palmer arrived.

'Why haven't you visited?' Muir yelled, still infuriated by Watt and his own error of judgement.

'We were told you didn't want company.'

'By Watt?'

'Yes. Why?'

'That devious scoundrel... Palmer, you must tell the others. He's a traitor to the cause. He has been spying on us all this time. I've heard it from his own mouth.'

Palmer couldn't quite believe it. That morning he'd given Watt letters to post so he could make it to Leith in time.

'What's been going on with the Society?'

'Crowds greater than ever before have gathered for you.'

'I thought I'd been forgotten.'

'We thought you wanted to be left alone. We sent another petition to Parliament but they ignored it. So, we wrote an Address. Hundreds of us gathered in the meetinghouse. I've brought it for you to see.'

He strained to read it in the terrible light.

The Reverend brought a candle closer.

'Dear friends and fellow citizens, you by your loyal and steady conduct in these days of adversity have shown that you are worthy of at least some small portion of liberty. Unto you we address our fears...'

Palmer interrupted. 'The crowds were silent as I read it to them.'

'Then offer me the same, Palmer! Where was I? ...In spite of the virulent scandal or malicious efforts of the people's enemies, we will tell you whole truths of a kind to alarm and arouse you out of your lethargy...'

'I don't think I've ever addressed so many people. Read on, Mr Muir.'

'...That portion of liberty you once enjoyed is fast setting, we fear, in the darkness of despotism and tyranny. Too soon, perhaps, you who were the world's envy as possessed of some small portion of liberty, will be sunk in the depth of slavery and misery if you prevent it not by your well timed efforts. Is not every new day adding a new link to your chains? Is not the executive branch daily seizing new, unprecedented, and unwarrantable powers? Has not the House of Commons, your only security from the evils of tyranny and aristocracy, joined the coalition against you?'

Putting down the Address for a second Muir found his mind still preoccupied, 'Palmer, this is fine news but you must alert the others to Robert Watt.'

'I will, don't you worry.'

'There's cause to worry. You're in grave danger.'

'When we wrote this Address I remember looking out the window towards the law courts and the old Parliament. I wondered what their reaction would be and whether there was an agent provocateur amongst the crowds. I'd never have suspected Watt, though.'

'I was just as naive. Perhaps more so.' Muir continued reading. '...Is not the House of Parliament's independence gone, while it's made up of pensioners and placemen? We've done our duty and are determined to keep our posts, ever ready to assert our just rights and privileges as men, the chief of which we account the right of universal suffrage in the choice of those who serve in the Commons House of Parliament and a frequent renewal of such power. We aren't deterred or disappointed by the late decision of the House of Commons concerning our petition. Far from being discouraged, we're more and more convinced that nothing can save this nation from ruin and give to the people that happiness which they've a right to look for under Government, but a reform in the House of Commons founded upon the eternal basis of fair, free and equal justice.'

'Fellow citizens…' Muir read, '…the time has now come when you must either gather round the fabric of liberty to support it or with your external infamy let if fall to the ground to rise no more, hurling along with it everything that is valuable and dear to an enlightened people.'

'The register of signatories went into the thousands,' said Palmer.

Although impressed, Muir thought it wise to advise, 'I don't think you should be using phrases like 'fabric of liberty' or words like 'citizen.' It's too…'

'French?'

'Well… yes.' Muir read on. 'You're plunged into a war by a wicked ministry and a compliant parliament who seem careless and unconcerned for your interest the end and design of which is almost too horrid to relate; the destruction of a whole people, merely because they want to be free. By it your commerce is fore cramped and almost ruined. Thousands and ten thousands of your fellow citizens from being in a state of prosperity are reduced to a state of poverty, misery and wretchedness. A list of bankruptcies unequalled in any former times forms a part of the retinue in this quixotic expedition. Your taxes, great and burdensome as they are, must soon be greatly augmented. Your treasure is wasting fast. The blood of your brethren is pouring out, and all this to forge chains for a free people, and eventually to rivet them forever on yourselves…'

'...To the loss of the invaluable rights and privileges, which our fathers enjoyed, we impute this barbarous and calamitous war, our ruinous and still growing taxation, and all the miseries and oppressions which we labour under... Fellow citizens - the Friends of Liberty call upon you by all that is dear and worthy of possessing as men, by your own oppressions, by the miseries and sorrow of your suffering brethren, by all that you dread, by the sweet remembrance of your patriotic ancestors, and all that your posterity has a right to expect from you, to join us in our exertions for the preservation of our perishing liberty, and the recovery of our long lost rights.'

Muir was nearly in tears, tearful for what he had been deprived of, tearful with hope for what had continued from his efforts, tearful that he had suspected that his old friend, the Reverend, had plotted against him and tearful for Watt's ongoing works of darkness.

'Thousands came, Mr Muir. They haven't forgotten you. We also have support from The London Corresponding Society.'

He knew how proud Palmer was of his Address. So much so, he sensed he'd have written it in his own blood.

Rejuvenated by Muir's oratory, Palmer declared, 'in Dundee, the weavers are very active. When I was there last they asked me to publish their own address, written by men and women not lucky enough to have had the education we've had, it was quite remarkable. Yet on my return to Edinburgh I passed Duphope Castle and saw that it had been turned into barracks. Hundreds of them have gone that way. A ship master I met on my way home told me of great distress in Glasgow, people starving on the streets who outside their parishes couldn't be helped by the poor law.'

Muir thought it his turn to listen to Palmer.

'Provisions, even hay, are being sent out of the kingdom to supply the German armies before our own cavalry are provided for. Foreign troops are in our pay while the number of fencibles has swollen to over four thousand. They fear foreign service but it is our poor I'm worried about. They're starving. Prices for meat, coal, candles, soap, sugar... they've never been so high. It's a sad world that you are confined from. The only good news is that the republicans have emerged the victors at Nantz.'

Muir smiled. 'I thought you weren't a republican.'

'Things have changed.'

'So the revolution in France is still strong?'

'Yes, whilst conservatism entrenches itself here. We fear Habeas Corpus will be suspended.'

'Even with a trial you aren't listened to...'

'I know but it's the principle.'

'No, I understand, I'm just furious with them that's all.'

Palmer didn't want to trouble him any more so shared only one final anxiety. 'A parliamentary act is to be passed to stop any societies from meeting.'

'It's to stop the United Irishmen. But it'll stop you here, too.'

Palmer moved closer. 'Skirving and Margarot intend to pass a motion for a secret committee.'

'They'll be playing into the authority's hands if they do.'

'And they intend to make a French invasion, qualification for a convention of emergency.'

Muir shook his head. 'That's madness. If the authorities hear of this they'll have all the excuses they need. Watt will pass on that information to Dundas. He's on the committee. Tell the others about Robert before any more of us are snared. Do you hear me?'

'Yes, I'll visit again tomorrow. I've lately been thinking of going to America. Priestley would help me settle. Despite the success of the petition, it's not the same without you.'

'I wish I'd gone. Go, but tell them about Watt first and visit tomorrow before you set sail.'

*

Tomorrow came but Palmer didn't. Muir imagined him on some bark following Tytler's wake across the Atlantic.

But come mid September Palmer arrived.

This time, in shackles.

'What happened?'

'They arrested me.' Palmer had caught a cold in the Tollbooth that whistled through his words.

'I can see that. Did you get chance to tell the others of Watt?'

'No, I'd barely left this hulk. It was the night I visited you. They marched me straight to prison.'

'So Skirving and Margarot are still in danger?'

'Yes. But what can we do? Hopefully they will visit us soon.'

'Did you get a fair trial?'

'I got a trial. They charged me with printing and distributing seditious pamphlets and sowing seeds of discontent. That address you read last they claimed was seditious.'

'Was Watt at the meeting house the day you wrote it?'

'Yes.'

'The scoundrel will have passed it onto Dundas.'

'My advocate, Mr Hagart, said the Address did imply censure but that was legal in the liberty of the press and the first principles of our government.'

'Well of course. It was for Parliament,' reasoned Muir.

'He quoted Burke, Richmond's and Pitt's reforming, as you did but the King's Advocate said, although freedom of argument and latitude of speech are permitted within Parliament, the same liberty would be extremely dangerous if permitted among the people.'

Nothing had changed. The same double standards existed.

'Hagart said, because Pitt said he might interfere with France's internal government, we had a right in Dundee to discuss this because it could cost us our lives. As a country,

Hagart said, we'd be mad to interfere with France
that Prussia and Russia had interfered with Poland.'

Palmer stopped to catch his breath but felt the
his chest. 'Hagart quoted Hume, saying the spi
people must frequently be roused to curb the ambition of the
court. I'd lost faith in advocates but this chap seemed, well he
went so far to say that the House of Commons had joined
with the King and Lords, against the people. He put up a
brilliant defence, Thomas.'

'So why are you shackled next to me then?'

Muir patted Palmer's shoulder to soften the gibe.

'Mr MacConcochie, for the prosecution, said, by
'asserting', we were doing something more than petitioning.
He said that universal suffrage was neither grounded in law
nor common sense and that the addressers of the petition
called their fellow citizens to gather round the Fabric of
Liberty.'

'I warned you about those French terms.'

'I know, I know... MacConcochie said we'd corrupted
the minds of the lower classes.'

'They've a right to learn just as much as Lords.'

'He said that had there been no Society for the Friends of
the People, the French would not have been hardy enough to
attack the British Nation.'

'That's entirely unfounded.'

'On the conflict with France he claimed that necessary
war must be supported.'

'Peace has always been as much of an option.'

'Said our Society was a little self elected parliament.'

'Ha! That's rich from coming from them.'

'Hagart refuted him nicely, though. He said if a law made
associations unlawful I would be in the wrong but without
such a law the practice of associations and petitioning was
legal... But then Lord Elksgrove butted in. He claimed it
would be a strange country if an attempt to raise the people
were not punishable. He also claimed my petition was

ɔmething more; an original measure to carry through what parliament had refused to grant.'

Palmer turned from facing the other side of the hulk to look directly at Muir. 'Can you remember when we talked of petitioning in Charlotte Square years back and you quoted Paine?'

'Who said petitioning was a waste of time? Yes, you disagreed with him.'

'Well, I don't any more. All they have to do is ignore you.'

'Tytler warned us and we've learnt the hard way.'

'They took me to the Tollbooth at Perth, seven years transportation for writing a petition to parliament. Abercrombie said I'd poisoned the minds of the lower classes and that, had those deluded men acted, I'd have been charged with high treason. If I return within my sentence, I shall suffer death. I told them that my politics was common justice, benevolence and humanity, to increase human happiness as far as I could.'

'What did they say to that?'

'They just walked out.'

Muir realised it was roughly a year since reading the Irish Address at the Edinburgh Convention. Still in his advocates' attire and Palmer still wearing the same vestment he'd worn in court, the two endured long freezing nights on the hulk with only glimmers of daylight.

Summer was a distant memory eclipsed by the December storms. Twice, their moorings had come untied at unholy hours and they'd nearly drifted out to sea. Thankfully, the actions of a local captain stopped such a misadventure.

Their first visit in a long while was not from Skirving but Maurice Margarot, the Londoner as he was known.

Muir whispered through the shivers.

'You're still a freeman, thank God.'

'And why shouldn't I be?' Margarot didn't give him chance to respond. 'Mr Muir, you should've seen the crowds we had gathering in Lady Lawson's Yard. As we made our way down King's Stables Road, no man could have passed in the other direction for the tide of citizens...'

'Maurice, you shouldn't use that word.'

'That's what we are. We organised the secret meeting at the carpenter's workshop. I have a transcript of what we said here.'

'Maurice, before we talk any further there's something you should know.'

Margarot interrupted. 'A real representation of the people and annual elections. That's what we asked for.'

'Maurice, please.'

'The speech went okay until I put my foot through the chair. Good job we was at a carpenter's.'

'Maurice, Watt is a spy! He's passing everything onto Dundas.'

'Watt, as in, Robert Watt? Our man on the committee? He's no spy. Good gracious me. No, he's an honest wine merchant like me, on hard times. Spare him a little respect, Mr Muir. Anyway, returning to my story... everyone's welcome, I said in the yard, Dundas, Braxfield even King George himself, for we've no secret which we dare not avow.'

Muir tried again. 'Maurice, the government are being informed of everything by someone within the committee. You must get Watt out and rein back anything that might land you in here.'

'Sure you aren't just frustrated cooped up in here? You know, looking for someone to blame?'

'No Maurice!'

'Let me tell you a little more about this meeting. I asked the crowds; why annual parliaments? Had to answer for them for there was no consensus. The same power that made them from annual to triennial, and from triennial to septennial, may very likely go on to make them for life, or even hereditary. So, I said, we must resist this assault on the democratic process.'

'Maurice, please get Watt out of the Society. I say this for your own safety.'

'Lord Kames says King David was commanded to compile his work with the council and advice of his whole realm, not the advice of representatives, not the advice of individuals but the advice of the whole realm.'

'Are you listening to a word I say?'

'Are you listening to me, more is the point? I said every man, including Mr Watt, is welcome to this Society for even some Lords speak sense from time to time. I said governance is one of the arts which necessity has suggested, which time and experience have ripened and which is susceptible of improvements without end. It must also be the privilege of every society to improve upon its government. Who said that, Mr Muir...? No? That was Lord Kames. The people did not know either!'

'Maurice, do not patronise the people. And listen to me. With Watt amongst you it's only a matter of time before you'll be shackled next to me and Palmer.'

'How do you know?'

'He told me himself.'

Margarot followed Muir's line of sight towards the depths of darkness where the other prisoners lay.

'You do hallucinate. So anyway as I was saying a scuffle broke out at the entrance to the yard. I continued to explain Kames when a tide of uniformed men swept in. I bound my hands to the chair. The Sheriff pulled at me but the chair and I were going nowhere. The crowds erupted with laughter.'

'One of the glories of our constitution is that it'll admit of repair without being thrown out of order and that repair must come from the people! The citizens! The Sheriff didn't like what I said and tried to cover my mouth but failed. Then he said, 'you call yourself citizens to infuriate me do you not?' I said he too was a citizen, that 'the word citizen is in all the student's cards. Even the pin makers of London are obliged to have the word citizen in their cards. It's therefore not the

adoption of anything new or dare I say it, French. It's
something very English and in our traditions"

At this Muir brewed inside. 'Margarot, why are you
antagonising the authorities? It'll do more harm than good as
Mr Palmer has found.'

Margarot did not take kindly to the suspected belittling
but tried to ignore it, continuing his saga until it was
interrupted by Palmer.

'Please Maurice, listen to Thomas.'

'Not you as well, Reverend. Did Watt confess to you
too?'

'No,' admitted Palmer.

'Well then.'

'Muir wouldn't lie; he's trying to help you...'

'No. He's jealous, Palmer, that other folk are now
running the Society.'

'Nonsense Maurice, I'm not.'

'So as I was saying, Reverend, this Sheriff grabbed me
by the collar, looked sternly into my eyes and declared, 'if
you persist in holding this meeting you'll be apprehended as
disorderly persons and dealt with accordingly.' So, I
dispersed the British Convention.'

Muir took his head out of his hands. 'The British what?'

'We've dropped the name; the Association of the Friends
of the Constitution and the People. It's far too wordy.'

'You've done what?'

'Unifying with the English cause,' Margarot asserted,
'will make the movement stronger.'

Muir was dumbstruck. All that he had done for Scotland
and all the efforts he'd made for the Irish state had succumbed
to British convention. Was there no escaping this
entanglement? He wished himself free of this degradation,
this rot that had made his Society a miserable plaything for
others.

He downed a quarter of Palmer's bottle of wine and
suffered more of the sorry tale having given up on convincing
Margarot of the dangers.

'We then met in Mason Lodge on Blackfriars Wynd,' Margarot recounted. 'The subject of your welfare came up in debate. Gerrald suggested your sentences would never be carried into execution as the French would be in the country before that was possible. Watt showed great surprise and enthusiasm for the eventuality. He's no spy.'

'But hear this,' invited Margarot.

Muir opened his eyes again.

'Within hours of your good friend, Skirving, acting as President and taking his seat at the meeting, soldiers on the authority of the magistrates, arrived to take him away. He refused to depart unless compelled to do so by force. The Provost forcibly drew him from his seat before anything was said.'

'Is he okay?' inquired Palmer.

'Later that day, Gerrald, Watt and I met with Skirving at his place. We were writing up the minutes of the meetings. Having bought a copy of the Edinburgh Gazetteer, Sinclair's suspicions that the Convention Bill in Ireland would be passed, was certified in print. Now that the government could suppress public assemblies Sinclair insisted we set up a secret committee of four including the secretary.'

'Maurice, this is absolute madness as I told you, Palmer.'

'There was madness in the room, Mr Muir, for just after the motion was passed we committed it to the flames but then decided to publish it. Stealing it from the fire I set my cuffs alight. Look you can see where they are blackened.'

'You are giving the authorities all the excuses they need.'

'Hear me out, Mr Muir, for you are ignorant of how this all ends.'

'No I'm not, Maurice. I know precisely how this'll all end.'

'We needed a convention of emergency to determine the meeting place of future gatherings because we could not meet in public any more. Times have changed. I can't expect either of you to understand that from in here but you must listen to what I have to say. All evening we tried to come to an agreement over how we'd circulate the news of the meeting to society members. We agreed each delegate should be entrusted with a sealed letter containing the name of the meeting place. This letter would be delivered, unopened, to the constituents, the receipt of which would be acknowledged by a letter to Skirving who was nominated the Secretary. Soon after Watt left we were disturbed by a bang at the door.'

'Say that again?'

Margarot repeated himself, a little perturbed.

'See Maurice! That is proof I know you herald bad news in this story. Watt will have informed on you, that much I can guess.'

'No, that was just coincidence. Watt signed the documents of the secret committee. I looked down from the upstairs window and saw officers. Whilst Skirving went downstairs we began to pile up papers. I could hear the altercation. Went something like, 'I want you to step outside.' 'Of my own house?' 'Yes, whilst we search it.' 'For what reason? Can you show me a warrant?' They couldn't. Skirving stood his ground, he said, 'then I must turn the door on you as an officious intruder for this is an unwarrantable, unconstitutional, and oppressive act, which you have no authority to emit.' I saw him try and close the door but an officer put his boot in the way and three other officers forced the door fully open.'

'So you were all arrested?'

'No Palmer. That's when Gerrald and I fled out of the attic window along the roof across two gable ends eventually into the Cowgate. There, we assumed the guise of tourists from England.'

That wouldn't have been hard, Muir thought.

'So where is Skirving?' asked Palmer.

'We watched him being marched to the Sheriff Substitute's office. But don't worry, he declined the declaration they had in store and they had to release him.'

'So he is still free?'

'We retired to a house in Flesh Market Close and resumed the meeting. He's fine Mr Muir. I'm more worried about the health of your mind. You seem not to trust anything or anyone any more.'

'Watt's a spy and only when you realise this will you be safe.'

Margarot walked out shaking his head.

That night, Muir talked with Palmer about the dangers facing Skirving on the outside.

The Reverend, however, drifted in and out of sleep.

He was exhausted too and latterly sensed Palmer's grumbles and acknowledgements were not in fact his but another prisoner's.

He silenced himself and through the darkness tried to discern whether Palmer was indeed asleep.

The day's candles were burned through.

It was no easy task.

How long had he been talking to someone else's cues, he wondered.

Then suddenly the hollow silence was intruded upon.

'I gave you a second life, Mr Muir, but you didn't stick to your side of the bargain.'

Muir leant forward as far as his shackles would allow.

'Who's that?'

'You've a short memory. They didn't do me for robbing the coach you passed. Only you know about that, Mr Muir. You never dealt with the handful of rogues that did this to us, though. Did you?'

The black voice acknowledged Palmer's stirring.

'There'll be no more second chances from now on.'

'Who are you?'

'No more deals.'

Palmer woke to Muir's shouting. 'Muir, what is it?'

'Did you hear that voice?'

'No…'

'Were you sleeping?'

'No, I was listening to your concerns… about Skirving.'

'You were asleep just a moment ago though?'

'No. I think you could do with some sleep. Perhaps Margarot is right about one thing. This place conjures imaginings.'

Muir stared into the darkness but the figure was as concealed now as he had been behind the muffler. He was certain it wasn't his mind deluding him. He was sure he was amongst bad company.

VI
55° 59' N
003° 10' W

Six days later Skirving arrived at the prison hulk not as visitor but fellow prisoner. Out of his overcoat pocket peered the white tufted head of what had turned out to be a dove after all.

Skirving relayed the events of that last week.

'I was over at the Gazetteer office talking to William Ross, the clerk. There was talk of foreign invasion, everywhere. The French were mobilising in the channel. I passed him details of an advert I wanted publishing for a meeting in my own home.'

'There wasn't much time. Ross told me they were going to suspend Habeas corpus. If they did there'd be no protection against wrongful imprisonment. I handed over a couple of shilling for the advert, but Ross wouldn't accept anything.'

'Back home I cleared the front room and was about to welcome the first member of the Society when I opened the door to a pair of constables. They marched me up to the magistrates again. Crowds hung down from windows watching me as if I was being taken to the executioner. The magistrate told me he'd ordered an interdict to stop all future meetings. They tried to disperse my supporters who'd walked up with me. But they failed. Leaving the magistrates I walked down to the Cockpit.'

'All the time I carried with me a note I'd the fortune to have with me when I was detained. Supporters disappointed with the aborted meeting began to congregate around the Cockpit. Two weavers lifted me onto their shoulders and I delivered the notification.'

The dove flew from Skirving's hand and out of the hulk whilst Muir read the note.

'Members of the committee of the Friends of the People, the magistrates of the city have forbid your legal and constitutional meeting called this day by advertisement. By preventing it they have given occasion to a great concourse of people, which may issue in tumult, and hinder your deliberations. It is judged proper to adjourn the meeting and to lay the business of it before several societies for their separate determination. It's therefore proposed to you to give place to the violence used against you. You'll thereby convince the public that you did not deserve such treatment; and now that your delegates have a permanent existence, your societies will be multiplied greatly, and means will be used to lay the business before each society individually by printed bulletins.'

Skirving sat back down after watching the dove from the shutter. 'Whilst I read it, the magistrates, constables and peace officers attempted to take it from me by force. The crowds stopped them, though. William Coulter insisted that no force be used against me. Eventually I was taken back to the magistrates and later released. Returning home, by accident I bumped into my good friend Mr Charles Brown, from Sheffield. We noticed the authorities had put spies around the city to report any meetings of the Society. Your former lover, Elisabeth Andrews, is one I'm sorry to say. She was spotted passing on information to the magistrates.'

'You were saying, about Mr Brown...'

'Yes, Charles and I went to the meetinghouse to find it blocked up and guarded with an armed force. Seeing the people gathering fast I made haste for fear of tumult. Town officers and soldiers seized us. We were led as condemned criminals through the most public streets. The tumultuous running of people from all quarters was completely alarming. We were conducted to the guardhouse but Mr James Laing, one of the town clerks, countermanded the procession to the council chamber and after a consultation of the magistrates we were dismissed.'

'How the devil have you ended up here then?'

'I'll explain, Reverend. Searching through papers back at home I found a document I'd written two months earlier. The repeated arrests I'd experienced over the last few days made me realise that if the document was ever to be published it'd have to be that moment. I wondered whether the officers, who'd searched my home without a warrant, had taken it from my possession. I turned the place upside down and eventually recognised it by the location and date on the top of the first page. 'Mason's Lodge, Blackfriars Wynd, fourth October, 1793.' I could remember the exact day I'd written it. Without reading any more I dug my hand into a wooden box full of shillings and left for the Gazetteer office where I met George Ross again. As he proofed the statement he was flabbergasted by the content. He'd the paper's reputation to think about but was still willing to take the risk. And a risk it certainly was. As the first of a thousand copies went to press I took a deep breath and lay it out in front of me. I've still the copy they didn't detect.'

Muir moved the statement into one of the few shards of light.

'The landholder is called upon to coalesce with the friends of the people, lest his property be soon left untenanted: The merchant, lest the commerce of the country be annihilated: The manufacturer whose laudable industry has been arrested in its progress: The unemployed citizen - the great mass of labouring and now starving poor, and finally, all the rabble are called upon by the remembrance of their patriotic ancestors, who shed their blood in the cause of freedom, and to whose memories even the enemies of that cause are compelled to pay an involuntary tribute of applause. They are called upon by the endearing appellation of fathers, by the claims of their children, and in the name of unborn millions, to demand with the firm and energetic voice of justice, the peaceful restitution of their rights. The thanks of the meeting are due to Mr Skirving of Strathruddie, the Secretary, for his un-remitted attention to the duties of this house and the interests of his country, and particularly, for having invited societies of every denomination unto their exertions in the common cause, by sending delegates to the ensuing General Convention. Had certain gentlemen countenanced this association last year, instead of pledging their lives and fortunes to prompt a corrupt and ambitious minister to engage in a war, which could only bring guilt and ruin on the nation, we might still be enjoying uncommon prosperity, and a happy understanding amongst ourselves as brethren. If they will not manfully retract that very impolitic step, and immediately join their influence to the only measure which can prevent further calamity, there will be anarchy and the Friends of the People will be blameless.'

'Ross told me if this was perceived by the authorities to be inflammatory, there's no mistaking its author. I had had a drink and told him that if you're going to be put on trial for something, you may as well make that something worthwhile. The next day it went to press and by the evening...'

'You'd been arrested?'

'Yes.'

By bribing the hulk keeper, Muir had asked Erskine to represent the Fife farmer. But they heard nothing back. No doubt he had enough to do celebrating the New Year. Favours it seemed extended only to the legal fraternity. It was looking increasingly likely that Skirving, a man who'd never been in a courtroom, would tomorrow on the seventh of January, be his own counsel and advocate.

Despite his arrival, the rats were still more numerous than the hulk's prisoners. Occasionally, a tail or twitching whisker would glimmer in the darkness. Meanwhile, on Palmer's shoulder, the dove, back from its flight, lit up his face with its snow white plumage.

Whilst they inspected the bird, Muir asked the hulk keeper to be escorted to the courtroom under armed guard so he could represent his friend. The request was refused. And so it was that the infested hulk became their legal chambers.

Skirving's pupillage was grounded on the first principle.

Pleading not guilty.

113

'Then establish that the indictment is vague, that sedition is not in any statute of our law and that the jury cannot decide upon a sedition charge if they do not know what it means to be seditious... Do you hear me, Skirving?'

'Yes.'

The other prisoners were intrigued by such confidence but sullen that it offered no hope to them. Palmer thought it a waste of breath but the legal shadow boxing required for tomorrow's fight was relentless.

'Argue also that since the British Convention has not been found to be illegal you can't be found guilty on the basis of being a member. State your position and the legal precedents that you have for behaving as you did. And explain how currently the constitutional infrastructure is breaching the people's rights set out in the Glorious Revolution of 1688, to the extent that the government is acting illegally.'

Muir paraphrased clauses of the revolution down on paper whilst Skirving basked in his advice, until that was, a guard ordered him to make his way to court. They wanted Skirving that evening.

*

At the doorway to the court Skirving stood trying to figure out where the defendant and his counsel were supposed to be. He thought it wise to let the others sit first. That way, by deduction his position would become clear. Dundas was the first to arrive, then Lords Swinton, Elksgrove, Dunsinnan and Abercrombie. He seemed to have half emptied the House of Lords for the day, which he supposed, wasn't such a bad thing.

Then the jury filed in. They weren't so much Skirving's peers as they should have been. He knew for a fact that Andrew Lauder-Dick and Hew Dalrymple, amongst them, were knights of the garter. Skirving wondered whether they had ever so much as tilled a field or drawn a plough. Yet in this place they held more power than he despite his towering frame.

Now with only one table vacant in the crucible of the court, he walked down the wooden steps and stood with his hand on the bible.

The Solicitor General addressed the court. 'To George, by the Grace of God, King of Great Britain, France, and Ireland, Defender of the Faith.'

The King of France, Skirving thought. For proceedings to open with an all out lie did not bode well.

'To makers of our court, messengers at arms, our sheriffs, greetings all. It is humbly meant and complained to us, by our right trusty Robert Dundas, esquire of Arniston, our advocate accuses William Skirving in June, July and August of the year, 1793, of writing and distributing seditious and inflammatory writing, calculating to excite the people to acts of outrage and violence, by insidiously calumniating and misrepresenting the measures of Government, and seditiously justifying the enemies of our country, with whom we are at open war. How do you plead?'

'Not guilty.'

Skirving then moved to the bar where his advocate would normally stand.

'Fellow countrymen, for I may not call you fellow citizens, the following trial is founded upon an indictment of so general a nature that it renders it impossible to provide an adequate defence. The public Prosecutor has deprived me of the use of some hundreds of papers out of which he selected what he thought proper without previous intimation. Under these circumstances it is hoped that the public above me in the gallery and those who'll read of this trial, will make proportional allowances, and as none of the papers have been returned the reader will also execute some blanks.'

He looked up at the public gallery. Margarot could be spotted in his distinctive wine merchant's jacket with his wife, Betsy. Next to him was Gerrald. Further along was

Skirving's wife and their eight sons and daughters, squeezed onto the end of the bench.

'My Lord,' said Skirving, 'a long time ago I perceived the public mind in this country was in a remarkable state of irritation. I fought to direct this irritation into some channel that might make it more moderate and regulated. I urged to the utmost of my influence, the association of the people and subjected the public irritation to the control of delegates, chosen by the people themselves because of their greater wisdom and prudence.'

'If the magistrates of Edinburgh shall prevail to break up these meetings which have for a long time shown themselves to be orderly and peaceable, and shall prevent the public discontent from flowing, you'll pent up that irritation until it breaks forth in tumult and bring upon this place the evils you hoped to prevent.'

'My earnest desire has been a union which I've been seeking among the people that could moderate the evils which are coming upon the world.'

Having listened to Skirving, the Solicitor General read out the Address and then pointed out, 'Mr Skirving, you signed it as the Secretary General of the Friends of the People.'

Proudly, Skirving declared, 'I agree with every word as too, it seems, do those in the public gallery.'

The Solicitor General then read out the handbill bearing the location and date, 'Masons Lodge Blackfriars Wynd, fourth October, 1793' adding the prefix, 'inflammatory'.

'This is also signed in your name.'

Skirving nodded.

After going on for some time, the Solicitor General concluded, 'the Friends of the People have seditiously arrogated themselves the name of The British Convention of the Delegates of the People and have associated to obtain universal suffrage, and annual parliaments. Under the specious pretext of reform their real purposes were of the most dangerous and destructive tendency, hostile to the peace and happiness as well as to the constitution of this realm. From October, November and December 1793, you called yourselves 'citizens' modelling yourself on the French and you divided yourselves into committees, amongst them, finance and secrecy. Mr Skirving you were an active ringleader and part of that secret committee.'

As his own advocate, Skirving returned to the bar. 'Not being accustomed to speak in public, I'm not able to follow the Solicitor General in the long speech that he has made, but I've thrown my thoughts together, and shall beg leave to read them to your Lordships, from the paper in my hand, if I'm permitted. There's nothing said against me in particular that is worth the noticing. Surely the prosecutor ought to have specified the crime as defined, in some one or other of the statutes to which he refers, and which are presently cognizable in this court; and in the transgression of which he wishes to prove that I have been guilty.'

The Lords didn't bat an eyelid. Their wigs lolled over their heads like the dust covers to time wearied statues, which is what Skirving thought they would eventually become.

'Sedition!' continued Skirving, 'I know not what the prosecutor means by sedition. He doesn't attribute to it a single quality either of mind or action. I'm not called on to declare any opinion of sedition. He is. But he only says 'whereas' where he talks of it and says no more. Surely, whatever idea he has of sedition, after describing it as a crime so heinous and so severely punishable, he should also be able to define it? It would be unjust of the court to admit such an unprecedented attack on any man, and it's hoped, they won't indulge the public prosecutor in this particularly given that this business is to be brought under the review of parliament.'

He hoped this was a warning to the Lords that they were also, theoretically, answerable to scrutiny. Skirving added, 'I ask you to remember an approbation of the Glorious Revolution goes still farther. It declares that if by any means, by force or by fraud, by violence or by corruption, the necessary constitutional provisions should be taken away, the same objectives would again justify the same national struggle, and the same extremities, unless they could be recovered and re-obtained by more gentle, peaceful, and therefore more happy means. All that was valuable to the people of this country, all the provisions which were stipulated to procure the peace and prosperity, the individual liberty, and the general property of the people of this land, have all been, since the revolution, taken away - All!'

'This country,' hailed Skirving, 'was established by the revolution to avoid all future mistakes. The contract between prince and people was made clear to understand. The revolutionists began by altering the oaths of the contracting parties, the Coronation Oath for all future sovereigns and the Oath of Allegiance for all future subjects.'

'They cut up by the roots the damnable doctrine of passive obedience and non-resistance by emphatically specifying and ordaining, that the following words of their former oath; First William and Mary, Chapter Eight, should not be required or enjoined.'

'Thus, the oath 'I declare that it is not lawful upon any pretence whatever to take up arms against the King', was removed from the constitution.'

'No oath of slavery ever ought to bind a nation or an individual. This alteration was made to prevent the future sovereigns of this country from being misled, as the four preceding sovereigns had been, to trust to a senseless superstition about royalty, which though many persons for their interests have professed, no man of common sense ever entertained.'

'Their next care was to provide for the due administration of the executive power and the responsibility of its confidential advisers. They stated, 'all matters and things relating to the well governing of this kingdom shall be transacted and signed by the privy council, thereby guarding, as far as laws could guard, against that accursed engine of despotism, a cabinet council, or that more accursed instrument, an interior cabinet.'

'They established that no person who receives a pension from the Crown, or has an office and place of profit under the King is allowed to serve as a member of the House of Commons. This is outlined in Section Twelve. W.III. Chapter Two, entitled: Securing the purity and independence of the people's representatives in parliament.'

Skirving then addressed the jury, particularly the knights of the garter. 'Those who wrote the revolution settlement also decreed that juries should be fairly taken, without partiality, and should act freely, without influence.'

Not one juryman looked up to face him.

He continued. 'Now, all these objects and consequences of the Glorious Revolution would have no value, they would be nugatory and worthless, they would be a mockery unless they went effectually to obtain and secure to the people of this land these three important points…'

'First, an honest and responsible exercise of the executive authority, secondly, real, independent, and faithful representatives of the Commons in parliament and thirdly, a fair and impartial administration of justice in the courts of law.'

'We, in the words of our ancestors, at the time of the revolution, do now again claim, demand, and insist upon all of these as our undoubted rights: the true, ancient and indubitable rights, and liberties of this kingdom.'

'If then by various means it has happened that this provisional responsibility of the privy council no longer remains the election of the House of Commons, its election is neither fair, nor free, or frequent.'

'The provisional independence of its members is gone. The House of Commons, at present, swarms with persons having offices and places of profit under the King, and receiving pensions from the Crown.'

'Juries are not fairly and impartially taken. They do not act freely and without influence. Bail money requested by courts is excessive. Excessive fines are imposed. Illegal and cruel punishments are inflicted. Judges are not independent of the Crown as royal pensions and lucrative offices have been granted to some of them.'

'Because of this, a committee should be appointed to inquire and consider whether any invalidated provisions may be fit to be restored in order that the people of this land may recover the situation and security in which they were placed by the Glorious Revolution in sixteen eighty eight.'

A rapture of applause came from the public gallery, led by Margarot and Gerrald. In its midst, Skirving declared, 'by opposing the Friends of the People, the opposers have brought their country to the very brink of ruin. I am ready to answer for The Association of the Friends of the People, and for all their proceedings from first to last. But at present, I am indicted, only as an individual.'

When the cheers receded, no immediate reply was made by anyone in the court.

Eventually, the Solicitor General raised the accusation, 'when the civil magistrate requested to search your property, you resisted.'

'No idea of guilt, or even of fault, can arise in any man's mind on my conduct towards the civil magistrate, in that particular case. If the officer of a civil magistrate shall come to me and desire me to go out of my own house I have a right to ask the reason, and if he can show me no warrant I may turn him to the door as an officious intruder. It's false that I, in anyway, contravened the proclamation of the sheriff and provost, though indeed I did consider it an unwarrantable, unconstitutional, and oppressive act which they'd no authority to emit.'

'If the matters charged in the libel amount to the crime of sedition then sedition must be a very innocent thing indeed. Nay, if my conduct from beginning to end is sedition, I glory in it as the highest service of my life and judge such sedition the highest virtue because I disinterestedly pursued it to promote the public welfare.'

'But, I must insist, that as neither the crime itself, nor the law defining it are stated in my indictment then that indictment is illegal, and ought therefore to be discharged.'

'If the term, sedition, is in any statute of our law then it will speak for itself. But if no such law is stated upon then in this case the indictment must be declared without foundation. For, no libel is relevant which is not a transcript of some statute.'

'Surely, your Lordships will not support the doctrine that the exchange of sentiment between people, or the mutual discussion of argument in society is sedition or any sort of crime.'

'Association is the natural inheritance of creation. Arbitrary tyrannical power separates man from his brother and infuses the selfish unfeeling principle more and more in the heart. But the principle of liberty, that true principle which Christianity implants in the soul, the principle of liberty which Christ has restored and by which he makes men free, is the load stone which draws souls together and establishes the social band which is the source of all morality.'

'As a certain token of those halcyon days which we hope for, the influence of the uniting principle shall be remarkable. It was the signal and the means of our father's deliverance from Popish domination. It promises a still more glorious deliverance, a deliverance not from one tyranny to embrace another but a deliverance from the principle of tyranny itself, to establish the love of mankind. You would do well therefore not to counteract the work of Christ on this earth.'

'I cannot be tried upon accusations made against a long allowed society which has not as yet been tried and legally convicted. The present indictment against me is illegal, and must be dismissed.'

'As the jury know not the idea of sedition, by proceeding they might be guilty of the grossest injustice. The original intention of trial by jury was to guard against the partiality and injustice of magistrates and judges. The county courts became so corrupt that juries were created as a remedy.

Formerly, the juries of Scotland were empanelled in civil as well as in criminal actions. Juries are now limited to the trial of high crimes and misdemeanours, an injustice in itself. It's a common notion that jurymen are judges of the fact only, and not the law. It's exceedingly natural that jurymen should look up with veneration to the high rank of those dispensing justice over the nation.'

He looked at the jury. 'I cannot be incriminated merely for being a member of the British Convention unless that Convention was found guilty, which cannot be found in this present trial. I am not before the court as responsible from the charges brought against the British Convention because none have been brought. You, the jury, are my sole and independent judges. You are my countrymen. No court can restrict or control you.'

Looking seaward, Muir's parents reached out to their son's shackled hands. He was ready to walk along the gangplank aboard the *Royal George*, a revenues cutter constructed to apprehend smugglers in the past. Sailors walked the yardarm whilst at the transom younger recruits assembled the yawl rig as it hung over the stern waters.

On this fine April day Muir felt alienated from the cutter's idiosyncrasies for it too was an adversary tearing him from the people he loved and the country he strove to liberate.

Muir's father told him that most people spent their entire lives in the county they were born but it seemed God had something else in store for him. He then slipped a bible into his son's pocket and placed two heavy packages attached by string around his son's neck.

'Rabbits?'

'Yes, Tom, from the falconer. A gift. He didn't charge. Used to have them when you were a boy.'

'That's why I renewed the order.'

His father's eyes welled up as he waved goodbye but weighed down by the chain and shackles Muir could not wave back. The sailors seemed to judge him from on high. He tried to look back at his mother and father just before he went below deck but they were lost behind the cortège of convicts. Terribly alone, it was only the sight of Palmer that stopped him from breaking down.

When his eyes had adjusted to the darkness below deck, he opened the bible and read:

'To Thomas Muir, from your afflicted parents.'

Soon though, he sensed the man next to Palmer had his eyes on him. Muir recognised his lantern jaw from the Tollbooth prison. Now offshore and out of chains he held out his hand in which was a good portion of rabbit meat wrapped in paper, with the intention of curtailing his suspicions. The man postponed finishing off the letter he was writing, accepted the gift and returned the handshake.

'Kidlaw. Pleased to meet you.'

As Muir introduced himself, he was almost certain this man, Kidlaw, spoke in the same tongue as the voice he'd heard in the hulk. With saurian movements the man arced back up the slope of the hull and camouflaged all but the whites of his eyes.

Where had he heard that name? A recent court case sprung up in his mind. Drawn from the ship's confines to the moral dankness of the High Court, he recalled Kidlaw's forgery case. Widely reported in legal circles, the accused had narrowly avoided the death sentence and instead was sentenced to life in the colonies.

He recalled that the man in the hulk had stated that it wasn't for the coach robbery that he was imprisoned. It was all starting to fit together but he still couldn't recognise him from any of the Society meetings. That said, he was reassured he wasn't hallucinating after all.

Fives hours into the journey and now up on deck, Palmer confided with Muir, an anomaly.

'If his name's Kidlaw what's he doing signing that letter as Ogilvie?'

He remained as bewildered as Palmer as they watched the captain take a bearing off a yellow speck of light. He thought it wise to keep what he knew of Kidlaw to himself for now. As the ship sailed south, that speck of light turned out to be a flaming beacon on Lindisfarne castle.

The captain had followed their trials with intrigue. Had he not been bound by his occupation he would perhaps have seen the advocate and the Reverend as something more than just livestock he had to deliver in less than two weeks to the south coast.

Whilst they finished scavenging meat from the rabbit carcasses, their heads turned to a call from the crow's nest.

'Captain Ogilvie, a naval ship approaches three leagues to the south.'

Muir and Palmer looked at each other realising Kidlaw's plan. The naval ship passed within five boat lengths to windward. Their ship slouched in its wind shadow. As it passed, crewmen could be seen being whipped. Their backs were striped red like butchered pigs. Muir made a note of the cruelty fearing it was just a fleeting glimpse of things to come whilst Palmer enacted the sign of the cross to ward off the devil. The others just grinned.

*

At four in the morning the *Royal George* arrived into Southampton Water. They had been at sea for ten days. An enormous naval warship passed as they drifted onto their quay. Navigating the stern, the name, *Irresistible,* towered above them.

Lamplight lit up a conversation on deck, between what looked like the captain and a subservient. Palmer took a second look as they drifted past. He was almost certain it was Dr Martins. But Muir thought it couldn't be. He'd joined the Society after all. What was he doing in the Royal Navy? The ship's surgeon perhaps. He remembered Palmer's diminishing eyesight and discounted the possibility.

Passing *Irresistible's* bow, the black shore acquired the silhouettes of smaller ships, rowing boats, pontoons, warehouses and yardarms. The tail of the moon lit a strip of silted bank. Whilst in other areas, dockers waved amber fire torches at Ogilvie and the sleep deprived crew.

Now alongside, the Commander of the colony studied the convicts as they passed his lantern. Until, that was, he spotted the Reverend's vestment and the advocate's gown.

'To one side.'

'We don't want preferential treatment.'

'You won't get it. Soldiers take the Reverend to the *Stanilaus* hulk on the outer most quay.'

'We're sailing on the same boat aren't we?'

'Take Mr Muir, to the transport *Canada* without delay. It disembarks at dawn.'

'Palmer, I will write.'

*

A week later Palmer was dragged from the *Stanilaus* to a transport ship called the *Surprise*. In keeping with its name, Margarot welcomed him aboard as if he were its owner.

'It's slightly better than Newgate Prison.'

'I didn't know you'd been sentenced, Margarot?'

'It seems Muir wasn't deluded. He deserves my apology. I'll tell you of it later but first some good news. I'll let Skirving tell you.'

The farmer embraced Palmer, 'the Earl of Lauderdale has petitioned the House of Lords on our behalf.'

Margarot interjected, 'but let's not get our hopes up too much, Viscount Stormont is opposing Lauderdale. He claims there are no grounds for interfering with the established courts of criminal justice.'

'Established perhaps, legitimate? I don't think so. They were nothing but show trials,' Palmer remarked.

'The leader of the opposition, Fox, is supporting Mr Adams' motion for our release.'

'Where's Gerrald?'

'Newgate.'

'We won't be released but Mr Adams hopes to commute the sentence from transportation to fine and imprisonment. He believes the current sentence to be illegal. He has support from Mr Whitbread, Mr Sheridan and Mr Grey. If the motion's passed, we won't have to endure this voyage to New South Wales'

'But William, it's too late for Muir. The transport ship, *Canada's*, already left port.'

'Good God. They'd no right to send him yet, not before the parliamentary motion's been voted on…'

'Well they have.'

'Many die of dysentery; they are ex-slave ships reeking with pestilence.'

They dwelt on the sad truth that they might never see him again whilst Skirving read the beginning of a copy of Godwin's novel entitled, *Things As They Are*. Muir seemed the protagonist more so than the fictional character, Caleb Williams.

For hours they took turns to look out of the tiny shutter. Nothing but a dead cormorant tapping against the hull with every sway of the swell was of note, leaving them depressed and dreary. They had not been given access to the sea stores yet and Palmer considered how they might cook the bird.

Now alone, the clattering of someone walking up the gangplank did little to withdraw Palmer from his melancholy. He just stared into the waters. The tide seemed to be rising higher than the quay could cope with and it was this drawn out process that had preoccupied him for hours as the quay had dipped below sea level.

When Palmer finally returned his attentions to the cabin, he couldn't quite believe his eyes. The Muir he'd imagined famishing mid Atlantic was stood before him looking tubbier than ever.

'Palmer!'

'Are you wearing two jackets? You're as fat as a goose.'

'We raided the sea stores when the voyage was cancelled. The ship was full of rot so the captain turned back fearing we'd sink if we encountered a storm.'

'Aha! Saved by the woodworm!' celebrated Palmer.

'We seem to have nature on our side!'

'But what of the woodworm in parliament?' inquired Skirving.

'It seems unlikely we'll be supported by a house we've been steadfastly trying to reform for years.'

'Have faith...'

'The Society's no more. The voyage we're about to endure will be horrendous if it's anything like my time on the *Canada*, before we raided the sea stores, that is. I was surrounded by street robbers, murderers and villains. If dysentery doesn't get you, your cabin mates will. Present company excluded.'

'Have faith. If Parliament votes in our favour, we'll only have a short prison sentence to endure.' Muir looked at the approaching black storm clouds and doubted Palmer's optimism.

On Monday morning all but Palmer, who was suffering from influenza, left the prison ship in chain gangs. Last week's unusually high spring tides coupled with the storms had washed parts of the harbour road into the drainage ditch below.

The other convicts in Muir's gang, including Kidlaw and Ellis, longed to go down into the ditch water but not to rebuild the road.

Fish had been stranded by the ebbing tide.

The convicts sunk their hands in and pulled out stones to throw back onto the road. Blinded by the lifted silt, occasionally, a fish would knock into their hands and the convicts would become frantic to have their catch. But they were as blind as the fish.

During this expedition Kidlaw whispered to Ellis that he believed there was a design among the soldiers to mutiny and carry the ship into some part of France once they set sail. Ellis told him to hold his tongue. Muir overheard as did Draper, a soldier, who considered the idea utter nonsense.

In an effort to build alliances, particularly with Kidlaw, who was a worry, Muir used the sun rising over the eastern side of the town as a pretext to remove his shirt.

Handing one sleeve to the convict in front, each tied a knot at the cuffs and then dropped stones down the arms before trawling it upstream.

Becoming progressively heavier, first with the silt then with prodding weights that had a life of their own, the other convicts stopped passing up stones onto the road and watched in expectation of a fresh breakfast when they returned to the hulk.

'Work as normal or they'll suspect something.'

The back of the shirt was now creased with the sides of fish. Moments later, Ellis called to Muir and pointed further down the road to a prison guard inspecting the work of another gang.

'Tie up the shirt and sink it.'

'They'll escape…'

'… Then put it up onto the bank and get back to work.' They lifted the shirt, now a full bladder, and flung it onto the ground.

A surge of water flattened the long grass.

The prison guard was closer now.

'Get back to work.'

They all sunk their arms into the mud and before long were throwing stones aplenty. From up on the road, however, the prison guard noticed a patch of progress and the convict wearing the soaked shirt.

Dragged to the Commander's office, Muir saw a hand tied recruit like those he'd seen press ganged in the taverns of Edinburgh, being lowered on a rope head first into the dock water. The superior officers found it hilarious. The prison guard asked whether they wanted to dunk Muir but thankfully he was under the Commander's jurisdiction.

Now in his lookout post, a lengthy pause hung like a sea fret. Eventually, the Commander asked for an account of his journey aboard the *Royal George*. Muir gave a prosaic log of time below deck, his efforts with convicts like Kidlaw, the squall that hit them off The Wash and their navigation into Southampton Water.

The Commander became increasingly irritated.

'Silence! Captain Ogilvie has written to the Sheriff Pringle of Edinburgh charging you and fellow mutineer, Palmer, with conspiracy. He writes here that: 'Had he or Palmer obeyed the call of nature and ascended the deck during the course of it, the crew had orders to chop you down.' What've you to say about the matter?'

'This is news to me and would be to Palmer, would he hear of it.'

'You're a man of court. Lying to me is no different to lying under oath.'

Muir thought back to all the lawyers, now mostly Lords, who were as much trained liars as they were trained lawyers.

'I'm telling the whole truth. Our conversation with Ogilvie was amicable.'

'How could it have been? He's charged you with conspiracy and mutiny. You must be aware of what additional sentence awaits you?'

It was then that he remembered Palmer's observation the first night they were at sea. Kidlaw had signed his letter 'Ogilvie'.

'Before any sentencing is carried out I believe you must hear this from Captain Ogilvie in person.'

'I doubt that is possible. The *Royal George* has returned to Edinburgh. I believe it set off this morning.'

'The cutters were damaged against the quays during the storms and high tides. Please give me the liberty of searching for someone I believe would vouch for me, against this accusation. Commander, I believe the letter is forged.'

Across the way from the Commander's office, that morning Palmer had woken into an illness from the suffocating heat of twenty four convicts sleeping head to toe, shoulder to shoulder, beneath a closed wooden hatchway perforated with only a single hole.

Now back from the drainage ditch, Kidlaw and another man were helping themselves to Palmer's wine store.

'Caught us some very fine fish did Mr Muir but suffered for it,' Kidlaw recounted.

The other man laughed. The Reverend didn't know him and hadn't been introduced. He seemed well spoken and well dressed. What need he had leeching off others, Palmer could not quite fathom and the sight of them eating raw un-gutted fish that still twitched with life, made his stomach turn.

As Skirving helped Palmer down the gangplank to find a doctor they passed a young lad with a walking stick in one hand and a lurcher on a lead in the other.

Nearly out of earshot Palmer heard a faint, 'Uncle Thomas?'

'Ah, Richard! William, this is my nephew, Richard Fysche-Palmer.'

The young lad tried to hide the sadness of not immediately recognising his uncle. Whilst Skirving searched for a doctor, Palmer examined what was soon to be his hunting dog.

'You'll need fresh meat to stay healthy out there and they say a lurcher can outrun a kangaroo.'

'Is it broken to the gun?'

Richard nodded, 'but not to the sea. I'll leave that to you and your friend.'

They held his muzzle.

'He has the nose of a pointer...'

'... But the speed of a greyhound.'

The Commander had deliberated for some time on Muir's life but eventually conceded, 'if you are not back here with or without Captain Ogilvie, within the hour, I will bring your sentencing forward a week. Do you hear?'

Muir sprinted along the quayside and down the pontoon he arrived on, hurdling over barrels and fracturing boards on landing all the time knowing that Kidlaw, his opponent, would be eating the fish he sought to provide in retrospect only for the other men in his gang. All that the scoundrel had brought him was a looming death sentence. Palmer would surely know of the possible fate that also awaited him too. Had they interrogated him with the same ill placed certainty?

Southampton Water was clogged with vessels leaving on the ebbing tide taking advantage of the storm's end. But the winds now were too light. Finally he reached the pier, utterly exhausted. The *Royal George* had gone.

Three pontoons along, oblivious to Muir's troubles, Palmer kneeled down to study the hound. A few moments later it began to growl. Palmer peered upwards to see Joseph Draper and Kidlaw. They kept their distance. The dog had something against them. Palmer registered its sixth sense.

During a lull in the conversation he pointed out to Richard that Draper was the person who had lately attempted to assassinate Prince Edward.

'Mr Palmer's correct,' confirmed Draper, 'we attempted to raise an insurrection in Quebec amongst the troops. Some of the other insurgents are aboard too but I led the operation. That, I'm proud to say.'

'Despite its ultimate failure. But you turn your hands to less violent trades these days.'

Kidlaw grinned and answered for his friend. 'He stitches people up does Mr Draper.'

Palmer hoped to clarify Kidlaw's sinister turn of phrase for his nephew. 'We employ him. Ex-assassins make very effective tailors.'

He showed Richard the shoulder of his jacket.

'You can't see that it has been stitched up can you?'

Draper held a smile but sensed Palmer was mocking him earlier. As he left, Richard slipped a shilling into Draper's hand. 'You'll not go far wrong in his company, Uncle Thomas.'

Palmer noticed the dog's discomfort easing as Draper left and wondered who to believe, his nephew or his hound?

'Oh, Uncle, before I forget, the walking stick's a present from father. God bless.'

And it was with the walking stick and his dog that he made his way back to the hulk.

Meanwhile, Muir scanned the fleet and in the near distance recognised the *Royal George's* yawl rig.

It was only perhaps two hundred yards away.

'Captain Ogilvie!'

The flogging sails deafened the call to those on board. He called again whilst his mind raced through the implications of not talking to the captain. He believed him to be a man of principle and was sure of Palmer to believe his suspicions about Kidlaw.

With the cutter moving into a lull before the darker windier patches of open water he called for a third time but the sail's stillness made no difference to him being heard. There was only one option; he had to reach the cutter before it reached the darker waters.

He squelched out of his muddy shoes, pulled down his over trousers and in just his undergarments stepped down a jetty ladder. Slipping into the water like a tubby rat, the bladder wrack clawed at him but eventually he made it to freer waters.

With the lurcher on the lead Palmer and Skirving walked the ship's deck looking for somewhere to read the Morning Chronicle.

News of Adam's motion was imminent, they suspected.

Turning the page, Palmer lowered it to reveal a swimmer heading straight out to sea.

'What is that man doing?'

Skirving welcomed Palmer's comment as for the second time that day Draper was pestering him for money to buy stock to sell in New South Wales. Palmer had flatly refused valuing the lurcher's judgement. Skirving, though, was a soft touch.

'Looks like he's trying to reach that ship.'

'That's what we sailed here on.'

The swimmer changed the side he came up for air on and presented his face to them.

'Palmer, that's Mr Muir. I didn't know he could swim.'

'Trying to escape and we haven't even got to Botany Bay!'

*

'Intending to hold the rudder all the way to Scotland are we?'

In bursts of clarity and muteness, Muir explained, 'Captain Ogilvie! A man's been pretending to be you. He's written to the Sheriff in Edinburgh claiming I tried to mutiny whilst we were at sea.'

'I'll have to log this escape attempt.'

Muir coughed as he accidentally swallowed some salt water. 'The Commander... has given me an hour to find you... and I have worked within his remit ...he said nothing of the illegality of swimming. Please... Captain Ogilvie, I need your word in my favour ...or I'll be hanged.'

His head went under.

Ogilvie lowered a pole.

Palmer's influenza had left him irritable.

'What on earth had you in mind?'

Muir held his temper in check knowing Palmer was oblivious to Kidlaw's grander design.

He tried to warm himself up next to the lurcher.

'I was trying to save your bacon as well as mine.'

'It'll be construed as attempting to escape.'

'Sometimes you have to take risks. Ogilvie and the Commander are discussing our fates now.'

Skirving was counting shillings from a trunk under his bed whilst Draper was trying to hide the transaction with his back to Palmer who now considered him nothing but a parasite.

Skirving approached them, 'it will keep him off my back and give him something to do.'

Palmer was lost for words.

134

He went over to his store to pour three glasses of port but the bottle was empty thanks to Draper and Kidlaw.

Seeing this, Margarot opened a flagon of claret for all.

'How was your trial?'

Palmer quaffed a mouthful. Disappointed with Skirving and Muir, he welcomed Margarot's company.

'My advocate, Mr Hagart, encouraged me to declare that I wasn't the person charged with the indictment!'

'Why so?'

'They'd spelt my name F I S C H E and not F Y S C H E. The objection was sustained in 1791 when Mr Low was indicted as Mr Law, in 1790 when Mr Anderson was indicted as Mr Adderson and in Deacon Brodie's case.'

'Clever Mr Hagart!'

'Oh yes, he quoted the 1672 Regulations that required the true name of the panel, for the trial to commence.'

Speedily necking his claret, Margarot's eyes widened followed by his mouth. 'I can better that, Reverend'. He filled everyone's glasses including Draper and Kidlaw's who had returned hearing the uncorking of another bottle.

Finding even his friends annoying, Muir slipped out on deck and set his paper, pen and ink on a piece of cargo to indulge in a bout of letter writing:

'Dear Mr Dyer, what I long dreaded has now occurred; I now certainly know that the whole vengeance of the Scotch judges has been exerted. I advise you to meet Mr Moffat in London. There you can be protected by a greater horror of independent men. Thomas Muir. Portsmouth. Sixth April, 1794.'

After rereading the letter he found himself staring meaninglessly into the cargo's surface. He felt thoroughly depressed until, that was, he found his name etched into the rusty ironwork.

He looked around it and also found Anderson's name. Lifting the covers he realised it was Tytler's printing press. The professor must have had it sent down all the way from

Edinburgh. Between the names was a note scored with something like the sharp end of a nail.

He collected together all the bagged fonts, boards, frames and clamps, anything that could be washed overboard and took them down to the cabin.

With a renewed sense of purpose he caught the tail end of Margarot's case for his court speech being more superior to Palmer's.

'I told the judge, Pitt had plundered the poor to help the rich, that the attempt to pay off the national debt by tax rises was one of the most barefaced robberies committed on the people that ever was attempted in any civilized nation, enriching only stockholders, moneyed men and gamblers.'

'I told him every war this country has been engaged in has nearly doubled the former debt and raised taxes. And this present war with France is no different. The faithful historian, I said, will show these events to be most disastrous to constitutional liberty, science, morals and trade ever since England established freedom. I insisted our society provided the unemployed with daytime meetings to have political debates and air ideals and that attacking our society attacked the cause for parliamentary reform.'

'I aired my thoughts on the court too. It was not the spelling of my name I objected to as in your case Reverend Palmer, but that the court was not fit to try me! The Lord Justice General was not there to do his duty. I said, how's this the High Court if it lacks the principal officer and representative of the King? I demanded I be discharged forthwith having done my duty.'

Margarot's tale now had the attention not just of Palmer but the other cabin mates and of a man who was loitering by the half closed cabin door with a bulldog.

'I said a man is presumed innocent till he is found guilty but this court presumes me to be criminal until my innocence is clearly proved. I said a judge ought to be like Caesar's wife, not only spotless but even unsuspected and that was not the case with the Lords present.'

'What did they say?'

'I hadn't finished. I reminded them that in one year of Alfred's reign forty four judges were hanged and that Judge Jeffreys had been torn to pieces by the people.'

The man at the door smiled, stifling a laugh. Margarot's humour refreshed Muir's interest in his fellow reformer.

'I clarified I did not mean to say the judges before me were guilty. I said that remained the judgement of a higher being. I told them the right to bring witnesses had been denied me and that the jury, the brightest privilege of Englishmen, who stand between those in power and those accused had been selected by those in power.'

Sealing his letters, Muir imagined Scotland's meeting places receding back to drinking, praying and law making. A deep freeze would return, a chronic hibernation now that the last of the reformers had been dealt with by Dundas.

'Wise words...'

Everyone turned.

The last two words were not Margarot's but those of the tall well built man who'd been listening by the door.

'Do you reside in this cabin because...'

Muir frowned at Skirving and stemmed his pending cack-handedness with his own words. 'Captain Campbell, what a pleasure it is to finally meet you.'

'Mr Muir isn't it. Your reputation precedes you. Mr Margarot, whilst you spoke with reverence they still found you guilty. Sometimes you have to work with the powerful to get what you want. But to deal with practicalities first, you owe me forty pounds each for your passage.'

'Captain Campbell our transportation isn't a foregone conclusion. In parliament, men who you answer to are debating our sentences.'

'Reverend, that was my other reason for visiting...'

Campbell handed Muir an issue of the Daily Chronicle, folded in quarter with one of the back pages facing up. In the drab light he read out the 'Parliamentary vote to review the sentences of Muir, Palmer, Skirving, Margarot and Gerrald.

Outcome. Thirty two votes, for. One hundred and seventy eight, against.'

It was not what any of them wanted to hear but Muir half expected such news.

'But what of the petition in the House of Lords?'

Palmer looked a little further down the same page.

'The committee of the House of Lords, attended by Lords Thurso and Kennison, reported that the appeal was incompetent and that before the Court of Judiciary, the relevancy of the late indictments and the power of the court to inflict the sentence of transportation, in the 1703 Act, is fully upheld and supported.'

Muir imagined Dundas celebrating Mr Adam's failed attempt to undermine his power.

Palmer's disappointment spilled into the second issue.

'We've to pay to be transported? Are you sure? Doesn't the government pay you?'

'Reverend, they've made no such payment. You're wealthier than most and they expect you to pay.'

'Have you spoken to the Commander about the mutiny charges?'

'He's let them pass. Now, the money gentlemen, if you will.'

Coins were counted into three bags and handed over.

They knew Captain Campbell was being paid twice.

'Can we have receipts for our payments?'

'Mr Palmer, you are required to pay for Mr Ellis' cabin too.'

'Why?'

'Because you've the money and I make the rules.'

'I've nothing against Ellis but why out of everyone should I pay?'

'If you don't pay you will be denied access to the sea stores.' Campbell tied another bag of forty pound coins around his bulging mid-rift.

'We leave this evening. Make sure you've everything on board.'

Palmer tried to suppress the desired thought that Campbell might slip overboard whilst up on deck with all that coinage on him and sink to the bottom of the dock. Such thoughts were not normally acquainted with the Reverend but Palmer had many sides to him.

VIII
35° 12' N
020° 40' W

Half in half out of sleep having spent several weeks at sea Palmer revisited the events of the last evening. Captain Campbell had invited them to dinner. Muir had declined. The Reverend wished he had too.

The host's apparent goodwill had turned quickly for in a very short space of time he'd drunk half a bottle of rum and proceeded to tell Mr Boston that he had begun to tire of 'the Reverend'. They were well within earshot of Palmer who sensed in Margarot agreement with the captain's views. It hurt him deeply and made him reassess his companion.

Barely had they finished the main course when Campbell ordered Skirving and Palmer down to the steerage, much to the amusement of Margarot and Campbell's first mate, McPherson.

And now, having napped early, wakefulness would plague him all night. Sharing his bunk with Kidlaw made things even worse. He had come to dislike him intensely, aware as Muir had made him, of the forger's letter stating that they were mutineers.

Stopping himself from mindlessly studying the bunk above he looked across the cabin, to find that he was not the only one awake.

Kidlaw had left the bunk and was rummaging through chests undisturbed by Draper who was sewing one of Muir's shirts. Palmer's already tested temper was now devoid of patience.

He ordered Kidlaw to get out of their belongings.

The forger snarled at Palmer's cold ridden face.

'Do as he says.'

Like a cornered fox, Kidlaw turned to the other voice.

The glow of a flame lit pipe reeled back the shadows.

Skirving had been keeping watch all along.

Draper put his shears back in his ditty bag. 'Gentlemen, our friend here, Mr Kidlaw, was merely looking for more clothes I could mend and meant no harm to Mr Muir.'

Balancing his pipe on a ledge, Skirving dropped down from his bunk and by both lapels, grabbed Kidlaw.

The bang woke Muir.

'Check your moneybags.'

Skirving found two gold and five silver coins on Kidlaw.

'What' you short of, Mr Muir?'

'Two guineas and four... no five shillings.'

Skirving handed the coins over very pleased with his intervention and wrote down what had already been taken, ready to report the crimes to Captain Campbell whilst Palmer made his way to his own belongings and found one of his boxes had been broken open.

Kidlaw slipped out.

Palmer broke down. 'I can't sleep in the same room never mind the same bunk as someone who's thieved from me. He'll come back.'

Palmer looked at Muir with utter terror in his eyes.

'We'll work something out.'

'This is worse than my first year at Eton.'

He put a hand on Palmer's shoulder envisaging him in the quadrangle, a boy in gowns and tails not an old man in sweat yellowed clothes. Memories of his enthusiasm with Tytler in the pub when the Society was just an idea between them, came to the forefront of his mind. Would they have been so keen knowing what they now knew, he wondered.

'Palmer, why don't you study Tytler's Encyclopaedia again? There's another section on boat building in the index. Skirving, pour us all a drink. I'll finish that report on Kidlaw.'

Before doing so, he checked the bags of printing press equipment. He didn't really know what had been in each in the first instance but thought it wise.

At the bottom of one he found a leather sphere. It fitted into the palm of his hand. He pressed a latch and the case opened to reveal a globe of the world.

Pure serendipity, he thought. Until, that was, he found a note from Professor Millar. The gift was intended to guide him in his most troubled hours.

Made by Miller's Instruments of Edinburgh, the professor wrote how it was one of the first globes ever to be made in Edinburgh perhaps, he hoped, the entire world.

Inspired, he returned to the report. Palmer suspected it would fall on deaf ears given that Campbell had treated him roughly at dinner. He placed the enormous encyclopaedia on his bunk and flicked through the page ends in search of papers he'd used as bookmarks.

They had gone. It wasn't just that he'd lost the pages of interest. The papers were letters of recommendation from England, crucial references for future business in Botany Bay. He remembered lending the encyclopaedia to Margarot earlier so he could read up on wine fermentation in hot climates. He hoped they'd been misplaced by accident but wondered about Margarot's intentions given his alliances at dinner.

*

Having given Palmer his bed so he didn't have to share with Kidlaw, Muir half awoke on deck the next day.

Something had been slipped beneath his head.

His eyes opened to lines of what seemed like barley, whereupon he slipped back into a dark groundless sleep.

An hour later, the globe prodded him as he rolled on his side. He awoke properly this time.

Sitting upright, he couldn't help but notice the number of women on board. Skirving had counted the passengers as if they were livestock. Sixty women. Only twenty three men. As he looked down the ship it seemed the farmer wasn't exaggerating the imbalance.

One woman had stood out from the others. She had sandy hair, a petit stature and a smile like the crescent moon. On boarding she'd caught his eye but he'd made no impression that he knew of.

As far as he was aware she was without a husband and by her demeanour, she seemed to care little for the ex-soldiers and sailors on board. As his heart stirred he studied the globe to work out their bearings. Somewhere between Britain and Rio. It was anyone's guess.

A little later, Palmer could be seen clambering towards him with two bags and the lurcher on a long lead.

'That thief can't take my valuables if I keep them on me.'

'I've handed the complaint in to Captain Campbell. In addition, the ship's steward and his wife tell me that they've also issued a complaint.'

'Against Kidlaw?'

Muir nodded.

'They saw him trying to steal my purse yesterday morning.'

'More witnesses, the better. Any response from Campbell?'

'No. Not yet. If truth be told he took little notice. He looked…'

'Drunk?'

'You said it not me, Reverend.'

'Thank you for giving me your bunk. Whose is that pillow?'

Muir looked where his head rested earlier and noticed for the first time, a pillow with an embroidered cotton cover. Picking it up he read the name sewed above the hem.

'Jane's I suppose. Perhaps not all the tailors on this ship are rogues like Draper.'

'I'm glad I resisted his requests for money, wish Mr Skirving had been more sensible.'

'So I bet does he given his reaction last night.'

The lurcher smelt the pillow's lavender fragrance. Muir's interest in scoundrels waned as he desired to meet the pillow's owner. No doubt, she would return.

'You know he gave that villain somewhere between thirty and forty shillings,' commented Palmer, 'a small fortune! This hound can't be in the same room as Draper.

143

Seen much of Margarot? I suspect he'll be with his wife if he's any sense.'

Muir hesitated. He didn't want to say anything that might broach the fellowship but he struggled to keep his observation from Palmer. 'When I delivered the complaint he was sharing breakfast with the captain.'

'You know he has asked Skirving to pay for the copies of 'An Englishman's Right addressed to Juries', which we distributed in Edinburgh. I suspect also he's taken my letters of recommendation from the Encyclopaedia, though that's only a suspicion at present.'

'There seems to have been a sea change in him. He still hasn't apologised for ignoring my warnings about Robert Watt. But I forgive his naivety. Good morning, Skirving.'

'Morning Tom… Captain wants to see us.'

'I hoped to wait here until Jane returned for the pillow.'

'It's starting to rain. We've business to attend to. Your little romance can wait.'

Soldiers manned the doorway as they entered the roundhouse. Kidlaw and Draper sat either side of the captain. As the ship lilted over they grasped their goblets of rum propelling Captain Campbell into his indictment.

'John Kidlaw tells me you, William Skirving, bribed him with thirty shillings to entice him into an attempted mutiny.'

'What? That's absolute rubbish.'

'Remember who you're talking to.'

'Captain Campbell, I gifted that money to Mr Kidlaw so he could buy goods to trade in Botany Bay.'

Kidlaw's eyes roll upwards as Skirving stated his good will.

'And Joseph Draper here also accuses you of mutiny from what he heard whilst fixing your clothes.'

'We've employed him for his trade and that alone.'

'Yes. Precisely.' The captain celebrated his supposed unravelling, 'not his abilities as a tailor but his abilities as an assassin. I'm glad to have him by my side not yours.'

'No, his abilities as a tailor, sir. You can see his handiwork in Mr Muir's shirt.'

'Thinks you had plans to assassinate me, to take the ship.'

'None of us can sail,' explained Skirving.

'So you considered it! Write that down, Kidlaw.'

'You're ordering a convicted forger to keep records?'

'There is not a shred of evidence against us.'

'Have these convicts put in irons!'

The soldiers led them up on deck.

As Muir turned back at his accusers he saw someone loitering in the drinks store wearing a long crimson jacket.

Ochre drips stained their ankles as the drizzle mixed with the salt corroded irons that shackled them to the stern castle. When shivers turned sporadically to convulsions the drips released like blood. Hearing boot steps they looked up to find a middle aged soldier.

'I'm Sergeant Reddish. I'll do my utmost to vindicate you.'

Palmer recognised him as the man that helped himself to his wine back in Southampton. Perhaps he wanted to repay his debts by lobbying for them. The Reverend was therefore encouraging until Muir butted in.

'We can do our own vindicating.'

'I'm the brother of Mr Canning.'

'And?'

'He's a Member of Parliament.'

'We're in the middle of the Atlantic!'

'What use is a connection with an MP out here? They're barely much use on land.'

He remembered the MP for Inverness who had attended the first meeting and wondered what part he had played in his sentencing.

Palmer apologised. 'Mr Muir doesn't mean to be so abrupt. We're grateful for your concerns. Write down your observations. We'd be glad to have you as a witness if this comes to court.'

When Sergeant Reddish finally left, Muir mumbled, 'Palmer, he's most possibly a spy employed by the government to keep us in check. Last thing I want is to be relying upon him to certify our innocence. That, he will not do.'

Looking out to sea, the sound of what Muir supposed was Reddish's returning footsteps fermented his anger some more until he yelled, 'what do you want now? I'm unable to sign over my allegiance! I am in irons!'

'That's no way to speak to a woman.'

Muir looked across. It was the person who'd lit up his face when joining the ship. He tried to undo his error by wriggling his backside off the flattened, half soaked cushion and dared to guess her name. 'Jane, thank you for making last night's sleep better than it might have been.'

'That's not my pillow.'

'Oh.'

That smile he so loved bridged her cheeks. 'I'm joking. We haven't much time. Keep it for now. Before Campbell sees me, there's food for tonight and sheets for you and your friends.'

'Mr Palmer. Pleased to meet you. That man asleep is Mr Skirving.'

'Keep them hidden till dark or you'll have them confiscated.' As she emptied her gifts inside their jackets, their irons stained her cotton white cuffs.

She then broke some bread and split it between them.

Boot steps could be heard behind. In a flash she lost herself between the deck dwellers despite being very much present in Muir's mind having made a rather dreadful day end rather jubilantly.

With his full mouth and a cheeky façade, Palmer garbled, 'she's a spy too is she?'

Muir stuffed his mouth some more to be excused from answering and envisaged a future with her. But just as this

146

new ray of hope emerged in his mind he caught sight of someone wearing a red jacket liaising with Captain Campbell by the door of the roundhouse. Palmer's jovial spirit became overcast.

'He's turned on us. He laughed with the captain when they belittled me at dinner. His conviction's corroded.'

'Palmer, your eyes aren't what they used to be. That's the captain's first mate, McPherson. Besides, we've Skirving, Jane and your Sergeant friend to help us, the MP's brother.'

'I'll be charged with bribing Draper for the purpose of murdering the captain. I gave him money for fixing my clothes.'

The unfairness coupled with Palmer's ill health pulled him briefly under. He was in no fit state to spend the night on deck.

'So, he's not sided with the captain?'

'No. Don't worry, Reverend. We aren't alone.'

*

Out of the bleak darkness, the sun, still deep beneath the horizon, blued the night sky. An hour from dawn the sea regained its darkness relative to the under lit clouds.

Eventually, the first specks of the sun's corona emerged.

Muir's eyelids rose with the new day.

Shaking off his sleepy logic he wondered how the sea always failed to drown the sun and how it always managed to keep burning amid the depths.

'Beautiful isn't it.'

Muir was startled.

He had been leaning on Jane.

'I brought you breakfast. You think Botany Bay's as bad as they say?'

'Must be some reason why it's been a deterrent against crime for the last decade. I don't know, Jane. Don't know what world awaits us. Are my friends asleep?'

'Yes.'

147

'I fear we've lost one of our companions to the captain. Are you willing to take his place?'

They looked across at Skirving. He was twitching. Dreaming of his orchard, so Muir imagined. It was ripe time for picking. The cold winds of dawn that had drenched his side had knocked some of the fruit to the ground and no one was there to pick them up, to stop them going to waste. Eventually, he awoke when flashes of a strangled orchard and weed choked field began to haunt his mind.

Jane and Muir noticed how their hair had bleached during the voyage. As they looked into each others eyes their minds learned for the first time where their hearts beat inside.

A few hours later Captain Campbell had everyone on deck; the hundred or so convicts, half that number of ex-soldiers and a handful of free people going over to start a new life in New South Wales.

Riddled with influenza, Palmer suffered the indignity of having a second set of irons placed around his wrists and ankles. But when fitting them, the soldier demanded a reason. Captain Campbell walked across, pulled out his pistol, held it against the soldier's temple and asked whether that was a good enough reason.

He then walked up to the bridge, knocking over a few children before declaring that he had uncovered a dangerous and bloody plot among the soldiers to excite a mutiny.

Those in the crowd pointed at each other jovially supposing their compatriots as mutineers. Arresting the mockery, Campbell fired his pistol in the air, insisting that soldiers had planned to murder him and the principal officers so they could take the ship to France or America.

Laughs and groans surfaced and amplified when a convict pointed upwards. Captain Campbell had blown a hole through the sail canvas. It was beginning to tear in the wind. Silence spread, however, when he pointed his pistol through the crowds.

'That man, his title, 'Reverend', is so ill placed. That man conspired to murder me.'

Palmer opened his eyes. In the same moment, Margarot stepped onto the bridge. He was furnished with some of the captain's arms, far more accurate pistols, Muir conceded, than their own.

'Even the Reverend's once close compatriots have warned against him,' claimed Campbell. 'Mr Margarot here told me two days ago to keep a watchful eye on the old gentleman.'

Palmer murmured, half to himself, that he was not so old.

Muir put his handkerchief to Palmer's mouth. 'Rest. You'll do no good aggravating yourself. Jane's with us now.'

The comforting words were interrupted by banging from above and behind. They looked around. Peeking out of the roundhouse were two blunderbusses mounted from the inside, swivelling from port to starboard.

Skirving, Palmer and he were done for, Muir thought.

'Draper? Where are you Draper?'

Campbell looked around the ship. One of the blunderbusses skied its aim and out stepped the tailor.

'Stay where you are. Tell those aboard what you told me last night.'

'Skirving and Palmer intended to murder you and the principal officers and run away with the ship. Palmer gave me money, tea, sugar, rum and clothes. He promised much more for the purpose of throwing you overboard.'

Palmer strained with rage.

'I readily agree to be hung up at the yard arm if it can be proved by a single credible witness that I have ever given Joseph Draper any one thing but a single glass of rum.'

Campbell grinned whilst looking for witnesses. Muir watched Kidlaw with contempt. Perhaps though the implications of speaking against Palmer this time were too serious even for him. The life affirming silence was broken by Palmer once again,

'I employed him as a tailor and paid him rather scantily for his work but never gave him a penny for any other purpose.'

149

This reminded Draper.

'Skirving gave me money, lots of money for the same purpose.'

The farmer was sickened by how Draper had treacherously converted charity into bribery. He noticed that his dove had left their cabin and landed on deck. He longed for its freedom. Slipping back inside the roundhouse, Draper dipped the blunderbuss barrel down at Skirving and Palmer like a crow's beak about to mutilate a worm.

As if given the nod by Draper, Kidlaw stepped forward.

'I heard them talking Erse, Irish Gaelic that is, to disguise their talk of mutiny.'

Muir reflected on the blind threat he'd heard in the prison hulk back in Leith. This is what Kidlaw had in mind for him.

Palmer couldn't believe what he was hearing.

'None of us know any Erse. Do you, Kidlaw?'

'No, Mr Palmer.'

'Reverend, to you... If you don't know any Erse how do you know when someone's speaking of mutiny in that tongue?'

Kidlaw seemed troubled, a robber and forger he might be, a clear thinker he was not.

Ellis was stirred by such lies. 'Kidlaw, back in Portsmouth you said the soldiers were going to mutiny. They've not. Only you seem to know their designs.'

'Shut up, young Ellis,' ordered Campbell. 'I believe you to be in a lewd relationship with that lifelong bachelor, the Reverend!'

As Ellis shook his head in disbelief. Campbell ordered his crew to arrest McPherson, which they did, circling around him like vultures.

'As of this moment you're stripped of your rank as first mate. Take him into custody.'

And on that order the crew carried down their one time superior in shackles to his cabin where he was made a prisoner.

Campbell justified his actions.

'I've it on good authority from this woman who's been a servant to McPherson that he was at the head of the mutiny plot.'

Muir and Palmer looked up trying to work out whom Campbell was pointing his near empty bottle of whisky, towards.

'Betsy.'

'Betsy?'

'Yes Palmer, Margarot's wife has also turned against us.'

By the judgement of a now emptied bottle of whisky, Campbell selected six soldiers. Muir hazarded a guess that it was fewer than he initially intended because he stumbled with his counting at around five. Along with the reformers, they were led towards the weather deck and placed in irons.

The soldiers had their shirts torn open whilst Campbell gave orders to various sailors and settlers to set up watches around the ship before returning with his whip.

Skirving was particularly disturbed by what followed.

Within half an hour the deck was awash with blood.

Amidst this cacophony of cruelty appeared an angel in Palmer's delirium that came to him with hugs from her father. It was the Boston's little girl. Only four years old. Palmer sought solace in her little shoulder that he gently rested his chin upon.

He then ushered her to be gone from this unholy place.

Ceaseless suffering specked the rigging and sails in more blood. The soldiers lay contorted and defeated as on a battlefield.

Later, a tempestuous storm came from the south west as if God himself was disgusted. The once blood red decks were awash with wave after wave of sea spray. All were baptised with a second chance apart from Campbell who whilst still covered in blood had sought shelter from the storm below.

Muir was sure a soldier had been lost over the side and thanked the Lord for the shackles that kept him and his friends aboard. He could tolerate being punch drunk from the relentless pummelling but if they were to go overboard, coral they would become. Beside him, Palmer lost the rhythm in taking gasps of breath between the soakings and looked at times as if he was drowning.

Eventually, during a lull in the storm Boston's little girl arrived again to hug the Reverend. Muir couldn't believe his eyes. Aware that Palmer might be too weak to hold onto her if the storms intensified, he grabbed her as she passed by.

'Be gone. This is no place for you.'

Mr and Mrs Boston appeared on the quarterdeck ready to retrieve their daughter. But she was swept off her feet. Not by a wave but by the newly arrived Captain Campbell who hauled her up by one arm like a rag doll.

'Are you handing that scoundrel messages?'

The little girl shook her head. Mr and Mrs Boston ran over.

'Have her flogged.'

'She's not five years old,' shouted Muir.

Campbell's drunk recruits each pulled up an arm lifting her off the deck again. The winds strengthened.

From their clutches Mrs Boston tried to claim her little girl.

'I will suffer for her.'

The soldiers dropped the child like a sack of spuds.

A wave washed the decks sending her sliding.

Muir reached out as far as his shackles would allow and by the grace of God grabbed her ankle.

'Go to your father after these waves have passed.'

The resurgent deck wash seemed to be building with the latest squall. He held her ankle, wishing for a cessation of the elements.

Meanwhile on the stern castle, away from the deck wash, Campbell ripped off Mrs Boston's blouse and took a step back to fly his whip. Each lashing cut into her and all who had the misfortune of seeing what took place.

The ordeal lasted an hour until the storm briefly relented and Mrs Boston was left nearly unconscious half naked on the deck, her bloom of youth and elegance violated but resilient. The only grace for her was that, part way through her assault, she was able to watch her girl return to her husband, unharmed.

Campbell then turned the whip on the Reverend. When it was all over Palmer looked unconscious. The irons were taking all his weight and as the storm built up on itself again, Muir feared the chains might snap.

A few hours later conditions became so torrential that two sailors crawled their way towards the Reverend and unclamped the irons before taking him down to his cabin.

Muir called out to them.

'I feared he would be lost overboard. Thank you.'

'Don't thank us. Thank the woman who bribed Campbell. She doesn't believe a man as ill as he should weather this.'

On his way to the less exposed deck, Palmer emerged from his inner retreat with the Lord, no longer needing to seek refuge within himself. Nearly every sailor and settler he passed was now armed. Unlike before, watches kept lookout at the bow, the bridge and the stern castle. The settlers had turned out volunteers to aid Captain Campbell in his extremity and for him they were willing to weather storms.

Back in his cabin, despite being close to death Palmer got straight to work drawing up a petition of those few sailors, settlers and passengers who were against Campbell's actions. He could hardly hold the quill at first but after severe exigencies he checked over his writing:

'Friday the thirty first of May 1794. The signatories below are concerned at the unhappy difference that has taken place between the first mate and yourself. They hope that Captain Campbell is not forgetful of the frailties of human nature arising from liquor or passion. They hope Captain Campbell will recollect the character he wishes to bear onshore, and that an instance of generous forgiveness, or of a temporary suspension, will not lessen him in the esteem of his numerous friends. There is none on board who is acquainted with the passage who possesses the nautical skill of Mr McPherson.'

Palmer nearly baulked at the polite language he was required to use. He wanted to tell the captain he was an insult to the human race but thought better of it.

Before he slept, he went about collecting signatories and remembered to give his walking stick to Mrs Boston. That, he did before collapsing in his bunk only to find that once again he was sharing it with his assailant, Kidlaw.

The next morning, a very drunk Captain Campbell dragged Palmer to the back of the ship before tearing up the petition and throwing the papers in his face.

Muir and Skirving had been released at sunrise. He was alone with the thought that he'd laboured hard to gain the signatures of many on the ship before dawn and it had come to nothing.

The power of one fool had overruled the sense of the majority. He came close to losing his temper, a potentially fatal mistake. It was hauled in only by the sight of something very welcome. Confused by what Palmer was looking at, Campbell turned to the bow and cursed that no one had informed him they were approaching Rio.

*

The *Swift*, a British sloop of war, fired a cannon on their arrival. Campbell moored to leeward. His oarsmen rowed him across. Palmer squatted at the stern, hands bound and hooded.

An officer helped them aboard.

'I'm seeking a court martial for this convict.'

After acknowledging Campbell, the officer threw back the hood. Palmer looked at his boots, contemplating the possible implications.

Utterly unexpectedly however, he heard his name and title. 'You do remember me, Reverend Palmer? I came to your services every Sunday.'

Palmer didn't. 'Of course I do.'

'Harting, I was just a boy then.'

'Yes, Harting. You have gone far.'

The coincidence was an incendiary inside Campbell's head.

His eyes bulged with anger.

'Why do you want Reverend Palmer under court martial?'

'Attempted mutiny.'

'And the evidence is?'

'Back aboard the *Surprise*.'

'Perhaps you could recount the evidence?'

Campbell spluttered. 'I have it on good authority from Mr Kidlaw and Mr Draper.'

'Officers of the ship?'

'Oh no, Harting. They are convicts. One is a lifer. The other is an assassin.'

Now below deck and having finished a lavish breakfast enjoyed as much by Palmer as by the others, the captain of the *Swift* pronounced that he believed Officer Harting's account of Palmer's character more than he did Captain Campbell and the convict's.

Campbell banged his hand on the table.

'Campbell, a captain of a naval ship overrules the authority of a transport ship captain. Do you hear me?'

Campbell was silent.

'Trouble me again whilst you're in Rio, I'll inflict on you twice the lashes you've inflicted on Palmer. What have you suffered, Reverend?'

'At least forty...'

'Then eighty it will be.'

Campbell clenched his jaw, swallowed his malice and left banging his head on the doorway.

'And remember you've no authority to try Reverend Palmer until you get to Botany Bay. I'll check you've obeyed this law when I arrive myself.'

Below deck Muir was warming himself against Jane. The thin sheets were the only things separating him from the debauchery of the cabin where linens seemed to be rising and falling as regularly as the white tops on the ocean.

Captain Campbell had, in the night, appeared from the roundhouse and whispered to him that it was Skirving and Palmer who he suspected as the ringleaders of the plot. Not himself. Classic divide and rule tactics in action. But sick of the suffering he had coalesced to gain a haven from the elements. He could in this sense understand Margarot's predicament. Perhaps he had wisely envisaged the captain's savagery.

A three quarters drank bottle of rum shielded him from the intimacies of the other cabin folk.

The copy of Godwin's book, *Things As They Are*, that Skirving had given him buckled his pillow. Gerrald's gift. He imagined his friend's circumstances. Latterly though, he indulged in Jane. She was reading furiously.

Further down the ship Skirving had been made to sleep in the same bed as Margarot, his accuser. Exhausted and cold he could not refuse. Had he, he would have been back in irons.

Earlier in the night Margarot had been woken by a figure Skirving thought might have been Draper. He went off to the roundhouse to speak to Captain Campbell. Skirving hoped Margarot would speak well of him and Palmer.

A good while later he returned.

Quite drunk.

As he clumsily got into bed with his blunderbuss, pistol and sword still on him, Skirving was pushed up against the hull.

Tormented, he asked Margarot why he hadn't told the captain that Palmer was in no fit state to mutiny given that his influenza had nearly made him unable to walk.

Swigging more wine, Margarot slipped into delirium.

*

Cries from above eventually woke Muir from Jane's side. He studied her lines as she came to the bottom of another page and retrieved Godwin's novel from beneath his pillow.

Escaping into the story would free him of his duties at least for a little while. But it was to be tested by the cries for help. He was however just too tired to deal with anything but fiction.

His reading however was punctured by old anxieties; Palmer and Skirving's suffering, born of the protagonist's predicament.

Now well into volume two, the anguish of Caleb's imprisonment with the wretched inmates was a shadow of realities aboard. For every one of Godwin's villains they had perhaps double that to keep their eyes on.

As far as the mutiny charges went he could remove himself from the allegations. For some reason Campbell had steered them away from him perhaps fearing his abilities as an advocate.

He slipped into Caleb's world. There was light at the end of the tunnel. A servant of the antagonist, Falkland, had supplied Caleb with tools to aid his escape into the wild.

Muir's own wilderness would be the woman by his side. And the text perhaps. The ocean as he had discovered last night provided no habitable wilderness in which to escape.

*

The convicts weren't allowed ashore in Rio but by bartering from on deck they could purchase goods from the dockside. It was during one such deal that Palmer found a note being slipped into his pocket.

Not wanting to lose what he had haggled for - a lime tree, a lemon tree and an orange tree for two shillings - he did not turn to identify the messenger.

Next to him was poor Mr Skirving, poor in spirits and in pocket. He had the misfortune of watching Kidlaw and

Draper, with his own money, outbid Palmer on some more fruit trees he was buying for Skirving.

As night fell Palmer was offered his cabin back under the outrageous conditions; sharing it solely with Kidlaw.

These were the games Campbell played.

Feverish, Palmer had no choice but to concede. What Kidlaw said in the cabin never registered in his mind, though. One of the unexpected benefits of the fever was delirium. It was as much a sedative to the taunts of his accuser as death was a protector from the excesses of pain.

Undressing, he remembered the note that had been slipped in his pocket. It was from Muir. He promised to join hand and heart with him in the vindication of his innocence.

He would bring his oppressors to justice.

Palmer almost wanted to show it to Kidlaw to make it clear what he was up against but thought concealment far wiser. He and Muir had not been on the best of terms since his retreat into rum and romance but Palmer was prepared to forgive him with his usual magnanimity. Kidlaw couldn't compute the confidence Palmer had found and slept uneasily.

In the early hours Campbell burst into the cabin. The lurcher bolted. Crewmen smashed the chest locks as Palmer tried to demonstrate that they were in fact open, emptying the chest's contents everywhere.

Campbell was satisfied when a pistol, a gun and a sword banged onto the cabin floor unravelling out of rolled up trousers and shirts. He confiscated them along with the lurcher. It gave out a reluctant whine, dragging its paws along the deck until it could no longer be seen or heard.

'God save the King! Everyone on deck!'

A thunderous bang ringed in Muir's ears as the explosion of gunpowder pervaded every one of the ship's timbers.

He put down the novel and scratched the back of his head.

After a few minutes he realised it was George III's birthday.

Whatever despotic rituals Campbell had in mind, he considered it only fair that he should go up on deck alongside Jane with the novel in his hand. Written by Godwin, the well known anarchist of the day, it was a small act of defiance. He suspected it would be lost on Campbell. He might even promise him the book after reading it himself.

Out on deck, Rio was close to slipping under the horizon.

Botany Bay would be their next sight of land.

As they sang the national anthem Skirving put Muir in the picture.

'Yesterday, Bet Carter, the McPherson lass and Gilthorpe's girl, were all put in irons. Girls for God's sake, put in irons.'

Jane shook her head and looked out to sea. 'Throw a stone and you get sent to Botany Bay. Shoot a protester and you get a new pair of socks.'

Muir remembered what Skirving had told him years back and asked her whether she was referring to the weavers' riots.

'I lost my father that day. He was one of the six shot dead.'

He tried to see the riots through the prism of Jane's loss but this was overshadowed by more recent atrocities.

'I've never heard anything like it,' whispered Skirving. 'Bet fainted on deck after denying the plot. When she came to, they hoisted her up and flogged her. There she is now being dragged out of her cabin for this nonsense. They tried to get McPherson's lass to testify against her own father, the first mate.'

A pessimism brought on by the rum from last night dogged Muir. Campbell was looking straight at him. He clenched Jane's hand in his and mimed 'God save the King'. Then he leant behind Skirving and patted Palmer on the shoulder.

The King's Birthday riots of 1792 were on both their minds. Standing in George Square, conceiving of the Society, asserting its pacifist and constitutional remit, meeting Tytler that night in the pub... look where it had got them.

Tytler had fled to America and after two years of promoting reform, they were miming the national anthem to celebrate a King who had brought inexcusable misery on their lives and the lives of their countrymen.

Perhaps Godwin's anarchism would have been more productive. Maybe they should have taken up arms against the King. After the national anthem, Skirving left and returned with a tray of glasses and a bottle of port.

Muir needed cheering up. Glasses were offered to Mr and Mrs Boston. Holding the walking stick in one hand and her little girl's hand in the other, she leant against her husband and returned the stick to Mr Palmer so she could take a glass. She'd clearly learned from someone that he had been dispossessed that morning.

To finish the bottle, Skirving gave the last two glasses to the sentinels nearby and then returned to the ship's store to dispose of the tray.

For the first time there was an air of joviality aboard.

Few genuinely liked the King but it was an excuse to lift the mood that had suffered since Campbell had announced his discovery of the supposed plot. The goats roaming the deck were a perpetual amusement as they chewed on skirts, dresses and anything else at their level.

Skirving returned on deck with a cask of strong ale for all to enjoy. Friendships were made between the unacquainted. Cabel Williams became a point of interest. Muir and Jane made their mutual interest in each other public.

The journey had become almost enjoyable. Until, that was, Captain Campbell arrived from the bow carrying a chewed up fruit tree.

'Who gave port to these sentinels?'

'I did, Captain Campbell.'

'Why, Mr Skirving?'

'To celebrate the King's birthday.'

'Really.'

'Yes.'

'They're protecting the ship from mutineers like you.'

'I am no mutineer, Captain Campbell.'

'You hope they'll drop their guard if they're drunk.'

'No, Captain Campbell'

'And who brought this barrel on deck?'

'Me, also.'

Campbell shook his head swigging port straight from the bottle. 'Sentinels, take this barrel below deck and do not let Mr Skirving anywhere near it or, for that matter, any of the ship's stores.'

'He meant no harm, Captain Campbell.'

Barely had one of the young sentinels finished uttering the captain's name, when Campbell had him by the throat and was pushing him to the stern castle, still holding the trunk of the fruit tree in his other clenched fist. They all knew what awaited him.

Campbell returned with just the tree. 'I have it on Kidlaw's authority that you, Palmer, maliciously destroyed his fruit trees. You came out here in the middle of the night to destroy them because he outbid you for them. Is this true?'

'Captain Campbell, they look like the claw marks of a cat and the teeth marks of a goat. You really think I'd chew on the leaves of a tree all night?'

Campbell didn't like being made to look stupid. Palmer pointed to one of two goats chewing on the hem of Jane's dress.

Skirving helped the remaining sentinel take the barrel below deck before guilt seeped into his soul. The ship's store was directly below where the young sentinel was being flogged and as they waddled the barrel down the corridor, his screams grew louder, stealing from them the port's warmth.

Muir and Jane had left when Skirving returned. Just as Campbell was walking back from the stern, Palmer confronted the captain.

'I paid for mine and Mr Ellis' cabin in Portsmouth. He never received his. You gave it to some convict woman who served you in it and now you are taking Mr Skirving's cabin, too?'

'You and Skirving will sleep together. I'll show you the bed myself.'

They followed Campbell flanked by three soldiers whose uniforms didn't quite fit. Then Palmer realised why. They were once the property of the accused. On the way they past the sentinel who was creased double lying in his own blood.

Below deck, Palmer and Skirving were thrown into a hovel of a cabin. Judging by the damp, it was below the waterline. Palmer was aghast. 'The bed is not two feet wide. How can two bulky men like us, sleep together in that?'

'Consider it practice. You'll soon be sleeping in narrower ones.'

They both knew Campbell was facetiously referring to coffins. The soldiers didn't laugh despite being ushered to do so.

But neither did they object.

'I demand a speedy and vigorous trial.'

'Mr Skirving, you'll be kept prisoner till I say any different. If that's the five months it takes to get to Botany Bay, so be it.'

Now alone, they sat with their backs against the hull. 'We purchased cabins and we were made to live with the soldiers. Now we are being made to live like felons. Where is the rule of law?'

Before Palmer could answer the question a spout of water poured through a gap in the hull where the oakum had deteriorated.

It went straight down Skirving's back.

'They have deprived me of the ship's stores. It was precisely what he threatened me with if I didn't pay for Ellis' cabin.'

'I'll share my food with you.'

Inspecting the mutineers chained to the hindmost part of the ship, Campbell listened to their groaning. The sun was relentless and the winds were fickle. Their skin was nearly as red as their lashes and a gnawing hunger tormented their innards.

'Punishment will be inflicted weekly till such time as you are hanged at the yardarm.'

'We know of no plot,' they shouted.

'How much are you feeding them?'

The corporal left his conversation with the gunners in the roundhouse.

'A biscuit and a half per day and three ounces of salt meat.'

'And how much water?'

'A quart.'

'Reduce it to a fifth.'

Casswell, one of the enchained men, lost it.

'You can't do this. You don't have the authority of any court, civil or military. A court martial that sits on life or death should consist of at least seven officers. We demand a lawyer.' He raised his voice. 'Muir! Help us!'

Campbell clamped Casswell's mouth.

'One more word out of you and I'll have the corporal run you through. I am always here, Casswell, even when I'm not on deck I am below you listening, waiting for you to cry or rattle one link in your chains, waiting to fire my pistols through the top of my cabin. I might hit anyone of you so don't endanger your accomplices with your whining. Four nights on deck should drill some sense into all of you. Wake me and I'll send you to sleep for a lifetime. Has Gilthorpe been flogged? Have him flogged if not. Whip the truth out of him if need be.'

*

Taking his midday walk down the ship, Muir spotted the accused doubled up with their chins and knees close together. He asked them whether they knew of Skirving and Palmer's whereabouts. They couldn't help.

163

Three floors below them Palmer was worrying about his lurcher. Skirving and he were taking turns sitting next to the locked cabin door where the draft eased the rotten heat of the stagnant little stowage space.

Palmer sensed another illness hibernating inside. Both were furious they had been forbidden books, papers, pens and ink. The gaps in the hull had spouted more water. Their bed sheets were perpetually wet with salt water that never dried.

The captain brought down dinner himself as if to revel in their suffering. The lurcher heaved towards Palmer when it saw its master but Campbell belted it hard for its disobedience.

Palmer asked whether they could have fresh bed sheets.

'What've you done crapped yourself old man?'

Palmer lifted the drenched cotton linens off the floorboards.

'No, Captain Campbell, I haven't.'

'Pissed yourself then? You live like animals.'

'Holes in the ship soak us.'

'They'll be repaired in Botany Bay. Don't worry about that.'

Palmer stood holding the sheet like a drowned ghost.

'I want my clothes, Captain Campbell. I've worn this vestment for a month now.'

Campbell left without even so much as muttering a response.

An hour later the door rattled against the frame. Palmer hobbled over bracing himself against his walking stick. Kidlaw appeared. The room took on an even more sinister feel than when Campbell was there.

'All your belongings are mine now, gentlemen. The captain has sent me to…'

Kidlaw seemed to treasure the orders he'd been given, so much so that he couldn't finish his remark. His hands were greyed with dirt from a whetstone he'd used to sharpen his cutlass blade.

'Finish us off?'

'Aye.'

Again Kidlaw couldn't understand Palmer's confidence. Neither could Skirving who was still resting on the boards and trying to get up as quickly as possible, seeing that his friend would soon receive a fatal blade wound.

'Has he now,' Palmer murmured.

The floorboards creaked above them as Muir, armed to the hilt, searched cabin by cabin for his friends. A dulled 'Palmer?' and an even duller, 'Skirving?' made their soundings through the oakum.

'Here, Thomas.'

'Shut up. He's in the wilderness. You don't have a hope in hell's chance.'

Working his way back through the bowels of the ship Muir realised that to save money Captain Campbell had reduced two messes to one. It was heaving with freemen and their families eating dinner.

In the twilight he studied every face hoping it was either Palmer's or Skirving's but all he saw was gluttony and greed. One figure stayed fixed on his plate. Muir recognised his portly build. As he sat next to him on the bench he remained fixed on his dinner.

'Mr Muir you do yourself no favours haranguing on behalf of Palmer and Skirving. You don't understand the world they're now in.'

'I know that innocent men shouldn't succumb to injustice.'

'Leave Palmer and Skirving to their fate. They're sure to be hanged. The convict cook, Gilthorpe, confessed and signed the declaration. The evidence amounting doesn't bode well for them.'

At the head of the table was Captain Campbell. Muir approached. The captain cleared his throat but spoke quietly. 'If you can find them, tell your friends I've fixed today as the day they'll be hanged. That's if they've not been finished off already.'

As the intruder lunged towards Palmer there was a desperate exhalation of breath.

From whom, Skirving couldn't quite determine.

He was at a loss to fathom what had just happened.

Until, that was, Kidlaw tumbled out of the cabin half folded in on himself. Palmer turned to reveal a long thin blade.

'The sword is mightier than the knife. Or certainly longer!'

'Where did you get that from?'

'This isn't any old walking stick.'

IX
30° 12' S
065° 54' E

Frustrated by another search of the ship and unable to do anything until his friends showed up, Muir read volume three of Godwin's book, *Things As They Are.*

Caleb Williams had so far lived a life of evasion from Falkland's attempts to find and silence him but he had been robbed by a band of criminals and physically attacked by one of them.

He looked down the gangway at Kidlaw, Captain Campbell and Draper, whom he modelled the criminals on in his mind.

As he read on, Caleb's saviour turned out to be the captain of the thieves. Would such a sea change occur in Campbell he wondered?

Watching James Gilthorpe place down the captain's dinner whilst still suffering from the flogging, he thought it a little late in the day for enlightenment.

Walking past the volunteer watches out on deck he saw something to windward that had eluded them entirely. Too busy suspecting enemies within they'd failed to notice a huge ship bearing down on them from the west.

Smoke then bellowed from a cannon.

Campbell went aboard HMS *Suffolk.*

Within an hour the tender had returned through the huge South Atlantic swell. To collect whom, he wondered.

Muir feared for Palmer and Skirving. He would be of no use here if they were taken prisoner aboard one of His Majesty's naval ships.

The oarsmen listened to his demands to go with Palmer and Skirving to act as their advocate but then explained that it was McPherson whom Commodore Captain Rainier had agreed to detain.

Palmer and Skirving would remain aboard, thankfully. Hearing from the oarsman that storms were expected, Muir reminded himself to check the security of the printing press.

Up on deck and with night beckoning, Manila hemp part mummified Palmer around the foremast. Each coil restricted his breathing. The captain had collared him after his escape from the ship's dungeon, but not Skirving. Yet.

The Reverend marked the ship's progress against the rate at which waves broke over the foredeck, the spray whipping his ankles as the torrents surged across the deck.

Loneliness was broken only by bad company. Captain Campbell walked the lurcher and his bulldog the length of the ship from the stern castle.

His own dog pulled like a fool. The lurcher dragged itself back. Until, that was, it caught sight of its loving owner.

Now competing to reach the foremast first, the bulldog took a chunk out of the lurcher's shoulder to which it retaliated with a bite to the bulldog's ear.

Sea spray seemed to separate the dogs momentarily. Palmer considered shouting at his hound but conceded that this would only draw it further into the bulldog's domain.

As the seawater streamed along the deck both dogs lost their footing and slid on their sides pulling Captain Campbell with them towards the leeward gunwale and into the ensuing dogfight.

As the ship levelled, drips of blood mushroomed diluting with the wet deck. The lurcher's left eye socket was spilling blood. The bulldog was panting with a bloody tongue. Captain Campbell was using his cuff as a bandage to put pressure on his own wound.

'Your dog just bit me.'

'It's yours that has blood down its jowls.'

'My own dog wouldn't bite me. Yours will have to go.'

'No!'

Campbell grabbed the lurcher and lifted it over the gunwale into the unforgiving sea. The wind heeled the ship angrily as if objecting to the injustice.

'I had to do it. This would never heal had that devil stayed aboard.'

Palmer yelled, not to Campbell but to God and as the ship broached, violently heeling over, his disbelieving eyes witnessed the ship cut deep into the black ocean to haul the lurcher back aboard.

Its rod like legs caught themselves in the shrouds.

The bulldog licked its master's wounds.

'I understand, Campbell. You'd never have recovered. You did what you had to.'

As they talked, Palmer saw Muir appear from behind the printing press. He was stamping all over the deck in an attempt to stand on the lurcher's lead. The Reverend kept Campbell talking and tried not to smile whilst he watched his dog being led below deck before the next broach.

Later that night, with only days until they expected to dock at Botany Bay, Campbell hoped to trial Palmer and Skirving before reaching dry land. That way he wouldn't be compromised by the governor's power. But the arrival of the *Swift* into Botany Bay haunted his mind. Chained to the benches of the roundhouse, the two prisoners demanded a copy of the charges and Muir as their counsel.

Campbell remembered his last sighting of the advocate, drunk with Jane. 'Mr Muir is incapable of acting as counsel.' He then reflected on the implications of running a trial without declaring the charges.

The governor knew about Skirving and Palmer. If they arrived hanged men he would want to see evidence of a legitimate trial having taken place. Breaching the law could terminate his transportation contracts with the government.

Further down the ship, Jane and Muir were asleep. That was until he found something licking his face. With no light coming in from the shutter it took him some time to realise that it was the lurcher.

The cabin was dark but the other women were collecting their possessions together. The lurcher bolted to the bang of Jane's oaken travelling chest landing where moments ago it had lay.

'Thank you,' muttered Muir.

The obstinate woman, who he had seen welcome no fewer than five men to her bunk on one evening, smiled debunking his sarcasm.

A few dark minutes past before he accepted sleep was no longer possible in the cabin. Opening his eyes again one eye looked at the blur of the pillow, the other ebbed in and out of focus on Jane's trunk. It was marked with a large 'J'.

Then, to his astonishment, the surname; Lambert.

He couldn't believe that their paths had crossed.

Inside his jacket pocket was her letter that he'd kept close to him all this time. The woman sleeping by his side had inspired him to set up the Society in the first place. She must have been caught boarding a ship on the west coast or unable to pay the rising fares.

He wanted to wake her to find out the nature of her capture but she was deep in sleep, a freedom he did not want to take from her.

Why didn't she say she'd come to be his client? She knew his surname after all. He, Palmer and Skirving weren't quite famous on the ship but they had established a degree of unwarranted infamy. She may have been embarrassed by her failed escape, perhaps.

He went out on deck and looked at the stars considering the forces of his own destiny. Something had driven Jane and him together, a providence divine not mere circumstance.

Something ethereal consecrated their union.

He thought back to Elisabeth, the only other woman he'd attempted in any sense to love.

Only betrayal had been harvested in that union.

When Muir returned Campbell was inside the cabin.

Jane had pulled the sheets up to her chin.

Her eyes were closed to his lewd gaze.

Muir checked the dog was still under the bunk and donned his jacket.

'It concerns Palmer's conduct.'

At first he doubted the Captain's reason for going into his cabin suspecting he had gone in purposely when Jane was alone.

But he couldn't say as much.

'Captain Campbell, I think it proper to say that Palmer is entitled to a copy of all the charges brought against him in order that he may be able to make out his defence.'

'No defence is necessary. No court of justice exists aboard. I'm not his prosecutor.'

'Then why have you confined Palmer?'

'He was not confined by me.'

'But you retain him in custody?'

Campbell's nose lifted as he reluctantly nodded.

'Then it's the same thing,' Muir reasoned. 'Every jailer is obliged to give a copy of the charges against the person he's charge of. But you are accountable for your own actions and you know best how to act.'

He seemed quite tactfully to have curbed the captain's powers but as Jane lowered her legs over, she stood on a paw protruding from under the bed. A sallow yelp muffled by the overhanging sheets caught Captain Campbell's ear at the door. Muir inhaled a deep breath and buried his head in his hands.

The captain undid the collar and looped it through a hoop on the end of a long pole then reattached it two holes further up the leather. Kicking the lurcher over the side, he let the pole slip past his hand's half healed lacerations until the dog hit the water.

Just as it looked up at Campbell, he forced the pole downwards submerging its head deep underwater. Palmer prayed hopelessly as its back legs kicked in a fury. Then, as if his prayers were answered the dog seemed to cork out of the water.

The collar floated by the dog's side.

But as the dog paddled yards away from the ship still choking from its ordeal, Campbell ordered the sails to be filled and turned to Palmer and Skirving.

'Consider yourselves very lucky. Your trial will now have to take place on land.'

Palmer was cut by the indecent grimaces from many on board but soothed by Jane Lambert's tears and comforted by Muir who watched the seemingly infinite eye contact between him and the lurcher as it drifted towards his horizon and into the inescapable ocean.

'I shouldn't have sent Campbell to your cabin. It wasn't your fault, Jane. I should have remembered about the dog. I couldn't reason. I was just so tired.'

Taking Jane's mind off the dog's suffering and sympathising with her own, Muir asked about the circumstances of her capture. Through the sobs she explained that she had been in a safe house for months when she finally made it to the west coast. They were out of sight of land when a naval frigate searched the ship. Freedom was in their grasp. Back on land, Gathersby tried to help all he could with the court case.

'He said you were abroad,' Jane murmured.

'I was in France. It must've been when I was on bail.'

'Gathersby said a trial might be possible if he could persuade Martin-Shore to represent me. It came to nothing.'

'He'd have made you pay. You were better off without him.'

'You know him?'

'He was the prosecutor at my trial. My fiancé knew him intimately.'

X
34° 00' S
151° 14' E

By hand signals from Kidlaw in the crow's nest, Campbell steered between the rocky outcrops to port and starboard. Fog had hidden the open water leading to the penal colony making it seem necessary to navigate past the rocks on the southern shore.

Muir knew they were close when he spotted a convict stranded on one such rock. Burned red and peeling, cooled only by the intermittent clap of sea spray springing up from the shelf below, the convict tried to divide his last piece of bread for now and later but it broke up into crumbs and he ended up struggling to salvage it from the rock face.

It was then that he noticed the convict ship passing silently by and decided to risk leaving the rock that he had been stricken on for the last two weeks, his punishment for assaulting a soldier of the colony. Only Muir had noticed the convict slipping into the water.

Leaving the company of Palmer and Skirving he kept one eye on the convict, the other eye on his own route to the back of the ship.

Captain Campbell was too busy looking at Kidlaw's arm signals to notice him aft of the wheel and luckily for the convict, the eddying currents had drawn the ship closer to him.

It would be a close call and now leaning over the ship's fantail, Muir agonised that the convict wasn't going to grasp hold of the rudder below. He flung a rope over the side that unravelled itself as the ship sailed away from its landing spot.

Increasingly, the coils were straightening out and frantically the convict kicked his way towards the rope's bitter end but he was still some way off and the ship's progress was beginning to take up nearly all of the rope's slack.

Muir cheered when finally the convict grabbed the rope and when questioned by Campbell for his outburst he defiantly exclaimed that he was simply pleased to have made it alive to New Holland.

The mist swallowed up the *Surprise's* customary two gun salute but in time a two storey government house with gardens down to the water's edge, punctured the blank visage.

As they docked, Governor Grose left his chair under the veranda and approached soon covering his nose with a handkerchief, from the ship's petulant stench.

Muir was keen to see who he had defied by helping the convict. He studied with great amusement, how the governor's large backside filled the loosely cut seat of his skin tight breeches, how his dimpled double chin slopped over his tight collar and how he used his cane as a walking stick.

Having raided the sea stores after the *Canada's* aborted voyage, he'd once been as large but this voyage had left him with a lean figure comparable to that of his youth. He could see why this man needed a small army to achieve his ends and wondered how long he would be his master.

Up the banks were one storey brick houses that looked onto orderly vegetable gardens tendered to by the diligent wives of soldiers.

As they neared it was apparent that the mist was seaborne and had not encroached upon the hinterland. A network of small wooden bridges joined areas separated by rivers. Palmer was first to point out natives at the top of the mound where some of the indigenous trees had been felled.

They longed to trek around the colony that afternoon. It was not quite the hell they had come to expect from rumours back in Scotland but all that was possibly about to change when they noticed Captain Campbell pacing to the governor's house with a monstrous bag of charges principally against Skirving and Palmer, which if unchallenged would lead them to the gallows.

Settled on their possessions by the quayside beneath the bow of the huge convict ship with the saffron sun easing their woes, they found a quill, paper and a pot of ink.

Palmer leant against the *Encyclopaedia Britannica* to begin scrolling a new petition in which they asserted that their accuser, Captain Patrick Campbell, was the principal conspirator who had black and malignant motives and had attempted to extort evidence against them using promises, bribes, threats and torture.

The Reverend and Skirving agreed that they meant without delay to institute a criminal charge against Campbell for subornation of perjury and for attempting to deprive them of their characters and lives, demanding his immediate arrest until such time as his trial could be concluded. Slipping a clean vestment over his head, Palmer marched up to the governor's house.

As they waited, a colony officer dropped a bagful of post at Muir's feet. Cracking one of the envelope's wax seals, an elaborately written letter revealed itself.

'Well, what does it say?'

He started again from the beginning, this time reading it aloud for Skirving. 'The cause in which you are embarked and to which you have born an honourable testimony is worthy of every exertion, and its importance to the world is too great to expect its accomplishment without opposition. Men may perish but truth will prevail.'

He skipped a long winded section.

'Our best wishes will ever attend you and we do believe that the day is not very distant when we shall again receive you on British shores, the welcome children of a free and happy country. By order of The Society.'

Skirving laughed. 'We haven't been granted official permission onto these shores yet.'

Looking up from the letter, Muir found Palmer returning in a state of flux. Patches of sweat had appeared under each armpit and his forehead was bedewed with frustration.

The governor was clearly in two minds.

175

As they waited, the shadows of their heaped possessions grew longer encroaching up the bank to the governor's house. As the evening drew on, settlers who had heard of their efforts for parliamentary reform, stopped to talk to them. Scots in the colony had a reputation for being the hardest, most dangerous and most feared but the reformers were different.

Muir made idle chat but soon felt gawped upon like a caged parrot and grew sick of their exotic status so went through his post to avoid any more introductions.

One letter was from Gathersby. He'd not seen or heard from him for two years.

To his amazement their chambers had recently folded.

Checking the address he noted the letter was from America.

His former clerk relayed how the ruling judges, favourites of the Tory government, had become so corrupt they were prejudicing against clients with Whig and reformist lawyers, so much so that guilty sentences were being handed out regardless of the evidence.

None of Muir's former colleagues could find anyone to represent because the barristers had been tarred with guilty verdicts and no one would go near them.

Some moved to Tory chambers. Those with backbones changed professions. He'd believed that Edinburgh, the court and the offices he'd shared with his colleagues had been lost to him. Now it seemed that world had changed for all liberal minded people.

Gathersby also reported how Henry Erskine had been deposed from his position of Dean of the Law Faculty for opposing the war against France.

The establishment was being cleansed of 'disagreeables' so the government could continue doing as it pleased regardless of public opinion and common sense.

Palmer noticed Kidlaw walking out of the governor's house. He took a wide arc back to the convict ship trying to avoid them at the quayside.

The Reverend was furious at the injustice he'd caused.

'What lies did you spout in there, you scoundrel?'

'Just truths, that the high court received a letter from Captain Ogilvie, stating you were mutinous not only on the *Surprise* but also aboard the *Royal George*.'

The altercation withdrew Muir from his imaginings of a Scottish establishment tearing at itself over the decision to fight the French.

Jane and Skirving, who had been watching the sunset under the arc of the ship's cut-water, were now as alert as he to the ensuing disagreement between Palmer and Kidlaw.

'That letter to the high court in Edinburgh was forged by you. I know your plan. You're a lifer but you hope to be pardoned for your services to the state. I saw you sign the letter in Ogilvie's hand.'

Palmer's voice was beginning to falter so Muir stepped in.

'We've asked Captain Ogilvie to write to Governor Grose to clarify that we were fine company on the *Royal George*. No doubt he has a bag of mail to get through as extensive as ours. But eventually the truth will be known. It's telling you're without any letters. You've adopted so many identities in your pitiful little life I suspect nobody knows to whom your post should be addressed! You've perhaps forgotten who you are, a Christian sin if ever there was one.'

Kidlaw boiled inside.

'I was Sheriff Clerk Depute of Inverness Shire'.

The others laughed.

He slipped his hand into one of his pockets. Fear consumed them all as the sun dropped below the horizon and dusk settled. They wondered what Kidlaw had in mind, what darkness he intended to cause.

But behind them, on the bow of the *Surprise* a figure loomed out of sight of all but Kidlaw.

Momentarily distracted, he looked up to see who it was but only the man's outline was visible. Ignoring the figure, he pulled out a nine inch blade and moved towards Muir.

Suddenly, the figure on the deck moved erratically and with his eyes on the others, Kidlaw didn't catch sight of the projectile flying down from the bow.

As the others saw it come into view, he took a step back but it wasn't enough. It smacked his arm with a cracking sound, flinging the blade onto the ground before shattering into three pieces of oak. It was some type of rigging block but Muir had his attention on the knife which he grabbed.

He then looked up to see who had come to his rescue.

But the ship's bow was now abandoned.

Muir looked back at his attacker but he was now clambering up the gangplank, tending to his injured if not broken arm. Eventually, as night fell a soldier came down the bank to tell them that Governor Grose had allowed them to go about the colony as they pleased. Relieved that they wouldn't have to stay aboard the convict ship, they took a box each, lit an oil lamp and walked over to their designated huts in the next cove.

*

Dreaming of the newly landed rogues of the colony in a perverse distortion of the forthcoming court case featuring Campbell as the prosecution, Kidlaw as the judge and Draper as a one man jury, Muir woke himself up and eventually emerged with his head on the mailbag that had doubled up as a pillow for the last few weeks.

Representing his friends against Campbell was foremost in his mind until he noticed an envelope that had spilled out during his disturbing night's sleep.

Inside was a letter from his parents. To his delight, they'd written to the President of the United States asking him to help their son. He wished he'd come across the letter earlier. It would have made adjusting to the colony so much easier. Lifting a shutter, he gazed out across Port Jackson and pictured an American ship at anchor, the star spangled ensign fluttering over the transom.

Just as he was fitting his braces, a man barged in to his cabin. A box concealed his face. He wondered whether it was one of the rogues. The intruder revealed himself to be Palmer. Slipping his hand into the box he unclenched his hand to reveal a mound of earth and at its peak, a disorientated worm.

'This is capital soil. Skirving will have a field day here. He's asked for a hundred acres. He'll be in his element. The climate is delicious. It has banished my influenza. The animals are grotesquely beautiful, not this worm but yonder up in that tree?'

Kaleidoscopically coloured lorikeets could be seen pruning each other.

'There are two of them in this, I bought it from one of the soldier's wives.'

Next to the soil sample, Palmer pointed to a pie. Pressed into the pastry were two beaks. Slipping a slice down his gizzard, he waited for the taste.

'Parrot for breakfast. Divine. Far better than cormorant I suspect! There is double the daylight hours compared to when I left Scotland. And they told us Botany Bay was a hell like no other, more fool them.'

'But we're not free,' Muir reminded Palmer.

'We're freer than we were on that blasted ship. That reminds me. I conversed with an artist in need of legal representation. What was his name? Watling! That's right. I pointed out your hut. He's in the woods finishing off a canvas. I should also mention I've expelled Margarot from our society. I intend to begin a narrative of my sufferings aboard the ship with the intention of having it heard in Westminster and published in England for the public to make their own minds regarding my character.'

Beyond the embankments where the trees had been felled and land levelled for the settlement, lay a cooler arbour of eucalyptus and gums.

Just into the woods lay all manner of workshops from a carpenter's shed to a blacksmith's forge, a wool shed and at the end, a hut with piles of grapes outside where Muir guessed, settlers were distilling wine.

The sporadic hammering, sawing and mulching was laced in a fugue of birdsong tantamount to an orchestra of the wilds.

Occasionally, when the hammering intensified and halted... ...so too would the wildlife... as if they were curious as to what was being made.

Muir stood at what seemed its epicentre until he noticed a walker surrounded by aboriginal children. Some of them had bone or straw through the middle cartilage of their noses. The man strolled with an easel and canvas, on which was a miniature world of the surrounding scenery.

'Watling!'

'Mr Muir? The advocate?'

'I need not ask your profession.'

'The painting's a commission from the governor.'

The natives ran off into the wilds.

'I've learned each of their surnames; Terribi-long, Benna-long, Bye-gong and Wye-gong. Did the Reverend tell you about my troubles?'

'I've my work cut out representing him. But I'll find time to help you too.'

'I'll pay you with my art if you please. I'm sure you wouldn't say no to a self portrait.'

'If you portray me as affably as I'll will you in court.'

'Deal. Mr Palmer seems to have put his court case to the back of his mind. He's in that last workshop. When I left he had his face in the biggest book I've ever seen. Said something about boat building.'

'That's news to me. I left him eating parrot pie in my hut. Whatever documents you have pertaining to the charges, put them under my bed. The hut's open. In fact, put them in the mail bag for safekeeping.'

Passing each workshop until Palmer's, Muir found the Reverend dragging a table outside into the light. Blueprints for a rowing boat baked in the sun. Boston's little girl studied them with curiosity.

'Thought we'd better start with a small project.'

Palmer pointed up to a board above the workshop doorway.

'Boston and Company' was written in white paint.

It hadn't yet dried.

'I thought I'd help the Boston family after what they suffered trying to help me in the storm. Though he is a republican, Mr Boston is a supporter of my friend, Joseph Priestley. He's hard working too and Jenny has agreed to be our secretary once she's learnt to write and add up.'

'I'm thinking of doing something piscatorial.'

Palmer looked up, utterly confused. 'Sorry?'

'I'm thinking of becoming a fisherman.'

'Wasn't our voyage enough to put you off such endeavours?'

'I like the sea, believe there's great fishing to be had.'

'And have you factored in the sharks?'

'It won't help Boston and Company if you put me off. I'm on the brink of offering you your first contract.'

'For what?'

'That boat!'

Muir pointed at the drawing.

'I'll have to check it's okay with Governor Grose so it's pending his agreement. Maybe add a few buoyancy tanks in case it turns turtle. And a rig, too, so it can be sailed and maybe a small keel. As a deposit I'll begin to collect evidence and testimonies. Agreed?'

'Agreed. There aren't so many sharks, so Watling says. Margarot terrified some witnesses from giving true testimonies. Act quickly. Offer them anonymity and security. Skirving tried to get the truth out of them. They closed like clams. Every one of them. Find someone who can offer them security. If Campbell's playing dirty, then...'

'We must too?'

Palmer looked down in shame.

'It is not the Christian way, but...'

'You have to survive, Reverend... Ever see Sergeant Reddish after that morning on deck?'

Palmer hesitated but failed to keep the secret.

'Your judgement was spot on. He made false allegations against the Bostons a few weeks after he spoke to us.'

*

It would be another month until the witnesses gained the confidence to speak against Captain Campbell. Casswell welcomed Muir inside. The others; Barton, Neale, Evans, Griffiths and McLean, stood by their bunks.

Muir cleared his throat.

'Gentlemen, I have to collect testimonies for the trials of William Skirving and Thomas Palmer. I understand your fears but I must ask you again, will your testimonies be forthcoming?'

They looked at each other.

'Can I ask each of you in turn, to join me outside?'

A general nodding of heads began the proceedings. Muir left the hut and sat down by the doorway, cross legged, looking out at the bay. The convict ship had been cleared from the quayside and hung heavily on its anchor in deeper water.

Having it in view would refresh their memories, he hoped. Muir was handed a cup of rum. It was after all, midday. He offered Casswell a place beside him so that he could see what he wrote but the man remained standing to Muir's puzzlement.

'I'll tell you what I told Campbell,' said Casswell.

'All I ask is you speak the truth without bias.'

'Skirving and Palmer never talked of the plot to me. Campbell tried to force lies out of me but failed. They...'

The breeze brushed Casswell's long hair across his face.

'They?'

When he tucked his hair back behind his ear, Muir noticed that he was crying.

'They flogged you?'

He lifted up his shirt.

Scar tissue shone in the sun all the way down his back.

'I've had to sleep on my front since.'

Muir stood up, lifted the shutter and placed the case notes on the ledge.

'The captain also threatened to kill me, to hang me at the yardarm.'

As Muir spoke to the others their accounts corroborated each other. No contradictions surfaced between statements and everything tallied with what he had seen happen aboard.

He was, however, astonished to learn that whilst in irons above where the captain slept, a heavy chain was run through their hands and leg irons, hastened to a staple at one end and led to the captain's bedside below deck. Campbell used it to torment them at his leisure through the night.

Although he felt he had the court cards of the pack, the accounts of this thug, Campbell, had left a bad taste in Muir's mouth so he downed the rum and checked his notes to see if he had missed anyone.

As McLean headed back into the shade, Muir asked him of Gilthorpe's whereabouts.

'They don't allow him in our hut. Brought shame on himself for what he did. Stays alone the other side of that dunny.'

McLean pointed to a rickety old dwelling where a man was shouldering his braces.

Muir bid farewell and walked into the thickening stench.

Once to windward the smell of human waste was replaced by stew which led him to Gilthorpe, the convict cook, tending to a pot over an open fire looking thoroughly depressed. He was a thick set man but his size ran contrary to his stamina, a man more attuned to culinary delights than adventurous heroics.

'Can I join you?'

Gilthorpe's face, beard and unkempt hair were dripping with steam from the pot, which could have fed all the men in the previous hut. Thankful for company, he went inside for another bowl and spoon. They ate ravenously. The rum had left him thirsty and the stew was watery enough to hydrate as much as anything else.

'Couldn't help it, Mr Muir. Couldn't take the flogging. On top of irons it was just too much.'

'Mr Gilthorpe…'

'James, please.'

'James, torture was made illegal in 1707. Campbell was in the wrong not you. You shouldn't feel any shame.'

Gilthorpe looked at his reflection in the stew and eventually looked up.

'Thank you. They're words I've waited some time to hear.'

'I need you to describe what happened.'

'After they…' Gilthorpe paused.

'…After they... ...tortured you?'

'Yes. I pretended I'd something to reveal so they'd take off my leg irons. I was carried down to the roundhouse. I...'

Gilthorpe hesitated.

'You signed a declaration?'

'Yes.'

'Stating Skirving and Palmer planned a mutiny?'

'May as well have signed their death warrant. Truly sorry, I am.'

'If it's forced by torture it's void.'

He didn't know whether this was actually the case within the jurisdiction of the penal colony. But saying such would at least calm Gilthorpe down.

'Would you like to write down what you heard them say?'

'They never spoke of mutiny. Skirving's a gentleman. Reverend Palmer's, well, true to his title. I couldn't take the flogging.'

Muir passed Gilthorpe his case notes and lowered a pen into his trembling hand. His thumb and first finger crushed it with determination.

Then he gave him a handkerchief to stop his tears from marring the other testimonies on the page and eventually Gilthorpe signed below what he had written.

Bidding farewell, he remembered that Campbell had harangued John Stirling as well.

But Muir was in two minds whether to bother collecting his testimony, now tired having written half a dozen or so. He wanted to test the printing press he'd had moved to one of the workshops. On the way back to his own hut he realised he would pass Stirling's cabin.

Approaching, the calls from the parrots in the trees seemed to become louder. The nearer he got though the more he realised that they were in fact cries for help. His instinct was to intervene but he slowed himself and slipped beneath the hut's shutters to eavesdrop.

Stirling's voice was desperate but defiant. 'My liberty's not yours to give me, Captain Campbell. It's the governor's.'

'You can have this rustled shirt...'

'I don't want your blasted shirt.'

'And this striped waistcoat.'

'I don't want your waistcoat either.'

Muir sensed Campbell wouldn't like Stirling's refusals but to his surprise, he continued with the bribes.

'And these three guineas, if you...'

'If I what?'

'Swear you heard Palmer and Skirving talking to Casswell about seizing the ship. Swear they said they intended to sail her to a foreign port.'

Stirling pleaded, 'I've told you... ...I heard no such plan.'

Muir scribbled down the conversation.

'Nonsense!' shouted Campbell. 'Swear also the ten guineas Palmer said he'd been robbed of, he gave to Casswell and Draper to carry out the mutiny. Say it and you can go free.'

'And what if I don't swear to these lies?'

'I'll blow your brains out with these pistols.'

Muir's heart began to race and he didn't know whether to intervene. But unarmed he was of no use and there was a risk that he might lose the testimonies.

'Kill me and you'll have nothing.'

Muir scribbled the death threats down and looked through the gaps in the wooden panels.

Campbell was circling Stirling with his pistol outstretched, like a clock's minute hand counting out time.

Given that the captain was subject to Governor Grose's jurisdiction Muir deduced that these were idol threats, but threats none the less.

He crouched back down and hoped he wouldn't hear gunshots. In his heightened alertness, he interpreted chairs scraping backwards and floorboards flexing as a retirement from interrogation. And he was right for in the corner of his eye, through the gaps in the panels, he could make out boot steps heading to the door.

Tucking himself well out of sight, he peered out once or twice. Four men walked along the path he had just walked. Campbell was recognisable in his ill placed captain's uniform, as was Draper in his self tailored jacket and pants. The man with his arm in a sling was the villain, John Kidlaw.

But what of the other man?

His heart hoped it was not who he thought it was. Looking away, up in the trees was a rainbow of lorikeets arcing over a branch. They almost seemed to pity him. As if they thought also that it might be Margarot waddling behind Captain Campbell having lost his way.

Suddenly, like a row of soldiers the birds turned their heads in sequence as they heard Campbell's orders.

'Come on, we'll see what more we can get out of Gilthorpe.'

The last man hurried his steps.

If only Campbell had used his name.

After untying Stirling, Muir returned with him to his own hut. Somerville and Watling were inside and had made their acquaintances.

'Ah, can I deal with Mr Somerville's testimony first, John?' asked Muir, 'and would you make my friend a drink?'

'Of Course,' said Watling who took care of Stirling who had been shocked into silence by the ordeal. 'The journey from Southampton was awful by all accounts,' he added. 'The French Bastille nor the Spanish Inquisition couldn't conjure more horrors!'

Muir looked towards Port Jackson. 'Only a romance got me through it. And Godwin's novel. But to business... Now, Mr Somerville, initially you refused to testify to the captain's accusations but then you did?'

'Only after I was tortured, Mr Muir. Only after I saw what they'd done to the others. Then they menaced me with double irons and left me languishing on the stern of the ship during the storm. It lasted for two days. You do remember the storm don't you?'

'I still have the nightmares, Mr Somerville, what with Boston's little girl nearly going overboard and her mother being flogged, too.'

Stunned by what he was hearing, Watling had to remember to draw breath.

Muir handed across the case notes.

'Write that you were tortured, made a false confession and would like to correct it with what you really heard.'

Somerville wrote frantically as if his conscience depended upon it for its liberation. But as he did, what the band of thugs were doing to the convict cook, drove Muir to action.

Once the testimony was complete they armed themselves and went in search of Gilthorpe. On the way, Somerville mentioned they'd read up in the *Encyclopaedia Britannica* on how to treat their wounds. Muir knew Tytler had written the sections on surgery and pharmacy. Though he didn't mention it, he was proud his old friend's influence was being felt around the world.

When they arrived Gilthorpe's hut was abandoned.

The fire was dead and the stew had grown cold.

Marks in the soil charted a recent struggle.

They looked towards the convict ship. A rowing boat was approaching. He watched each man clamber up the rope ladder. They were all slight and he was sure only four went up.

The convict cook had perhaps avoided persecution.

It had been a long day. Somerville and Stirling eventually left to join Casswell and the others. Watling was keen to take Gilthorpe off Muir's mind so suggested helping him scour the land for plots to set up home.

Climbing the highest headland to see the full scope of ground available, they looked inland towards a small settlement called Toongabbe.

Muir was struck by the similarities with the Glasgow of his childhood. Both had the mountains in the distance, both had developed around a waterway and both were changing rapidly in their lifetimes.

'What do you want to do here?'

'Fish.'

'Looking inland's no use then. Next bay along there's a derelict house feet from the water's edge. The bay forms an estuary of sorts. You'd have the choice of fresh or salt water depending on which way you row and the type of fish you want.'

Muir was inspired.

They hiked until dusk encountering what Watling explained were wombats and bandicoots, harmless marsupials that Muir studied with intrigue.

Springs and streams meandered through their journey. At times they had to take diversions around cordoned off holdings of pigs, sheep, turkeys and ducks. Awestruck by towering red gums, they were delayed further.

Out of breath, they looked down on the derelict house and noticed land across the other side that also seemed abandoned.

'You think that's available too?'

'Cockle Beach? Yes, I'd say cockles are pretty easy to catch, a good place to start.'

Muir grinned but seemed to have his thoughts on more distant shores. They looked out to sea, though Watling's thoughts were also elsewhere.

'I escaped at the Cape of Good Hope. Was within a whisker of boarding a ship back to Europe when they caught me. The penalty for attempting to escape here's much worse. You'd be mad to try.'

'What's that settlement up the coast?' asked Muir.

'Parramatta. That's out of bounds, too.'

Muir lowered his head in thought. Two footprints scored the sandy soil. Stepping into them, he trembled seeing that his shoes were dwarfed by the imprints.

'There are gorillas! I cannot buy land here.'

At that, Watling burst out laughing.

Sprinting back to civilisation, with relief Muir spotted a group of marines armed with bayonets, guarding the perimeter of the colony ready to shoot deserters.

'If we are attacked at least the soldiers will come to our defence. Come on...'

Watling's laughter was now coupled with tears of joy. Muir looked again at the soldiers who were also amused. Trying to find some composure, Watling explained.

'You're not the first to fall for this trick. You won't be the last. The soldiers like to amuse themselves by marking large footprints into the earth. It discourages the convicts from wandering too far.'

They walked back, Muir a little shorter, Watling a little taller but at least both now at the same casual pace.

Having picked up two cases of rum from their huts, they left to sell them at what had become the colony's only drinking hole.

Watling enlightened Muir. 'It's the remnants of a frigate that was washed up over a decade ago. Hasn't been as bad a storm since. One day that might change.'

Whilst they bartered a good price for their rum he noted how the landlord's face was the same shade as the ship's timber. Even his eyes appeared as knots in the wood, weathered and as unmoved as the wreck.

McLean had landed a job behind the bar. Muir was reminded to ask of Gilthorpe's fate. Rather pleased with himself, McLean relayed that he had rallied the lads behind him and confronted Campbell who was torturing Gilthorpe over the fire when they got to him.

'Casswell broke the captain's jaw. So quick was he that the captain was unable to reach for his pistol. The others circled Draper, Kidlaw and this other fellow until they managed to flee.'

'What did they call the other fellow?'

'I can't recall. It was all a blur. Our lives were on the line. They were armed to the hilt.'

Humbled by the turn of events, Muir wondered what had brought Gilthorpe back into their company. The offer of stew, perhaps. He had enough after all.

Whilst Watling bought the drinks, Muir searched for a free table. The soldiers drank on the leeward side of the frigate sheltered from the wind whilst the convicts gathered on the windward side, spending much of their time covering their drinks from the sand. He found a place between the two, by the stern. The frigate's interior was riddled with just as much prostitution as the convict ship. Occasional flashes of flesh would appear through the shutters to a raucous applause. A breast, a patch of hair, the raising and lowering of someone's backside, each would inspire the boozers turning some of them into customers. Muir seemed indifferent. That was, until he recognised one of the women.

Later, his attention was drawn to an altercation by the entrance of the brothel. A customer wasn't paying up. The prostitute had her back to Muir as she tried to stop the customer from leaving.

Muir looked up at the shutter from which he'd seen Jane and saw that another woman had taken that bunk. If it was Jane who was arguing for her money it was about time he helped her out. As he approached, his heart took over his head. Twisting the man's shirt in his grasp, he forced him down the beach.

'Do you mean to pay that woman for services rendered?'

The man was speechless. One of his arms was in a sling. He swung a punch with his other arm but had no foundation in his stance to make it anything more than a pathetic knock that came to nothing.

It was then that Muir realised who he was fighting. It was Kidlaw. Within seconds he had him on the ground and was searching him for coinage.

Watling, returning to an empty table, saw the commotion down the beach and on the way passed the ales to Jane.

Kidlaw was getting the better of Muir now and had his head locked inside his sling free arm. Until, that was, a rough looking man came to his aide and punched Kidlaw in the side of the mouth. His bleeding gums were thick with sand and the blow was enough to release the lock around Muir's neck.

Once he'd brushed himself off Muir realised the man helping him was the convict that had swam from the rock the day they arrived.

'Thank you, Mr?'

Muir waited.

'My name's Alasdair. Just returning the favour for passing me that rope. Might a drowned otherwise. I threw the block at this scoundrel when he had a knife at you as well.'

Kidlaw was now some way down the beach.

'Will you ever learn to give up?'

His mouth was hurting too much to answer.

Muir recalled the rigging block incident.

'That was you too, Alasdair?'

'I'll leave you alone now.'

'No!'

Palmer's desire for some form of security entered Muir's mind.

Alasdair was keen to maintain the conversation.

'See, the soldiers told me who you are.'

'They did?'

'The advocate?'

'And?'

'You might not remember me, but I remember you…'

'I remember passing the rope to you…'

'No. Before that. In Edinburgh.'

'You kept me from the scaffold.'

'I represented you?'

'Any trouble, Mr Muir, from Campbell and his cronies, just give me the nod. I hear he has a broken jaw but he doesn't need his jaw to wield a musket. Between you and me… I've weaponry. Been here six years. You make your own laws.'

Alasdair picked out a fragment of one of Kidlaw's rotten teeth. It had embedded itself between his knuckles. As the man walked back to the frigate, Muir realised who he'd encountered.

It was Alasdair Henderson.

His was the first ever case he'd won. He couldn't believe it. But he laughed to himself realising that in a roundabout way, he'd finally got his fee even if it had never been requested.

Back at the frigate, Jane was counting the bag of shillings they'd managed to separate from Kidlaw.

'Consider the excess a fine. Now, how much do you earn?'

'Three shillings on a good day.'

'It's not much of a reward given the risk of venereal disease. Watling, what've we in the colony?'

'French pox.'

'The Grand gore. Syphilis and gonorrhoea.'

'And I doubt there's mercury to cure it.'

'I'll pay you four shillings a day to be my servant.'

'And what do you want servicing for that?' asked Jane.

'A house and adjoining lands, pending their purchase. I'm not employing a strumpet if that's what you're alluding to. Doing so with funds from the Whig Party would be most improper though not unheard of. If you want to be my bed partner it will be without payment.'

Watling burst out laughing and passed Jane, Muir's drink.

'The only condition of employment is that you seek no other work. Are we agreed?'

'You'd have a monopoly over me, then?'

'In employment terms, yes. But no other.'

Jane gulped down Muir's entire drink, burped, smiled and shook his hand.

*

Weeks later, by the soldiered front gate of the governor's house, Muir waited putting his time to good use reordering a wad of papers ready for inspection. Ushered in by the soldier, he greeted Governor Grose as a prospective friend not as his master.

It was not reciprocated.

'If I'm to spend fourteen years here I think it wise to purchase some land and a house as Reverend Palmer intends to do.'

He unravelled a map showing the two plots of land divided by the mile wide estuary.

'This one already has a building I intend to renovate and name Hunters' Hill, the name of my family home in Scotland. By foot the plots are an hour apart. You have to walk down to the river bridge and back up the other side. I need your permission to purchase a small rowing boat. It'll halve the journey time.'

'I've another plot for sale on the same side as the building.'

'I considered that but it's in the lee of a hill and misses the morning light. I also want to sell fish so will be using the waters anyway.'

'You want to sell fish? Alongside your sales of rum, tobacco and sugar?'

'Stocks I bought in Rio are diminishing. I've been printing select passages from the Bible and selling them to the convicts. To better them, Governor Grose, to make them understand why they are here, and how they can be replenished through their punishment and why this confinement is necessary.'

'It is to be commended. I believe I'm right in saying that yours is the first printing press in the colony. Certainly the first since I've been here.'

The governor looked out of the window.

The ocean swell was rolling into the bay on the easterly wind.

'No cabin. No keel. If I find either, it'll be burned, you will be flogged.'

'It will be to cross the estuary only to reach Cockle Beach and return. I assure you governor that will be its only use.'

Muir had about turned when Grose remembered something.

'Before you go, you might want to pass on some good news to the Reverend. It concerns you also. I have it in writing from Captain Ogilvie that you were not mutinous aboard the *Royal George*. Seems I will have to watch John Kidlaw.'

'He has a track record of forgery. Clearly, he wrote the letter. Palmer's testimony also supports the fact. As does Kidlaw making public his knowledge of Ogilvie's supposed claim against us.'

'Precisely, how would he have known about the letter if he hadn't written it?'

'He tried to stab me a few weeks ago and brawled with me after that.'

'Really…'

'I'm not interested in pursuing charges but do bear it in mind when dealing with him.'

'Palmer and Skirving are not entirely off the hook, though. Captain Campbell's charges will still be considered in the colony court.'

He half bowed at the governor. They stepped out into the sunshine where convicts were constructing something.

'It's the colony's first theatre,' explained Grose.

Bidding farewell, Muir laughed to himself. The colony was riddled with enough drama without a theatre, he thought.

The post had arrived back at Hunters' Hill. Muir looked at the letter's date now outdated from the ocean long journey.

Seven months had passed since he'd arrived back in October. A chill awoke the April air. He was used to spring arriving at this time of year in Scotland. But here, with the world turned upside down autumn beckoned instead.

With respect to his friends' mutiny trials, they had been seven unproductive months. But in other ways life had regained some sense. He no longer had to deal with the ludicrous accusation made by Kidlaw regarding his conduct aboard the *Royal George.*

Hunters' Hill had new shutters and nearly a new roof. His skills as a fisherman had progressed such that he was in profit for his labours each Sunday at the colony market, despite the extortionate ground rent.

Returning to the letter, he hoped the paragraphs would bring news of a change of government in England, sincerely believing that a blatantly corrupt regime could not survive much longer. The arrival of the Whigs to power would lead to his sentence being quashed which in turn would precipitate their release and a new politics in their favour.

There was still a chance he might become MP for Cadder.

The package was from Newgate prison, London.

Enclosed was a copy of the first few sections of a political manifesto. The front page read:

'Convention. The only means of saving us from ruin. In a letter addressed to the people of England. By Joseph Gerrald.'

The dank stench of urine, almost tangible on the paper, reminded him of the Tollbooth. The perpetual damp, the monotonous grey, the cold helplessness it conjured.

Even on this waning day Botany Bay seemed like paradise compared to that place. He flicked through the first few pages, noting a quote from John Locke on the relationship between the governed and the government.

As he skim read, he learned that much of Gerrald's ideas were concerned with the pretexts and real motives behind England waging war against France. He would read it properly later. For now, he wanted to know how his dear friend was fairing.

His heart sank. Gerrald had consumption. In time it would be fatal. But it was testimony to his friend's modesty that he should overshadow news of his own suffering with worse news surrounding Robert Watt.

Muir couldn't quite believe that the man who had infiltrated the Society to the benefit of the government had himself been charged with treason.

Gerrald explained how Watt had confessed to plotting armed revolt against the state. Muir reflected on the dozens of testimonies that proved that a government employee, Captain Campbell, had used torture to gain confessions. He in no way accepted the authenticity of the confession.

It was to him, the state at its most vulgar. Watt's fate could have been his. It could so easily have been his. He trembled as he re-imagined him languishing in Edinburgh Castle where he had seen clients in days gone by.

Down at the waters edge, Muir waded out towards a row of large rocks that made a natural harbour to where his land met the sea. If he could keep on going he would be free. He mused there might be a time for that, remembering Gerrald's accounts of life as an advocate in Philadelphia.

But for now freedom would be something to muse upon not to pursue. In the detail of the pocket sized globe, New South Wales and America were not even a thumb's width apart. Studying the distant horizon, they may as well have been different worlds.

He had brought something to write with and rested within the undulating rock surface, meted out by centuries of weathering. His friends saw freedom by degree and were making progress in farming and boat building. For him though, freedom was an absolute that you either had or you didn't.

Challenged by Gerrald's letter, he began to doubt his earlier thought that progress had been made. It could so easily have been he that, like Watt, would never again hear the sound of the sea or feel the sun on his face. He remembered his pretence of being hard of hearing. It saddened him that Watt would be deaf for all the years that had been taken away from him.

The nature of his disposal was bad enough but the absence of experience afterwards haunted Muir's thoughts. No government that behaved like the current one could claim to understand the sanctity of life. He thought of Henry Dundas, the chief director of his current woes, and his son Robert, the Lord Advocate. They'd inflicted untold damage upon his relationship with his own father.

Angrily, he looked back at Hunters' Hill. He had tried to recreate their family home but his parents were missing thanks to the Dundas duo. It was just a house. Perhaps when Jane moved in that would change. Now though, he had to put all his energies into representing Palmer and Skirving.

Just one more week was left to construct their defence.

Despite their different views on the nature of freedom, he would do his utmost to stop them from being sentenced in the same way as Robert Watt.

XI
33° 59' S
151° 12' E

Campbell scowled at Muir and his clients as they approached the colony courtroom a week later. But something was amiss. The clerk then reiterated to the defence what he had already told the prosecution.

'Governor Grose's left the colony this very morning. Without the governor the case can't be heard.'

'Where's he gone to?' someone shouted.

'Wouldn't say. Wanted to leave New South Wales for some time, I'm told.'

The clerk took Muir to one side.

'Between you and me I don't think he'll return.'

Unforeseen circumstances had bought Skirving and Palmer more time. 'Whether the case will be heard in Grose's absence will be Mr Hunter's decision.'

'Mr Hunter?'

'Soon to be Governor Hunter. Until Grose returns that is. Will be arriving any day now.'

What a strange bit of luck. Though the government in Britain remained the same, a change in the colony administration had worked in their favour.

Skirving and Muir looked up to where they believed God to be and closed their eyes. Providence was at play. The thought passed from one to the other and back again until Skirving felt Campbell's shoulder dig into his own.

Palmer constrained his friend from retaliating whilst Muir encouraged the clerk to prevent any escalation of the situation. Addressing Campbell, the clerk clarified that he would inform Governor Hunter of this most recent act of aggression.

Returning to Hunters' Hill, Muir could now turn focus on printing a piece he'd given scant attention to so far. It was his own Treatise on the Libel Law of Scotland.

It seemed odd that it should flutter in the warm wind of the southern hemisphere as he read it for errors, remembering the cold Scottish winter in which it had been written.

But it was entirely fitting that it should have his attention so soon after the libellous incriminations of Campbell, Kidlaw and Draper. They had failed miserably so far and Kidlaw's plan to seek a pardon by supposedly helping the authorities was becoming a joke within the colony.

*

Days later, as Muir made his way to the governor's house he passed soldiers carrying a drinks cabinet from a newly docked ship. Inside the house, a tall man in his late fifties directed the soldiers into the correct rooms.

As they navigated doorways he helped from time to time.

Hoping to make a good impression, Muir took some of the cabinet's weight between the two struggling soldiers. He recalled being in the room with Governor Grose to buy his lands and argue his friends' innocence but the ambience, even in the midst of refurbishment, already seemed more relaxed.

The crotch mahogany chairs had eagles' heads at the ends of the arms. He remembered Anderson's furniture. He'd referred to them as American imports. How had a British governor got away with such furniture, Muir wondered. They would have been disallowed in Whitehall but permissible in such a distant colonial outposts as Botany Bay, perhaps.

A soldier who had directed the cabinet and writing table into place looked to the governor for orders to remove the convict but none were forthcoming.

Instead it was the soldiers who were ordered to leave.

In the corner of the room was a reading stand flanked by candle boards. Bellows, a hat rack and a large stand mounted globe were waiting for their positions.

Muir showed the governor his pocket globe to which he remarked that it was easier take around the world than his own. The statement lingered in Muir's mind as if it were almost a gesture of encouragement to breach his confinement.

'I would offer you a drink, Mr Muir, but the cabinet's empty.'

'It's not drink I seek, Governor, but my release.'

'Call me John. I'm a Leith man. On what grounds do you want to be released?'

'Lord Cockburn has declared that Lord Braxfield acted illegally during my trial. My society only ever acted constitutionally, peacefully and with recourse to the methods of petitioning permitted to the discontented, in the 1688 Bill of Rights.'

'I'm familiar with your society.'

Muir thought for a moment that he'd seen Hunter at one of his meetings. But so many hundreds had passed through the society it was impossible to be sure. He wanted to ask about the extent of that familiarity but thought it unwise and instead developed his argument.

'Lord Lauderdale stated in the House of Lords that we shouldn't be confined or prevented from going to any other place other than Britain.'

'As you can see I am busy. My time's as precious as yours but I will give it some attention.'

He believed Governor Hunter. It was introduction enough. As he walked out he noticed that the quay was free. The convict ship, *Surprise*, had left the colony. Hopefully, for good.

Campbell no longer haunted them but he knew nothing of Draper and Kidlaw's whereabouts. Though, even if they still plagued the settlement their powers would now be greatly diminished.

Muir put the last wooden latte over the hole in the outhouse roof. It was slowly taking the form of a fish and lobster store. But suddenly his attention was drawn from his tinkering to what lay beyond. A huge ship was passing by

Kirribili Point. He put down his hammer as it sailed past the mouth of the estuary on its way to the quayside.

Two guns fired. He squinted to try and make out what nationality it was, hoping it was American.

Calcutta was just readable along the transom.

He sighed as a union jack flapped into view.

Watling arrived later, still witness to the disappointment.

'I've come to sketch your property. To pay for your help?'

'Ah, Watling. Wonderful…'

Muir couldn't let others see his vulnerability to misfortune.

An American ship would arrive of that he was certain.

It was just a matter of time.

'Perfect timing. All the roofs are sound. You won't have to patch things up in your head.'

'I'll see what I can do from this shore first. Then, when you're off the roof we'll head over to Cockle Beach. How's Jane?'

'Sleeping, I believe. It's paradise compared to her communal hut.'

After half an hour over on the beach, Watling abandoned sketching Hunters' Hill from the water's edge and hoped to find a raised perspective from the headland.

With Muir's help they walked up into the eucalyptus woods. The lime green leaves drew the sting out of the midday sun and revealed more contrast in Watling's sketches than he had been aware of during their bleached conceptions.

'You should see Parramatta,' insisted Watling, 'Elysian scenery, Arcadian shades and classic bowers present themselves at every winding to the ravished eye. That's what I wrote to my aunt in a letter. She'll be over on the next ship, no doubt!'

'I thought it was out of bounds?'

'It is. The risk of death made it even more beautiful.'

After walking for some time, Watling became distracted by one particular area of wood. He creased over a new leaf and studied the part peeled sun parched trunks of alternating green, silver and sienna onto which he imagined the sun had imprinted an exact replica of foliage, branch and sky.

Muir tried to study with the same dedication but it seemed only a parody of Watling and before long he'd engaged with a far more curious sight a hundred yards further into the bush, what he could only initially describe as a man sized hare.

Only, its ears didn't droop like a hare's but pointed upwards. In a grinding motion it munched blades of grass. Lower down, a miniature version did exactly the same as clumps were passed from large paw to little paw. The curiosity took a step towards fresh grass and revealed its long feet.

'It's a Gangurru.'

'A Kangaroo, you mean?'

Watling nodded and returned to his sketch cutting in a line of charcoal onto the white page. In the same instance, a tumultuous black sound screeched through the depths.

Moments later, gunpowder smoke drifted in from the distance. More shots ripped bark from the tree that Watling was sketching, ruining his attempt at imitation. They protected themselves in the lee of the eucalyptus but feared for the creatures' safety as the yap of bloodhounds grew louder and louder.

Colony soldiers waded through the interior. No sounds came from the kangaroos. The sessile young would surely still be alive pouched beside its bleeding mother not knowing whether to flee for its own safety or be forever with its dying guardian and butchered in the same manner.

Had it learnt enough to survive by itself? Would it crawl out and escape? Muir wanted to know but as he slipped his head around the trunk more bark ripped away and the only brief glimpse he caught was a blur of gunpowder smoke and soldiers' hats.

Watling grasped his neck and pulled him out of range. Although curt, it was rightly prudent for almost in the same moment, two huge feet knocked against the exposed tree root next to Muir's hand.

With strident leaps the kangaroo paced towards the estuary, its grey hind collaborating with the tree trunks against the soldiers' aim. The young was still in the pouch infused by the pounding of its mother's hind feet, deafening out the distant ring of gunshot with her own increasingly victorious return fire.

Soldiers past like stretcher bearers.

A dead roo was bound to a carrying pole.

Spotting them, a soldier claimed they were outside the colony boundary and could be shot for desertion.

'Yes, if we were actually outside the colony boundary.'

Muir got up and gave Watling a hand, burdened under his drawing board that had doubled up as a shield.

They looked at the poor kangaroo laid out like a soldier. Such gentle creatures not used to modern weaponry and the stealth of the gun.

During Muir's inspection, he was grabbed and pushed forward.

'Put these men against the tree,' ordered one of the soldiers.

As they prepared to take aim, Muir clarified in a bout of sweat that the soldiers were trespassing.

'I purchased it four months ago from Governor Grose. The colony boundary includes this land and I'm within my rights as is Mr Watling who is a guest on my private property. You've no warrant to be here.'

The soldier leading the platoon walked out of sight where Muir realised he would shortly encounter a fence.

He eventually returned. 'Our mistake.'

Muir couldn't quite believe their aggression and stupidity. The soldiers looked at each other, rather dumbstruck by the reversal of power.

Begrudgingly, they picked up the kangaroo again and left. Muir walked home. The utter disrespect the soldiers had shown sickened him and when he saw on his desk, a letter headed with the Royal coat of arms of the United Kingdom, he came close to tearing it up. How could Scotland's unicorn face England's lion in anything that resembled democracy or common sense for that matter, he wondered.

Democracy as things were could only be had if Scotland partnered Ireland, he thought. On the verge of tearing it up he let his anger pass and opened the correspondence.

It was dated the twenty fifth October, 1795. Was it that late in the year? He'd completely forgotten about his thirtieth birthday exactly two months earlier. Perhaps he thought, it was better that way. The day might have been a very sad one indeed. The date was also a year on, to the day, from his arrival in Botany Bay, not an anniversary he could celebrate with much enthusiasm.

The letter was a duplicate of what the governor had sent the Duke of Portland, the British Home Secretary. Hunter stated that he could not be justified in forcibly detaining Muir and the other reformers in the colony against their consent.

Muir's world suddenly lightened.

Hunter had reported well of them, stating that they had not accepted provisions from the public store since their arrival and had lived in a retired and quiet manner.

In the conclusion of the letter, Hunter recommended continued banishment from Great Britain but possible sanctuary in Ireland at the instruction of His Majesty, King George III.

He reflected on the day. Never before had the spectre of death and the glimmer of freedom been experienced so closely.

Thankfully it was in that order and part of a trajectory he hoped to maintain, remembering that Palmer had earmarked tomorrow as the day of the launch.

Three quarters of the way along the two mile descent from Palmer's farm to the shore, the day so far had been occupied with moving the boat to the nearest piece of coastline. New premises would need to be purchased if a project of any greater size was to be undertaken.

Rolling the boat overland on three wooden posts was no easy task. More often than not they'd be lost down the embankment when they weren't prised in properly between the bow and the track.

Rather out of breath Palmer declared, 'I believe I may have found my vocation.'

'Boat building? What about spreading the word of God?'

'It seems everyone is doing that these days. Lawyers, convicts, the lot. You don't need to be a scholar in divinity any more. I have my mind on a ship far grander than this. A thirty-tonner. Been drawing up designs based on the ship out in the bay. It arrived a few days ago. The *Ceres* is its name. Look, in the lee of the headland. Goddess of fertility isn't it?'

Muir wished it had an American, not a British ensign.

'But this project has been very instructive. The jarrah wood, though not entirely seasoned, will serve its purpose. And the air tanks should save it from sinking should it capsize.'

'Sorry I had to make you saw off the keel. Grose was insistent.'

'Not a problem.'

'Although now with Hunter running the show, I'm sure we could have left it on. He's on our side, Palmer.'

'For the next project, I'll need a boatyard by the water's edge.'

'Don't invest too much here. You may be moving Boston & Co. to Ireland if we have our way.'

Palmer hesitated then thought he should tell Muir something. 'I spoke to Governor Hunter this morning about his petition.'

'To the home secretary? It's brilliant news isn't it. We will be free to go anywhere but Great Britain.'

'Yes, but you must understand, he said it'd be at least a year until King George decides. Even then, it could go either way.'

Heart sunk, Muir knew he couldn't wait that long. It was only trouble with the boat that snapped him out of his melancholy trance.

'The roller's slipping away.'

Before he could reach for it the post had careered down the embankment bouncing end on end down into the depths.

As Muir searched in the forest he caught sight of a tent between the branches. Intrigued, he approached. In the shade though he failed to spot the guy ropes and tripped into a fire pit.

A cloud of ash levitated above him.

Embarrassed, Muir tried to get up quickly submerging his hands into the hot coals beneath.

'Avez-vous froid?' asked someone from the tent. Long hair and an unkempt beard engulfed his eyes and nose, all but for a patch of skin on one cheekbone that had succumbed to the blade.

In one hand he held a knife, cross hatched in hair. In the other, he held out a cloth doused in cold water. Handing it to Muir, he regretted his earlier attempts at a joke.

'Francois Pierre Peron.'

'A Frenchman! Wonderful. Have you seen a wooden pole?'

Francois looked at the fallen wood all around them and picked one up nearby that he'd earmarked for the fire that evening.

Climbing back up the precipice to Muir's land stricken boat, they discussed Francois' adventures before spotting Palmer on the way with the actual roller they'd lost.

'Reverend, we've a helper. This is Francois.'

'Good day… Freeman, soldier or convict?'

'My story is a long one,' Francois said with a heavy mind.

'Well you can tell us on the way to Muir's plot. And you can give us a push too.'

Palmer grinned with pride as the estuary waters washed the dust away from the hull, revealing the knots and grains of the wooden panels he had so lovingly sanded and varnished.

'Since you're the only sailor amongst us Francois, can you take her on the maiden voyage, just to Cockle Beach and back?'

'D'accord.'

Muir and Palmer studied Francois' perfect rowing.

He was already halfway across the estuary.

'So, let me get this straight,' Palmer said, 'Francois has been stuck on Amsterdam Island, two thousand miles from the nearest land mass, slap bang in the depths of the Southern Ocean for the last five years with not another soul to speak with?'

'There was another French man,' Muir clarified, 'and two Englishmen. Francois was designated the mission leader. Their brief was to hunt seal until the return of their ship, the *Emilie*.'

'In China, fur seal skins are much in demand for fashioning high quality clothing and attract unbelievable prices,' Palmer noted.

'That was their market, so he said. They'd been on Amsterdam Island for a couple of years when the British arrived on the *Lion* and *Hindustan*.'

'Sounds like trouble...'

'Well yes, the British crew got Francois' compatriots drunk and whilst they were dozing, stole eight hundred of their seal skins. Despite the setback, Francois persevered and hunted every day. He said there were springs on the island and the water could be used to cook and drink but they mostly lived off seal meat. Eventually though, the food stocks ran out one winter. Despair led to an armed mutiny and he was seriously injured in what was a miniature Anglo French war, with just two on each side! The French forced the English to live in the Cave du Milieu. They lived in the hut by the jetty. But the next year, the other Frenchman died. The week before Christmas, Francois was praying over the Frenchman's grave when he looked up to see the first sail on the horizon for two years since the arrival of the English on *Hindustan*. It was the *Ceres*.'

'That has inspired my next boat? Well, true to its name I bet it brought much needed food.'

'I don't know about that. The same day it arrived, the Englishmen attempted to kill Francois but the plan was foiled by its arrival. It also provided them with their salvation. *Ceres*' captain, Hadley, told him that Francois' ship, the *Emilie*, had been stolen. Who by do you think by?'

'I don't know.'

'The crew of the *Lion*! Not only did they steal his seal skins, they took the only ship that knew of his isolation.'

'I thought we'd had it bad.'

'Did you hear what he said about the seal skins?'

'No.'

'Of course, he mentioned it when we were in the woods. Hadley didn't let him take the seal skins aboard. Francois had hunted seal every day for four years, and when he wasn't hunting he was skinning those he'd caught.'

Palmer calculated, 'even after the eight hundred that the English took from him, there would still be two and a half thousand! Lord! A small fortune.'

'Well,' recounted Muir, 'he said he had to make up his mind then and there on the jetty, should he risk waiting another four years for a ship to arrive that would let him take his fortune aboard or should he end his isolation and with it, his hold over the skins.'

They watched Francois turn the boat around and start the return leg.

'The next person to turn up at that jetty though, will have the best of both worlds, the skins and the transport.'

'Hmm. Perhaps the ship didn't live up to its name. What happened to the Englishmen?'

'He didn't say.'

With the boat trialled and fishing equipment on its way, Muir realised he would need to shift the old stock to turn the last of the outhouses into a facility for smoking fish.

Rum, sugar and printed sections from the bible, were not the most likely combined products of a tradesman but just after dawn in the colony, it seemed to be the winning formula. Alcohol and Christianity complimented each other, whilst the sugar was a favourite with the soldiers' wives.

Before noon, he'd knocked on nearly every door of the colony, starting with the freemen. He'd only missed Francois' habitation in the woods but sensed the Frenchman would have little interest in the bible.

Only his own bible remained.

The one his parents had given him.

He wouldn't sell that for all the days that he lived.

Returning home, Muir climbed the roof to inspect his handiwork. He looked at the ship, *Calcutta*, out in the bay and thinking he was still seeing double from the rum of the night before he concentrated his eyes to clarify that there was not another ship in the bay to windward.

No amount of focussing merged the two vessels. The new ship must have arrived before dawn. It was then that he recalled, at midnight, the flag being raised at Port Jackson to signal the arrival of a ship, when he was returning from the beached frigate with Francois.

The newly arrived ship had only two masts and was considerably shorter than the *Ceres*. Muir's heart nearly skipped a beat when he realised that it had an American flag. The day had finally arrived. He remembered the letter his parents had sent them and was convinced the Americans had come specifically to rescue him.

Disregarding the roof timbers, he jumped down onto the wood store and tumbled onto the ground below. The fall was painless and he only allowed the ship out of his sight to find his parents' letter.

Setting out in his rowing boat towards the American ship with a light breeze behind him he decided to test the rig and his sailing skills, saving his energy for the negotiations that he had planned.

He wondered what Governor Hunter would do to him if he found him outside the estuary but his destination was clear, he had no provisions and was only going a few hundred yards.

As he neared the stern, '*The Otter*' was written across the arch board. On deck, a man wearing a bleached American naval jacket was coiling sheets.

Having read the letters he welcomed Muir aboard.

'So you're an exiled Scot?' said the man, 'we've something in common already.'

'I recognise the accent.'

'I doubt it, Mr Muir. We went over to the Americas after the Forty Five. I was a bairn when the British troops attacked Culloden. You been there?'

'Yes. It was so desolate.' Muir felt uncomfortable lying about the proposed trip with Professor Anderson that never materialised. But the captain's recollections hid that unease.

'They smuggled me out to a ship on the west coast destined for America. No parents. Just a few well wishers who passed me around. Each taking turns to look after me.'

'Did George Washington send you? My parents wrote to him to help me as the letter shows...'

The man interrupted Muir, a little rattled that the account of his childhood had been interrupted.

'I'm master to no man, Mr Muir. I rarely step on dry land and on this ship I am the President. Well, Captain Ebenezer Dorr.'

'That's not very Scottish.'

210

'I left without a name or title. The Jewish man who took me in named me Ebenezer after his dear self.'

'And Dorr?'

'After what they locked me behind when I was old enough to roam.'

Ebenezer smiled whilst Muir tried to work out whether he was joking or being serious.

'You here to trade?'

'Not here, China maybe. I mean, I'll sell here if I can. But colony folk won't have money for what I'm selling.'

Muir remembered what Francois and Palmer had said about China. 'What are you selling? Seal skins?' He didn't mean it literally but the words stopped Ebenezer cold.

'How do you know?'

'What?'

'That I've seal skins?'

'I don't, I was just hypothesising.'

'Hypothesising?'

Below deck they were piled in their thousands.

'You hunt them yourself?'

'Some. Had labourers skin them on Amsterdam Island. Was Christmas Eve when I arrived. Most the skins had been abandoned. Christmas come a day early you might say.'

Muir wondered whether to mention his encounter with Francois. It would almost certainly create bad blood between him and Ebenezer. He couldn't afford to jeopardise the American connection and thought it wiser to let encounters run their own course.

Each night though, he found it almost impossible to sleep. To ease his conscience he brought Francois aboard his fishing enterprise. Being a fine rower, he was free to concentrate on trawling nets and setting out lines.

The Frenchman also helped construct the smoker. But the enjoyment was short lived for Francois would lament the whereabouts of his seal skins and Muir would struggle to maintain the secret hoping each day that Francois would find out from Ebenezer for himself, if they ever met that was.

A month into their business partnership, when Muir's conscience had got the better of his self interest, he finally revealed what was aboard *The Otter*.

Early the next morning Francois boarded the American ship whilst Muir rowed over to the *Ceres*. They'd heard that it was disembarking that day. Captain Hadley was an important witness to Francois' claim.

Below deck, the Frenchman stood dumbstruck. He hadn't entirely believed Muir but before him was his entire livelihood and a rather awkward Ebenezer Dorr.

In his mind, Francois constructed how the skins had been picked up a few days after his departure and had followed him for five thousand nautical miles.

He wondered whether there were times *The Otter* and *Ceres* might even have been in sight of each other. All the time he was mourning his loss, they were following him to Botany Bay.

Francois had brought aboard his oak hakapik as evidence of his profession. Its wooden grip delved inwards towards the darker decay resistant heartwood that his hands had clenched countless times.

The other end of the hakapik divided into a hammerhead and a hook. He thought of the thousands of seal skulls he had cracked, the number of journeys he had made dragging them over the rocks, the hook deep into their bleeding carcasses, the flocks of sea birds scavenging from the entrails spilt over the rocks.

He hadn't enjoyed killing them. Their last short cries woke him in his sleep. A recurring nightmare haunted him of going overboard and ending up on seal inhabited rocks without weaponry, pleading for their fish to avoid starvation. On every one of their heads appeared the injuries he had inflicted.

As he studied the skin piles he remembered the particularly large ones, the Herculean journeys their slaying precipitated and the newborn pups he'd had second thoughts of killing, leaving them amidst the trailing bloods of their ancestors.

His straight skinning edges were distinguishable from the jagged ones. These were made by his English underlings, Cook and Godwin. As a result of their perpetual alcoholic intoxication, their skinning was as messy as their attempt on his life.

Whilst he waited, their planned attack entered his mind. Looking into the galley, it merged with his view of Ebenezer who had the same tongue as his conspirators.

But this negativity was balanced against the seal skins being once again before his eyes. Despite the status of their disputed ownership, he admitted their re-emergence had to be accredited to the American captain. Ebenezer had a steak in his hand, cooked but oozing with blood. The Frenchman had eaten enough of them to know that it was seal meat.

Francois then remembered the last three kills he'd made. The arrival of the *Ceres* hadn't allowed him time to skin them so he'd piled them by the jetty. Ebenezer had not only taken his property, but was also feeding from the food store he'd left behind.

Up on deck, as Muir and Captain Hadley neared *The Otter* in the rowing boat, Francois recalled the relief he'd felt when the *Ceres* sailed towards Amsterdam Island.

Pigeon English had circled around his head, as well as the anxiety to strike the right note in his greeting with the captain and not come across as some mad lonely Frenchman persecuted by Englanders. It was not quite as swift as Ebenezer's introduction, however.

'Captain Hadley, of the *Ceres*.'

'Welcome aboard, Captain Ebenezer Dorr, of *The Otter*.'

Hadley hurried proceedings.

'Mr Muir has briefed me on the details of the dispute.'

'Nothing's disputed. The Frenchman can purchase these skins as he pleases. At market price,' insisted Ebenezer.

Francois exploded, 'I am not buying back what is mine.'

'What was yours. They were once God's. They were once the seal's. Might have once been yours but you were as careless with them as the seals were keeping them on their backs.'

'They are stolen goods. As it stands, you have stolen from my ship, the *Emilie*, and from me'.

Francois and Captain Hadley looked at each other. Hadley knew the *Emilie* had been ransacked and stolen by the English ship, the *Lion*. He also knew that Francois knew about the change of hands. Revealing such could have derailed Francois' argument at any moment but Hadley sensed that Ebenezer seemed oblivious to the fact.

Muir had his own well being to think about and tried to steer the conversation out of the diplomatic gridlock. He had a good friend in Francois but in Ebenezer, a means of escape with, he still believed, presidential backing.

'Men, you'd be best served to forget the *Emilie*. I have to declare I've learnt from Captain Hadley, it's been taken by the English ship, the *Lion*.'

Hadley tried to recall whether he'd told Muir this or not. He couldn't quite remember. The French man realised that in Muir's role play, he had avoided suggesting that Francois was lying to Ebenezer.

Muir continued, 'I'm not aware whether you've been told of this, Francois?'

The Frenchman hid his knowledge well, whilst Muir digressed. 'You're freemen. Francois, entangle yourself from old allegiances and strike new ones with America. You have far more in common than this altercation suggests.'

Hadley looked at the seal skins. 'Captain Dorr, I can vouch for Francois, these are the skins I prevented him from bringing aboard the *Ceres*. I'm partly responsible. Yet, Ebenezer, you wouldn't have profited at all had I not refused them aboard.'

Hadley was running out of time. Muir rowed him back to the *Ceres*. Fearing that Francois might strike Ebenezer's skull with the hakapik, he made haste on his return.

Ridding them of the English captain served another purpose for Muir. He was now in a stronger position to discuss the voyage from Botany Bay that might, he hoped, include a berth of his own.

He had Hadley's written testimony in his lapel pocket. It would work in the Frenchman's favour. But as he returned to *The Otter*, Ebenezer had Francois' head jammed between the shrouds. Only the collar of his sealskin jacket stopped the ropes from lacerating his neck.

Muir frantically climbed on deck, desperate to halt the tête-à-tête. Pulling Ebenezer away, he fell backwards and within seconds Francois had a grasp of the hakapik and was intent on finishing off the American captain for good.

It was only when Muir put himself between the two of them that the axe blow was redirected upwards, through Muir's hair and away before Francois settled it on the ground to take stock of how close he had come to killing his dear friend, Mr Muir.

'Gentlemen,' Muir half panted, 'agree to split the profits. Right down the middle. Sell them in Canton. Via America. Before one of us is killed. Business is about compromise. You've helped each other, thus far, more than you dare appreciate and providence has made you partners of business again. Please, Francois give me the hakapik. It has served its purpose to make you both rich men. But I fear it could kill one of you if this madness persists. The choice I believe is obvious.'

Francois let go of the weapon. It toppled onto the deck. Muir picked it up and, surprised by its weight, lowered it into his rowing boat gently enough to not crack the timbers.

Muir then led them to the shade of the captain's quarters believing it would quell their hotheadedness. They could draw out plans to serve both their interests though he would make little of his own aspirations for the time being.

After innumerable rums and ocean trekking tales, the Frenchman and the American grew to like each other. Only Muir could see the lunacy of how proximate their maligned fervency was to their newly found friendship.

By sunset, Ebenezer had offered the position of First Officer to Francois. He intended to sail to the west coast of America, then China and back to Boston. Muir sipped his rum. Every time 'America' was spoken, it seemed to Muir as heart warming as the liquor.

Returning on deck, Muir felt he'd achieved a great deal. Things were beginning to look up. Until, that was, he rowed back to Cockle Beach and caught sight of a ship tied to the quayside. The flag of St. George fluttered in front of the governor's house.

It was his nemesis, HMS *Providence*.

Muir wondered whether to return to *The Otter* and wait until dark to avoid being sighted. He didn't want to complicate the deal with Francois and Ebenezer though, or show them his vulnerability and the risk he posed.

As he rowed furiously, he told himself he must get back to the colony or face hanging for breaching the terms of his sentence. For this is how the captain of the Providence would consider his present voyage.

He calculated into the deal he'd just brokered, the damage HMS *Providence* could do to its success.

The future had gained another unwelcome uncertainty.

Prior to slipping into the estuary, he saw that someone on Providence's decks had a telescope pointing at him. He quickly turned his face the other way and dug in deep.

Pulling his boat up the beach, he couldn't be sure that he'd avoided detection.

XII
33° 50' S
151° 8' E

Muir arranged the typeface for the first two chapters of Gerrald's book. Every time, however, he came across a letter from the word, providence, the text lost Gerrald's intended meaning and appropriated that of his most recent experience. Such that, fears of a knock at the door breached his every second thought.

He looked over at the bible his parents had given him and decried the fact that the British Government could hijack a word of God, imbuing it with such cruel connotation, impregnating it with such ill intent. His Majesty's ship had nothing whatsoever to do with providence. Certainly not his own. That, he would insist upon.

His fury was such that he escaped this time successfully into Gerrald's text and made it his mission to have the first two chapters printed for his arrival, which was forecast any day soon.

Mornings were spent fishing, the evenings, printing.

That pattern was only broken when Palmer needed assistance moving oversize timbers. As his nautical curiosity took shape, Muir wondered whether he really should have granted him permission to construct the dry dock at Hunters' Hill and joked that it was fortunate for the Reverend that the *Ceres* had left Botany Bay. For, had it still been there, the asymmetry between it and his construction would have been visible for all to see. He was encouraging all the same, keeping his amusements to himself.

*

One Thursday afternoon an old face arrived at Hunters' Hill, stopping work invitingly early for Palmer and Muir. Gerrald seemed well enough at first glance. His West Indian upbringing on St Kitts had prepared him for the climate but it was internally, as Muir remembered from the letters, that he was suffering. The climate would ease the consumption but not offer a cure.

Muir handed him the first edition print of Convention's first two chapters and in return, Gerrald handed over two completed manuscripts that he struggled to contain in the antipodean wind.

One was entitled: 'The Voice of the People'. The second was a weightier and now complete handwritten edition entitled: 'Convention, the only means of saving us from ruin, in a letter addressed to the people of England.'

Muir placed them by the printing press, parting the pages where he estimated he'd read from already. Preparing the next page, he arranged the letters from right to left so that once printed they would read in the correct direction. His dear friend, meanwhile, rested in an easy chair out of the sun with Palmer. Both shared a flagon of wine as the landscape succumbed to shade and the sun dipped into the ocean.

'Leave Convention, what are your thoughts on The Voice of the People?'

'Gerrald, I've my own Treatise on Libel Law to print, I can't print this too.'

'Please, it's my only means of... I'm too ill to work.'

Muir daubed the brush in ink and spread it evenly over the typeface. Gerrald couldn't wait for a response. The illness had redefined his sense of time.

'It was published last month in London. Unfortunately, I spent the book launch chained to the decks of a convict ship somewhere in the Indian Ocean.'

Palmer laughed looking up at the clouds passing wildly overhead.

'It'll sell well here. I will offer you a good return. This is no juvenilia, Mr Muir! Its opening clearly defines the democrat as someone who maintains the rights of the people, an enemy to privileged orders and monarchical encroachments, an advocate of peace, economy and reform. It's clear with little room for ambiguity.'

As Muir leant over the letters for one last inspection, he acknowledged Gerrald's enthusiasm, taking care not to brush his hair against the ink, noticing too, the chunk of hair Francois had removed with the hakapik.

Trying to make sense of the writing in reverse was no easy task and left little intellectual space for considering the characteristics of a democrat.

'You will earn enough from Convention, I'm sure.'

Gerrald looked out distantly. 'It is not just about what it earns. It is what it states. I write that England and Scotland are still burdened under intolerable and still increasing taxes. Military barracks have been erected throughout the country. Foreign armies have been landed to fight the French. Taxes on Irish linen, shoes and other necessities are being pushed through to fund the war. The papers are filled with lists of bankrupts. The prisons are overcrowded with convicts. The streets swarm with beggars.'

Hunters' Hill in Glasgow, the fields and woods, the people at the meetings, they all flashed through Muir's mind but the ink was drying in the relentless heat and as a drip of sweat slipped from his temple down his cheek towards his chin and onto the typeface, he knew he had to soon press the paper or it would all have been a waste of time.

Gerrald studied Muir's house. 'Professor Millar has immigrated to America. He's another one sick of Scotland and England's descent into despotism. In my most recent writing, I've established long held precedents in England, for democracy.'

'What like?' asked Palmer.

'Every year, the Saxons convened the free men of the kingdom to compose the assembly of people. It was called Mycelgemot, Folk-mote or Convention. See where I found my work's title? It was their business to take care that the people received no wrong from the king, his queen or their children.'

Muir missed the second thing Gerrald said, as Millar's emigration returned to the forefront of his mind. He wondered if there was anyone left in Scotland and longed for the freedom America seemed to hold.

But before he knew it, the task in hand had to be addressed imminently. Quickly, he lowered the page border, placed the paper on top, dropped down the lid, slid it all under the press and turned the clamp handles until they'd tighten no more.

'That's what Mr Pitt's head needs to go under,' joked Gerrald. Muir burst out laughing, relieved that he'd made the drying deadline.

'Tell me about Mr Pitt, Gerrald?'

'When Mr Pitt was called into power, the death warrant of Old England's remaining liberties was signed. You can read the rest yourself if you decide to publish. It's all in The Voice of the People. Pitt's only part of the problem, though. It's about how we think of each other.'

'And how should we think about each other?' asked Palmer.

'The wolf's the natural enemy of the lamb, the vulture, the dove. But one people can never be the natural enemy of another, unless we consider mankind in the same savage light as the vulture and the wolf. A nation's no more than a member of that large family, the human race, and can only flourish in proportion with the felicity and welfare of the whole. That's a direct quote. Will you publish it?'

Muir saw in Gerrald a man untainted by suffering and in many ways he was suffering the most. He wished he'd been able to spend more time with him in Scotland. He knew he would publish it but he wanted to hear the pitch first.

'My handwriting's such a disgrace. I fear the meaning will be lost to all but myself. And when I'm gone, Mr Muir it will be lost to all mankind. There was no light in Newgate. Sometimes, I had to mix my own piss with grime when they stopped me acquiring ink.'

Humour protruded through Gerrald's shame. Thankfully, it was only the smell of onion, stale bread and linseed oil that Muir had to tolerate currently as he inspected the inked page for errors.

The beginning of one paragraph on the French Revolution was patched by the drop of sweat that had run through the oil based ink.

The words; 'an instructive lesson was conveyed to the tyrants of the earth,' were much fainter than the rest, as if his own exhaustion was curbing the struggle.

'I'll publish your second book. Much work's to be done.'

'Thank you, Thomas. It's the only way I can live here.'

Muir avoided eye contact knowing that one day consumption would contradict his friend's last utterance.

'What else's in it? Tell me. I'm tired of proof reading.'

Gerrald browsed through his own handwriting. 'What greater absurdity can be imagined, than that a people who owe all their prosperity to commerce, to their connections with other people, should call themselves the natural enemy of this or of that people!'

'Ah, so you provide an economic incentive for peace between nations. I like that. It's no longer an ideal but something actually in our own interest for a world economy.'

Gerrald ignored the extension of his own idea.

'Ah! Pitt again. In the old English dictionary, enquiry was a constitutional privilege derived from the Magna Carta and the Bill of Rights. People could enquire into the conduct of kings, their ministers and the errors of their governments. But now, according to Mr Pitt's new code, which is implicitly adopted by all the legal courts through the three kingdoms, enquiry implies disloyalty, sedition or treason.'

'This conveys precisely our plight. Quite brilliant.'

But again Gerrald trammelled over Muir's encouragement.

'They who are audacious enough to claim this ancient obsolete privilege expose themselves to the penalties of fine, pillory, or imprisonment, and if in Scotland, of transportation for fourteen years to Botany Bay.'

Muir mused on the extended injustice felt in Scotland derived from government policy to continue exile and banishment akin to the clearances of the past decades.

'Equal rights!' hailed Gerrald waking up Palmer who'd began to snooze, 'that's what I ask for, equal rights, including the right of every citizen to the protection and benefits of society, a right of voting for the election of those who are to make laws by which he himself is to be bound, by which his liberty, his property, his life are affected. And an equal right of exerting to advantage the genius and talents which he may possess, the equal rights of nature.'

With Palmer engrossed in measurements, calculations and the practicalities of boat building over the last year and Skirving attuning his farming to the New South Wales climate up on the heath, their collective cause had gone off the boil.

But the tide seemed to have turned with Gerrald's arrival to their shores. Talk of rights was refreshing for Muir who had spent months trying to prevent Palmer and Skirving from being hanged. Dark clouds of betrayal and injustice were now replaced by wisps of idealism and blue skies.

Further down, Gerrald called for 'Brothers' to arise and resume the sceptre of the world, to whom it is due and to hurl those sultans from their thrones and let laws and eternal morality fill their places. His global appeal was evident with reference to the sultanate tyrannies of Arabia.

On the last page was a satirical definition of sedition.

'Any thought,' Gerrald paused, 'word or action of your life, if brought into a court of justice and determined so by a corrupt judge and settled so by a packed jury. Dreams may be seditious!'

He was pleased Muir had decided to publish his work. He looked at the final page he had not handed over, a proof from the English edition which read: 'Just published. Price 4d. A faithful narrative of the last illness, death and internment of the right honourable William Pitt.'

He thought it was wise to keep this from Muir until the rest had gone to press. Gerrald slowly got to his feet.

'If I don't see you before, put January the sixteenth in your diary. Two weeks tomorrow. It's the opening night of the colony theatre. They're performing a revenge.'

'I'll do my utmost,' promised Gerrald.

Alone, Muir read through the sections of Convention, he'd not yet published. One paragraph rekindled a burning desire to escape. Now by the dry dock, he read it again to Palmer.

'In America, that country which God and man have concurred to render the blissful habitation of abundance and of peace, the poor are not broken down by taxes to support the expensive trappings of royalty, or to pamper the luxury of an insolent nobility. No lordly peer tramples down the corn of the husbandman. No proud prelate wrings from him the tythe of his industry.'

'Inspiring stuff. If you're willing to wait awhile you might find passage on this ship.'

Muir looked through where the hull should have been as Palmer made his offer. The internal cross sections reminded him of the ribs belonging to the skeleton in Tytler's room. He wondered whether he could wait for this phoenix to rise from the flames or whether a ticket to America was more likely aboard *The Otter*.

Strolling into the dry dock, Muir noticed it was awash with papers. Pointing this out to Palmer, the Reverend cursed.

'Gerrald distracted me. Have any pages gone in the drink?'

'Not that I can see. What is it?' asked Muir.

'Just a record.'

Muir collected the pages together eventually finding the title page. 'A Narrative of the sufferings of T.F. Palmer and W. Skirving during a voyage to New South Wales, 1794.'

'What about me?' Muir joked.

'You're mentioned as well.'

Muir reflected on his view that Palmer's ideals of freedom were waning. Perhaps, they just had different ways of dealing with their suffering.

*

Gerrald dropped by to see how the printing was coming on. Muir was in the rowing boat and Francois was about to launch it from the shallows when he asked if he could also come along.

Muir didn't think it wise given his health but unaware of his serious health condition, Francois welcomed him aboard. They'd trawled the eelgrass for prawns all morning. Now it was time to check on the lobster pots.

It wasn't long before he was lecturing Francois about his books hopeful of securing their first buyer.

His enthusiasms exacerbated his lungs.

'*Convention*, states that the English ministry has neither received injuries or had rights invaded by France and are acting with a spirit of conquest, barefaced usurpation and an eagerness to interfere with their internal government. Does this resonate with your experiences?'

'I have been on Amsterdam Island for four years.'

'Well, my books will put you in the picture.'

Muir looked up from the net he was retrieving before bringing into view, the claws and then the body of a furious lobster.

'France was not the first to strike.'

Francois found it refreshing to talk to an Englishman who wasn't conspiring to kill him.

'Holland,' Gerrald added, 'didn't seek aggression like England, who allied themselves with Prussia. Instead, the Dutch compromised through negotiation. Despotism has been extinguished in France, yet England has shown alacrity to adopt the system which for more than a century, she has loudly condemned and which she has renounced in the eyes of all Europe. England once criticised the old regime, now it war mongers on the pretext of restoring that which it so vehemently criticised.'

As Muir brought the lobster aboard, Francois meticulously clamped shut the pincers and then nodded to Gerrald to pass the string.

'But the British are finding it hard on the ground,' added Gerrald. Francois continued to point towards the string. 'They fled before Dunkirk whilst the French defeated the Hanoverians at Hoondfchoote. And the Austrians at Maubeuge, for that matter. Not only is the British war effort immoral, it's utterly fruitless.'

They were all in danger of losing the battle with the lobster and it was only after a second request that Gerrald put the European conflicts of the last few years to one side and addressed the conflict in hand by finally passing Francois the string.

Eventually, they dropped the disarmed creature into the box.

'So France's holding its own without me?' asked Francois.

Gerrald deliberated. 'Not exactly...' Pocketed by wheezing exacerbations that suppressed his passion for the unfolding events, he added, 'in some areas of your homeland, the German eagle, that emblem of tyranny and massacre, now flies in triumph over the walls of towns where lately waved the banners of freedom.'

'What's to be done in your opinion?'

'Instead of subsidizing half of the mercenaries in Europe, His Majesty's ministers would far better have employed those meek and diligent pastors, the learned doctors of Oxford, Cambridge and Gottingen, whose duty it is to preach peace and not the sword. But will diplomacy ever come before self interest, I ask you?'

Muir noticed tapping from inside the box. Gerrald's desire for reform had rekindled Muir's heartfelt beliefs and he saw in the lobster's plight, an analogy of his own circumstances. Botany Bay was to him, a box he was trapped inside. He longed to return to the country he had strove to reform and work for freedom once again.

Gerrald piped up again as they came closer to the shore.

'But the most recent news from a letter having arrived just this week is, French Republicans have defeated the French Royalists, who were attacking the newly formed government they call the Directory. A chap called Napoleon has swept to fame. He led the defence.'

'Never heard of him. Napoleon who?' asked Francois.

'Bonaparte. He's been made Commander of the Interior and the Army of Italy.'

'Well, he hasn't been stranded on a deserted island for four years has he? I've some catching up to do.'

They all laughed as they drifted into the shallows beneath Hunter's Hill. For Francois, a man of action, the advocates aboard engaged in a reality foreign to him.

With Muir, he lifted the box whilst Gerrald prepared to climb out and tie the boat up to the jetty post. Ill experienced, he misjudged the depth and subsequently ended up waist deep in water.

Then, as he lost his footing, he rocked the boat around and the others dropped the box over. Gerrald's head went underwater. Having got him to the beach, he coughed up stuff for some time. Muir knew he should have done the task instead. As he consoled Gerrald he watched Francois search the shallows for the escaping lobsters, grasping them before they made for the depths. Muir couldn't work out whom to support in the ordeal until a lobster bit Francois' finger causing it to bleed everywhere.

*

Twenty four hours later, it was Ebenezer Dorr and not Gerrald who Francois and Muir had inside the boat. Holding on nervously to both gunwales, Ebenezer's lanky physique was more suited to two hundred foot ships not twelve foot rowing boats.

He seemed incapable of keeping his weight in the centre and it was only Muir and Francois' dexterity that stopped them from capsizing. But the estuary was a safe place to discuss Muir's future and this was no innocent day's fishing.

'Why can't you stay here like the others?'

Muir turned to Ebenezer as he finished his question. Francois stopped rowing on his side. They let the tide push them behind the nearby headland, thick with gum trees, so that it hid them from the governor's house.

'I'm determined not to put a thing as precious as liberty in Governor Hunter's hands.'

As Muir spoke, Ebenezer looked out to sea. 'If they find you out there you'll be hung up by the yardarm.'

'I know.'

'Well, what kind of a freedom's that?'

They both stared bleakly at HMS *Providence*, anchored at the mouth of the bay until Ebenezer noticed his fishing line twitching along the gunwale. Life emerged from the depths. At first, just panicked glimmers piercing the sun's reflections. Later, ferocious rotations that swung the line under the boat.

Ebenezer perilously looked over the side but received a disapproving prod from Francois' oar. They all waited in anticipation until finally a modest silver bream broke the surface. Its tail occasionally slapped the hull.

They were relieved. The previous catch that day was a dwarf lion fish. They'd had to cut the line not wanting to touch its venomous dorsal fins, a mistake Muir had made before.

'If I'm found to be harbouring you, I'll be charged. We were searched by the patrol boats when we came into Port Jackson. It'll be no different going out,' warned Ebenezer.

'Then I'll meet you out there.'

'Out of sight of land?' said Francois.

'How?' added Ebenezer.

'You think I took up boating just to fish?'

'You'll drown out there in this.'

'If you were aboard, perhaps.'

Francois smiled and half nodded in agreement at Muir's response to Ebenezer. Muir removed the hook from the bream's mouth and as he leant forward to put it amongst the others, his miniature globe dropped out of his top pocket.

The Frenchman was quick to pick it up.

'I'd rather die trying to be free than live in this place.'

Francois saw the seriousness of Muir's statement. He studied the globe's detail. A little time passed. Enamoured by Muir's worldliness, he reached inside his shirt to pull out a hand held compass and then lifted the chain over Muir's head.

'I've confidence in you.'

The needle rotated onto the north south line.

Muir looked past the globe, past HMS *Providence*, due east.

'Thank you, Francois.'

But Ebenezer was still undecided.

'You'll be as much a liability in Boston.'

'I'll swim ashore before you enter port.'

Muir smiled persuasively. Francois turned to Ebenezer and muttered almost privately, 'he's still convinced the President of the United States sent you to retrieve him.'

Muir breached their privacy. 'It is meant to be. We didn't find each other by accident. You didn't have the good fortune of picking up Francois' seal skins, without providence playing its part.'

Ebenezer looked back at the British naval ship.

'That's what I fear, Muir, HMS *Providence* will play its part, and not in your favour.'

The bream was now basking on a bed of its own brethren. Whilst the other fish stared unknowingly, there was still a mind behind the most recent catch and it seemed to have its eye on Ebenezer who was now walking above it trying to make his way passed Francois and Muir. With clumsy footwork, he stepped momentarily on the gasping fish and sprayed its eggs over the decking. Francois saw this and tried to point it out but did not know the English words. Instead he muttered, 'attention aux oeufs de poisson!' to both Ebenezer and Muir's dismay.

Wrapped up in trying to convince the captain of his venture, Muir ignored Francois to support Ebenezer as he stepped onto the seat to examine the patrol boats guarding the entrance of the bay.

Ebenezer explained the plan.

'You'll leave on Wednesday evening after sunset. We'll leave on Thursday at dawn, eight hours later. You must stay on the same compass bearing. Due east. We'll find you out of sight of land, at dawn, on Friday. But first, you must pay me ten guineas.'

That was all Muir had left. Stepping back down, Francois again warned Ebenezer about the fish eggs but he was dumbfounded and as his first foot landed it slid along every one of the boat's clinkers and within a fraction of a second, the captain had fallen overboard into the depths of the estuary.

High on Ebenezer's decision to take him aboard, Muir couldn't quite believe what had just happened.

'You want your guineas now, Captain, or ashore to avoid sinking?'

Fortunately for Muir, Ebenezer's ears hadn't quite cleared properly. Francois' efforts to maintain a straight face crippled at this point and he hid his amusement only by picking up the pregnant, gasping half trodden fish.

Though its jaw was beginning to lock, it was still alive. Muir took it from Francois and slipped it back into the estuary where, he liked to think, it swam beside Ebenezer as he swam his way back to Cockle Beach, a mascot he would maintain in his mind on the day of the escape.

*

On Wednesday morning, Muir looked out across the estuary where Ebenezer had fallen overboard. Now overseen by soldiers, convicts trawled their nets from the shore into the depths. It wouldn't have been a good day for him to fish considering the disturbances they were making.

His rowing boat had lain upside down all day. By its sides, a few dead dogfish lay strewn around. They'd been used to sand the varnished hull to a matt finish in the hope that mud would stick to the sides. In the heat, the expression on Muir's face seemed as imperilled as the grimaces of the dead.

He looked again at the letter he would give to Palmer to post to the President of the United States, George Washington. It outlined a plan of escape and requested assistance if he reached Philadelphia.

In his other pocket was a letter to Governor Hunter he would also deliver in due course and a statement giving his lands to Palmer's Boston and Company.

Palmer would be furious at him sanding down the boat but perhaps acquiring Muir's lands would make amends. He'd kept both letters on his person in case his house was searched having heard that the Reverend's farm had been a few months back.

Looking down the coast by the quay, *The Otter* was being fitted out for departure. Many were surprised at how little trading Ebenezer Dorr had engaged in during his stay at Port Jackson. But Muir knew the reason for this and kept it well hidden. As the plan of escape raced around his mind, his solitude was breached by a figure standing over him.

It was Captain Broughton of the ship, HMS *Providence*. Muir pushed the letters deep into his trouser pockets and hoped a search was not on the cards.

'Strange to be sanding down a perfectly decent hull, Mr Muir.'

'Fish see their reflections in the glaze. It repels them. It's reducing my catch. An aborigine pointed it out to me.'

'Are you preparing this boat for a stealth operation?'

'Whatever do you mean? I've everything I could possibly ask for. Who would want to escape from a paradise like this?'

'Someone who believes in the principle of freedom.'

'Freedom's an ideal I left behind a long time ago. Compromise's the watchword of today.'

Broughton was almost convinced when an inkling of doubt trickled down into his mind like a bead of sweat. He was just about to mount a case for this disbelief and demand that Muir be searched when cries came from the other side of the estuary.

Officers fired into the depths.

Climbing up onto some nearby rocks to get a better view, a limbless soldier could be seen drifting face down.

Broughton raised his pistol and searched for a shark fin.

Muir knew that having been fed, the shark would be well below the surface. Broughton's efforts were pointless.

'Captain Broughton can I row you back to save you a walk down the estuary and back?'

The captain hesitated. Saying no would have implied he was scared. Saying yes could endanger them both.

'But you say they'll not be scared off by their reflections.'

'Sharks are the only fish not to be. They eat their own I'm told. But I suspect it'll not be feeding for a while yet.'

Protecting his pride, Broughton turned the boat upright and placed the paddles inside somewhat against his intuitions.

As they made their way towards the commotion on the other shore, Muir noticed an intruder entering Hunters' Hill. Not wanting to involve the captain, he did not point it out but instead engaged in conversation.

'I believe it's the opening night of the colony theatre. Have you a ticket?'

'What's being played out?'

'A revenge of some sort...'

'You believe in revenge, Mr Muir?'

'No. Justice and fairness, yes. But not revenge.'

They were nearing the shore. The convicts were still on the embankment. Soldiers waded in search of the shark but Captain Broughton was keen to get onto dry land.

'Thank you, Mr Muir. Remember the terms of your sentence. If I find you outside this colony, I'll hang you by the yardarm, myself. A British court's sentenced you; the Royal Navy will enforce that sentence if need be. Farewell.'

Muir rowed against the current towards his house, wondering what in God's name the intruder was up to. On the way he heard something slide against the hull. His heart raced. He paddled harder, fearing the shark's presence but he was corrected when the limb of the decapitated soldier bobbed up beside him.

Running up the embankment with an oar in his hands, he entered the ground floor. Nothing was unusual. He ran upstairs hearing muffled screams. Wood scraped against wood and banging shook the timber walls.

In the bedroom, Jane was pinned down beneath the convict. His breeches were around his ankles. Her nose was bleeding all over the sheets. Her dress was forced up to her midriff and her blouse was torn down the middle.

The sickening shunts of the bedstead halted only as Muir cracked the oar against the convict's skull sending him to the floor in convulsions of despair.

Throwing the covers over Jane and passing her a handkerchief, Muir inspected whether he'd killed the rogue. As he turned the man over he was astounded to find it was Kidlaw.

Looking out of the window, Muir watched Captain Broughton talking to the soldiers guarding the convicts by the shore. Kidlaw must have escaped during the shark attack.

Worried that Broughton would inspect Hunters' Hill, Muir thought it wise to hide the body in the fish store and having tied him up dragged him across the field all the time hoping Broughton was still talking to the soldiers.

Jane was too traumatised to help and Muir was surprised how heavy an unconscious body was, dragging its heals in the meadow grass.

Inside the fish store, Muir heaved Kidlaw up before tipping him face first into an old bath full of fish and lobsters. With the doors bolted, his back on the sun hot panels and his eyes closed, he caught his breath until he heard a voice.

'Mr Muir.'

Jesus, Muir thought. Broughton was here, he must have seen everything. His luck was up.

'You know, I think…'

Broughton prevaricated.

'Yes, captain, you think?'

'… I will join you at the colony theatre after all. Today seems a perfect day to muse on revenge.'

Muir thought of his oar splitting Kidlaw's skull, confusing the captain's comment with his own action.

'The shark attack on the fishermen, nature's vengeance?' clarified Broughton.

'Oh right, I see,' Muir tried desperately to get it together. 'Yes, that reminds me, I must get some fishing done before the tide turns.'

'The tide is always turning. Remember that.'

Muir didn't quite understand so just remained silent.

'The shark doesn't deter you?'

'No.'

Shaking his head, Muir walked over to his fishing boat. A muffled rasping sound emanated from the outhouse.

Broughton and Muir looked at each other.

'Livestock. Just livestock. The lobsters aren't quite dead,' explained Muir, 'the soldiers' wives like them as fresh as possible. Did you know they make that sound to deter predators?'

'No,' said Broughton.

'I wouldn't go inside. They're roaming all over. It's anarchy.'

'You said you hadn't been out today.'

'Yesterday's catch.'

Muir pushed out the fishing boat hoping his confidence would deter any further interest, hoping he would not hear the door bolt scrape across.

As he stepped aboard his boat he watched with relief, Broughton walking back to the quayside over the lee of the hill.

XIII
33° 50' S
151° 8' E

Now with a possible murder charge around his neck as well as fourteen years' transportation, Muir returned to the house. Jane wanted to be left alone. Her nose was no longer bleeding but she was still crying. Muir searched frantically for something to take their mind off the ordeal.

More post had arrived. He opened a small envelope. Inside, was a poem called *Liberty. An Ode inscribed to Thomas Muir esquire, younger of Hunters' Hill.*

He read through the verse that celebrated Isaac Newton, Sidney, and the Goddess Liberty, the bodies of Lauderdale, Fox, Sheridan, and Muir, the pride of the Scots.

The pride of the Scots, Muir thought. Clearly the poem wasn't judging his most recent action, the disposing of someone's body into a lobsters' lair. Even Jane found some amusement in the comparison.

Brave suffering son, the poem had him down as: 'In the glorious cause, see the goddess him crown, with the laurels of glory, of universal praise!' If they needed anything to lift their confidence after what had happened and after what Muir had just done, it was this poem.

*

Sydney's first theatre was selling tickets at one shilling for the gallery or flour, meat and spirits in lieu. Francois paid for Muir since he'd given all his money to Ebenezer.

As a Godly light lit up the amphitheatre they took to their seats beside two other gentlemen, who after spotting the fork lightning, tipped their caps to Francois.

With the ocean bay a backdrop to the stage, Muir enquired whether Francois had ever sought revenge against the men who had tried to kill him on Amsterdam Island.

235

'My dear friend,' explained Francois, 'when we arrived with Captain Hadley, I made Godwin and Cook freemen of the colony. I could've had them hanged but what use would that have been? They wouldn't be sitting next to you had I done that. Mr Muir, let me introduce to you to Mr Godwin and Mr Cook.'

Muir had become used to Francois' suave demeanour but the latest introduction epitomised him. To move on from his earlier slip up, Muir asked whether they were any relation to Godwin the great writer and Cook, the pioneering explorer who in their lifetime had been the first to voyage the Pacific. They both looked at him quizzically.

Francois leant towards Muir. 'Their ignorance makes me regret that decision!'

Muir laughed. 'Hopefully this performance will educate them in what they so narrowly avoided, the curse of revenge. Could Ebenezer not make the drama?'

'He's loading *The Otter*. This ocean going passage will be tough. I told him I'd eat anything but seal.'

Muir smiled. 'It's a wise time to depart. Some convicts, who escaped the colony, stole from the aborigines who retaliated against the colony taking crops and lives. Governor Hunter is to retaliate with soldiery. The aborigines will retaliate with spears. Seeking revenge by both sides will get us nowhere. I hope the governor is watching this drama. Perhaps he will learn something.'

As Muir finished speaking the theatre manager introduced the revenge tragedy to be nothing less than Shakespeare's play, *Julius Caesar*.

In the backdrop to the open air theatre, Muir noticed the latest element in his own revenge drama. HMS *Providence* had left its anchorage and was sailing out of the bay.

Like eels the Royal Navy could cross entire oceans to get what they wanted and for Captain Broughton this was more a priority than soaking up Shakespeare. Something had changed his plans and Muir hoped it had nothing to do with his intended escape.

Muir hoped *Providence* would be struck by the next fork of lightning but when he had controlled his passions he added the ship's departure to his calculations of the night's plans.

In the short term it was a benefit rather than a hindrance, for it would be difficult enough navigating past the frigates patrolling the bay.

The re-enactment of Caesar's collapse and foaming at the mouth from epilepsy reminded Muir of his concerns for Gerrald. He had brought the prints of *Convention* and *The Voice of the People*, with him. His friend was loyal and wouldn't miss an engagement, particularly given that he had his lifeworks to collect.

Something wasn't quite right and he wondered whether his fall into the shallows had adversely affected his condition.

Back in the theatre the players were making use of the deteriorating weather conditions, tallying them with Casca telling Cicero that the storm was a good sign of the evil he and his collaborators planned to carry out on Caesar.

To Muir each raindrop washed away his goodly plans but perhaps the storm arriving into Botany Bay had to be endured now so that it could be avoided later.

He looked around the theatre and wondered who would be his Cassius. Who would scupper his best laid plans? Was the man sitting to his left a future adversary as Godwin and Cook sat on his right had been to Francois in days gone by?

Should he be staying at home as Calphurnia was advising Caesar? He had protected Jane from foreknowledge of the escape plan for his sake also. He wondered whether he would be killed because he was too wanting of his own freedom in a world founded on chains.

Were he to die, would Palmer and Skirving incite the commoners to riot in protest of his death like Antony had for Caesar? His lands after all, on Palmer's instructions, would be left to the people, like Caesar's.

With the tragedy of revenge engrained in his mind Muir left the theatre before the last act and ran across to Palmer's farm. Speeches from the penultimate act rallied around his mind. He didn't much like Brutus for what he'd done and how he reminded him of both Watt and Dundas, in equal doses.

But one thing Brutus said he did agree with, that there was a tide in the affairs of men that when taken at the flood leads on to fortune and when omitted leads all the voyages of one's life bound for shallows and miseries.

Muir felt more than ever that on such a full sea as that evening, he must afloat and take the current when it served or else lose his venture. There would not be another *Otter*. That, he knew.

He knocked persistently at Palmer's but eventually gave up waiting and moved onto Gerrald's at Farm Cove. The front door was wide open, Muir guessed, to ventilate the bottom floor.

Palmer was nursing him at his bedside. Palsied, the consumption had made him bed bound for the last few weeks. He was on the verge of death. Palmer's bible, no longer read by the Reverend, was arched over Gerrald's chest, making the pages wet with sweat.

Deep down Muir wanted Gerrald to escape with him but knew that he was not strong enough for a night on land never mind a night at sea.

Instead, he dedicated the occasion to saying his goodbyes. Gerrald and he held each other until Muir remembered the prints of *Convention* and *The Voice of the People* in his satchel.

Trying to focus through the tears welling up in his eyes he read: *A Convention. The only means of saving us from ruin. In a letter addressed to the people of England. By Joseph Gerrald.*

Between sentencing and transportation writing the book had kept Gerrald sane. Hopefully, knowing, on his deathbed that his works were both in print would give additional meaning to his struggling last days.

Muir knew that soon it would be all that remained of this dutiful human being. In dedication he swept through

Convention murmuring sentences that were particularly poignant.

The pamphlet opened with a point made by the philosopher, John Locke, that people should endeavour to put governance into such hands, that may secure to them the ends for which Government was first erected.

Then Gerrald followed it with the assertion that, 'war declared by government must be supported by the people. For, it is the blood of the peasants that flows in battle not the King's and it is the purse of the tradesman that is emptied in the contest.'

Quoting Swift, he wrote that the war that preceded the peace of Rustic amounted to the loss of one hundred thousand men and a debt remaining of twenty millions.

Citing Dalrymple's *Memoirs of Great Britain and Ireland*, he made clear that eighty thousand poor people had died of want back at home because corn was exported to the continent to feed Dutch and German allies, doubling its price in England and quadrupling its price in Scotland.

Gerrald argued that this was all to give a king to another people. It was all 'to interfere in the internal government of another country, in order to prevent the people from choosing not only those whom they think proper to govern them, but also in what manner the people shall be governed.' The result was, 'a tyranny as insulting to their feelings, as it was destructive to their rights.'

Thinking about the present war that had extended from the Straits of Gibraltar to the bottom of the Baltic, Muir put into context events since the treaty of Rustic, a century earlier.

Gerrald had provided an account of The War of Jenkins' Ear. Its aim was to protect British commerce. But that purpose was soon usurped by the romantic folly of helping the Empress Queen of Hungary to preserve the dominions of the Elector of Hanover and fix the Imperial crown upon the head of a princess of the house of Austria.

The excitation of the civil war that was Culloden was next addressed. It was designed to fix The House of Hanover on the British throne, raping, pillaging and plundering in its wake.

Muir thought of Ebenezer Dorr and his suffering there. That sympathy imbued in him a confidence that the captain would stick to his side of the bargain when it came to the escape.

Concluding this sad history of recent British foreign policy, Gerrald declared, 'war then, you perceive, Fellow Citizens, is only a frightful enumeration of massacres, assassinations, proscriptions and devastations. And the mild and gentle methods by which we in Europe make a boast to conduct it, are nothing more than an improvement in the mystery of murder. ...Man was not naturally hostile to man. He was made for labour and not for war.'

They were the most satisfying parts to print and he realised that perhaps for the first time a writer had uncovered the pity of war. Concluding this brief exposition, Gerrald argued that the only justification for any war was the principle of self defence. In the present war between France and England this could only be applied by the French.

Watching the work's author slowly dying in front of him he wondered in future generations how many lives would be saved through the enactment of this principle.

As Muir searched for a handkerchief in his jacket pocket, he came across Godwin's book that Gerrald had leant him for the voyage.

'I want to return it.'

'Tomorrow to fresh woods and pastures new. That's what I told Godwin his book made me feel. And how did it affect you?' asked Gerrald.

'It got me through the ordeal on the convict ship.'

'That's what literature should do, get you through ordeals. Do you know, Godwin wrote the end of Caleb's adventure first?'

'I didn't.'

'If we could only know the end of our own adventures on their outset...'

Muir was about to comment but thought it better to remain silent. Gerrald unfolded the last page that he'd concealed the day he'd persuaded Muir to print *The Voice of the People*.

'A faithful narrative of the last illness, death and internment of the right honourable William Pitt.'

Muir ignored the sad irony.

But Gerrald didn't. 'And this is the faithful narrative of the last illness, death and internment of the right honourable Joseph Gerrald.'

His friend dying beside him was, to Muir, a man unafraid of putting his name beside his ideas and it was to Gerrald that he would now risk his life in the pursuit of personal and political freedom. He was perhaps the inspiration. In the morning they both might no longer be alive.

After a few minutes Palmer intimated that he, not just Gerrald, was too hot and took off his black vestment to reveal cotton slacks beneath.

He led Muir to the door.

'Take this.'

Muir hung the Reverend's vestment over his arm.

'Is it to bless my escape?'

Palmer looked to the ground. 'I'm no longer a man of cloth. More a man of science now. It's impracticable when boat building.'

'So why should I wear it?'

'To hide you in the night whilst you leave the bay.'

'Bless you, Palmer.'

'I still think you shouldn't go out in this storm.'

'It will have calmed by the time I set out.'

'I understand. A distant reason imparts your madness.'

'Pray for a sea change, Palmer.'

'Times on the convict ship made my prayers redundant.'

'You will write to Gerrald's wife? What is this book in the pocket?'

'Something to read aboard *The Otter*. But not before. Go dear friend and find your freedom. One day I'll follow in your wake.'

Racing back home to find Jane asleep, Muir tried to explain the plan. But she remained drowsy and defeated.

An emptied spirit bottle still claimed her grasp.

Packing up a handful of her clothes, he heard banging from outside. Ignoring it for now he carried her, still wrapped in linen, out of the house under the moonlight.

It was then that he realised the source of the banging. The doors to the fish store were rattling and it wasn't the winds. He looked across to where the boat was beached and decided to make a run for it. But half way across, a deep thud led to the splitting of wood panels. Laden with Jane over his shoulder, he made slow progress down the second half of the field all the time wondering when Kidlaw would be upon him.

Finally, he lowered her in the front of the boat. The sand scraped against the hull more than it normally did, with her weight at the bow, but eventually the water lapped alongside.

Knee deep he stepped inside. Turning backwards to begin rowing he heard the door bolt scrape across. Catching the stones on the bottom, he paddled hard. For against the moonlit sky, Kidlaw could be seen running straight towards them.

As the convict waded into the water Muir could see he was brandishing a gutting knife in one hand and an axe in the other. Closer still Muir could see his face and forearms lacerated from lobster bites.

Wading towards them, he was within an oar's length when suddenly the seabed fell away beneath him and he had to swim. But with an axe and a knife it proved impossible. Every stride Kidlaw took into the depths, Muir dug an oars' stroke through the water drawing him further towards Cockle Beach.

Kidlaw seemed to consider dumping the weapons and swimming after them. If he needed to Muir would strike him with the oar again. This time it would be fatal for he would drown. But their assailant returned to Hunters' Hill deterred, Muir thought, by fears of the shark.

Now halfway across, Muir realised that Kidlaw could take the river bridge and scupper his departure but as he saw him return to the shore of Hunters' Hill, he wondered whether the convict still thought Jane was home.

Oil lamps still flickered inside to give that impression. The wicks would be gone by the morning. Kidlaw appeared in the downstairs room and then disappeared only to reappear in the bedroom, to attack Jane again, Muir thought.

Muir laughed a pitying laugh and looked over his shoulder to where she was resting peacefully amongst the hypnotic ripples of waters dividing at the bow.

He looked back at the land he had purchased. It had provided a pretext for buying the boat five months earlier and remained a monument to what adventures lay ahead.

Landing on Cockle Beach for the last time, he touched the ground, marked his face with its sands and bid farewell to his other landlocked accomplice.

The river bridge inland was just visible. He looked again at the house. Kidlaw this time could not be seen either at the house or along the shore towards the bridge. No doubt he would be pillaging in one of the back rooms.

Muir had to put Kidlaw behind him and so walked the boat along the estuary shoreline until he was in sight of Kirribili Point, from where he would row out into the ocean.

Earlier fears were replaced in the darkness by imaginings of the soldier's footless leg and the shark's presence. However, as he felt his way passed the large stones and boulders, he was still rationally minded enough to distinguish between fears and likelihoods.

The shark was most likely digesting the limb not looking for another. That said, he had learned from his aboriginal friend that 'Kiarabilli' meant 'good fishing spot'. What was a good fishing spot for men may well be a good fishing spot for sharks too.

As he hugged the east facing shoreline the ocean between the two headlands opened up. When the shoreline he was on turned to face north he left it, set the compass and prepared to head due east into the open water.

Under the deep shadow of Kirribilli Point, he stepped into the boat. Apart from the two patrol ships, their route to the ocean was unhindered.

But what if he met *Providence* whilst waiting for *The Otter*? What then? As this seed of doubt gained light from the uncovering moon, the dark foresail at the bow ruffled a little.

A moment later, Jane poked her head out. Muir put his finger to his lips. She remained silent but behind him on the headland noticed a silhouette against the moon.

Had Kidlaw made such progress, Muir wondered, pursuing him all this way. Muir prepared to row into the depths again where he knew they would be safe.

But suddenly another silhouette appeared. The figures then removed their hats and waved briefly. Fear turned to hope. A tense jaw turned towards a smile. Though not wanting to show the whites of his teeth, Muir could discern from their different heights that it was First Mate, Francois Pierre Peron and Captain Ebenezer Dorr.

They disappeared as soon as they had appeared not wanting to draw attention to the voyagers. Alone again, Muir waded into the ocean looking for reassurance from Jane until, a moment later, Francois jumped through the surf to embrace his friend.

'I hope you will find us on the vast ocean out of sight of land. But if you should not then we shall have perished of a death much sweeter than the life we led here.'

Muir felt a tear roll down his face as he bid farewell, but it was not his own for his eyes were dry. Stepping into the boat he wondered whether he would ever again stand on the earth.

But the moment seemed to be exhaled into the past for before he knew it, Jane was demanding more starboard oar to counteract the northerly breeze and avoid Botany Bay's leeward shore.

With HMS *Providence* gone the patrol boats seemed less vigilant than the last few weeks, no longer under His Majesty's inspection. Muir hazarded a guess that one was in fact anchored a few miles along the southern shore.

Rowing across the expanse of Botany Bay, he faced backwards and noticed occasional trails of cloudy water on the outermost edge of the boat's port wake.

Wave after wave washed away the mud layer he'd added after sanding the hull. For any of his potential captors who searched the night waters, the light wood now glimmered in the moonlight.

Exhausted from several miles of rowing, they were now at the mouth of the bay near Bradley's Head. Muir had tried to not be too hasty, to allow time for the remaining patrol boat to tack up wind to the north shore, where he hoped they'd conduct their patrols heading west away from his intended course.

The patrol ship's moonlit sails, mere slivers as seen from the trailing edge to the mast, collapsed as they tacked. Then they filled again as they went along the northern shore, curiously obeying Muir's wishes.

Now presenting their entire sail canvass as they cut across the bay, they appeared like eyes without pupils. Fogged over, blind to that which they searched.

But Muir's attention was stolen by something else. Suddenly the ocean seemed to be falling away from underneath him. The boat then crashed into the trough below.

Beyond the bay, the surging ascents and descents of the ocean swell haunted them like ghosts from a storm that had ended long ago. He'd sensed nothing like this in the estuary and feared their escape too ambitious.

Out in the ocean, the waves reflected little moonlight. Against their intuitions, they set their course due east into the unknown.

As Muir looked back at the penal colony, now just the flickering of oil lamps and open fires, he inhaled deep breaths of satisfaction at being free from man's mastery over his fellow man, free from the crude mechanics of government, free from circumstances born out of corruption and despotic control.

But flung into what? He did not know. A fate decided by a jury of nature's elements? This time it was his eyes that were tearful. As he wiped them on Jane's sleeve, he looked back to see the patrol boat making its run downwind along the mouth of the bay.

It had suddenly advanced upon them in the wake of his time sapping thoughts. Drawn by his pursuit of freedom. Matters became graver still when he realised that now out of the confines of the penal colony their capture would result in hanging. He had saved Jane from Kidlaw but exposed her to death.

Ordering her to lie down, Muir pulled Palmer's vestment hood over his brow and suppressed his rowing to avoid creating any white water.

Since they had not turned directly towards him he could infer that they were still undetected, but as the patrol boat reached the south shore it came even closer.

Muir was exhausted and his eyes seemed to be failing him. Or was it simply the moon behind a cloud? He looked up but no clouds or stars could be seen. No stars, he thought.

He looked again at the patrol boat.

Nearer now but fainter, like a ship brushed into a watercolour.

'It's the sea fog, Tom.'

Muir turned around to Jane and realised she was right. As he looked beyond her and the bow, increasingly thicker banks of fog approached to swallow them up.

He turned back to the stern. The patrol boat was a ghost of its former self, turning into the wind as if heading into a tack. Still pointing straight at them, it disappeared like a daunting idea in an unpleasant dream extinguished by one's own waking.

But was it still heading straight at them or was it beating back upwind to the northern shore? The fog deprived him of this knowledge. He rowed due east waiting for its re-emergence wondering if he had been seen, rehearsing in his mind their hanging, but every thought was stolen by the damp wisps drifting in from the north east.

He looked behind him. Jane had fitted the sail to the mast and was binding it to the boom. Soon, perhaps, he could rest his arms.

Fine reaching across the wind, trying desperately with the tiller to hold a course due east, Muir's mind drifted to his saviours. Ebenezer and Francois would be loading their seal skins back aboard, settling debts and chasing payments.

He wondered whether his fish stall would be missed tomorrow afternoon and whether the alarm would be called before *The Otter's* departure.

His absence from church on Sunday would blow the whistle on his escape but by then *The Otter* would have left Port Jackson and Governor Hunter would be powerless to act.

But what if the patrol ship had seen him? What if they stopped *The Otter* from leaving at dawn? What then? They wouldn't need to be hanged at the yardarm they would be hung by the elements. He checked the compass. Their bearing was a few degrees south of east.

*

As the sea fog began to disperse and the dawn light emerged from over the transom, the wind also began to veer a few degrees to the east.

Now on the nose, he detached the sail and took to the oars again. They'd sailed for four hours.

He intended to row for another two.

As the sun burned the sea fog, a glistening sea emerged hemmed in by a thin dark coastline and a line of grey bellied clouds further out to sea.

Eight hours had passed from departure to dawn. He'd hoped that the coast would be out of sight. But it wasn't. So he drove himself to row some more but collapsed backwards and summarily collapsed.

For a few hours both Jane and Muir slept oblivious to the fact that the other was sleeping and not rowing. Occasionally, stirring apparitions that HMS *Providence* was towering over them would wake them whereupon they'd check the surrounds and fall a slumber once more.

Eventually, Jane awoke properly and scanned the coastline for any masts. *The Otter* should have left by now.

With the sun directly above her she kept rowing and guessed that it was around midday.

Rowing out, Muir had told her that the rendezvous was planned for dawn. A few hours later could be expected, but seven or eight? Had they drifted south out of view of *The Otter's* crow's nest? Had Ebenezer abandoned Muir's agreement with the silver in his possession? She couldn't wake Muir not after all he had done for her but the rowing was becoming fruitless as the winds and seas began to rise again.

Opening his eyes sometime later, Muir's world became no brighter. Then he realised, dusk had come and another night at sea was on their hands.

Between the buoyancy tanks and beneath the seat panel there was just enough room for them both to lie down but it was no welcome bed. More a coffin, he feared.

That said, with their weight so low, it was surprisingly stable against the growing ocean swell. They insulated themselves in the sail. But as the winds strengthened it would free itself from where they'd tucked it around them.

The sea spray left them soaking wet.

They knew they mustn't fall asleep.

It was becoming cold enough to die of exposure.

Time telescoped whilst they waited, with only the swell beating out what their minds had reconfigured to be the seconds of each minute and the minutes of each hour.

As the boat rocked, Muir caught sight of the sea around him. White horses broke on every other wave. A horizon of distant oceanic mountains and an atmosphere of perpetually uplifted haze confused the distinction between sea and air.

Then suddenly everything disappeared.

After a drenching, they lay within the cavity of the boat and lodged themselves in place against the underside of the seat.

It had turned turtle and made itself into a sea cave.

A finite air pocket was theirs but for how long?

At moments it was so quiet and so dark.

They had been flipped by a breaking wave.

Muir had worked out that much.

'We should stay in here for as long as we can, then climb onto the hull.'

'We'll suffocate, or drown,' feared Jane.

'We won't. I promise.'

It was as if a door had been closed on the storm outside. Although the waves smashed onto them from time to time, they were secure to the ocean in a way they had not been before when the boat was upright.

'Lodge your feet against the ledge and your shoulder against the bulkhead.'

They embraced each other to secure themselves further. The shark flashed through his mind and then through hers but they were too tired to react to it and had begun to fear nothing.

Feeling Palmer's vestment swaying in the depths, his mind drifted into the boat shed. The dry sawdust and the blueprints lay out like a still ocean. His boat had seemed enormous on land not the fraction of a wave face that it was now.

He wished he could trust Ebenezer like he could trust Palmer and he began to have doubts about any rendezvous whatsoever with *The Otter*.

The prospect of them finding an upturned hull with no sign of life haunted him. Occasionally, he would draw his head nearer to Jane's to check she was still breathing and hadn't succumbed to the cold.

Each time he checked, a welcome breath cooled him further.

The darkness did not intensify when he closed his eyes.

The only other things he could sense were the cold, the storm and the grain in the wood that Palmer had so meticulously sanded for him. In his mind he knew where every knot lay and where every piece of wood joined.

'What've you brought me to?'

Jane's voice cut into his mind. He had no answer. He did not know what was going to happen. It was then that he smelt blood. Jane's nose had begun to bleed again. The shark flashed through his mind again. But through hers, he hoped not.

That morning, the sun seemed to rise and fall a thousand times as the undulating swell redefined their horizon. Entwined in their mutual exhaustion, they'd become a chrysalis within the linen sheet that Jane had been sleeping innocently under days before.

He now hoped they'd turn into something that could leave this heartless place as they lay on top of the hull's unsettling cambers. As he turned his head to her, Muir noticed her bruise clad body purpling the wet sheets.

She awoke as the boat dragged down another wave face. The relentless crashing of white water consumed her. When she had climbed back on the hull, Muir used the time to feed her some of their rescued supplies.

As he did so, the compass slipped out from under her blouse. What was once their collaborator had now colluded against them. But the needle was unmoved by their change of perspective. Unconcerned by the wash of time eating away at their fates it pointed north towards its co-conspirator, the eye of the storm.

In what had Muir based his trust in Ebenezer and Francois? His own veiled hope of freedom, a pang of desperation and the belief in America?

Now all of these were shrouded under the coat of dried sea salt fixing his expression of fatality into what he feared would become his death mask.

The sun would then leather his face until the birds gouged out his eyes. The next sea surge would throw him into the ocean. He thought of the bream and like it, wished to survive the unfathomable depths. His right eye looked up, not at three men deliberating over the price of freedom but at God, the forces of nature and the jury deliberating over their fates.

Following a convulsion or two, Jane leaned over the side and vomited. As the wave licked the hull, the sick clung to the surface momentarily, before returning to the water. As the boat rolled she saw her broken reflection an arm's length away.

Then, something in the depths, a bloated carcass reduced in parts to just bone and ligament, a socket with an eye plucked out.

She reached into the water and prodded it but felt nothing.

In her peripheral vision she saw it further astern. Lying back and looking skyward, a fateful yelp ricocheted through her mind. She remembered standing on its paw, then part of the lurcher's coat washed flesh side up.

It was peppered with bite marks.

They'd turned turtle at some point in the night. Muir remembered that much but he couldn't remember clambering out of the air pocket onto the upturned hull.

Before sunrise he recollected the horned moon snarling at him and later, a cloud making a face for a moment as he too came close to fully fledged hallucinations.

What exactly was he hoping for? His companions had failed him and if found by any other they were to be hanged. They had lost their oars. He assumed the rigging would be ruined. He wondered whether the boat could be turned back upright or whether they had the energy for the task.

As the waters around him calmed momentarily he was able to see towards the horizon.

To his astonishment, a ship's sail bleached a patch of the sky.

Had it two masts like *The Otter*, or four like HMS *Providence*?

Was it their saviour or their nemesis?

Had it come to defend or prosecute them?

He didn't know whether to attract its attention, whether to fight their case. Lowering his body into the water, he dunked his head under.

Gasping for breath, he came back up inside the hull's air pocket. Dimmed by the ocean hue, as his eyes adjusted he followed a rope down into the depths where he felt for the end of the mast suspended below them in the darkness.

As he swam down and freed the rope from the mast cleat, he wondered whether its weight would drag him under forcing him to let go. But it didn't.

Clambering back on top of the capsized hull, Jane helped him drag the increasingly weighty mast out of the water. Shivering, she removed her crimson blouse and tied it to the top of the mast.

Holding the mast upright, Muir noticed that the upturned hull was sitting lower in the water. It was causing them to sink slightly. But it was a gamble they'd have to take if they had any chance of being seen.

For some time they watched the ship on the horizon and prayed that it would turn, present its foresails and perhaps fire a gun or two. But it did nothing. Instead, the back of their rowing boat slipped underwater with each passing wave, raising the bow and making it unstable to rest upon.

Muir hazarded a guess that the weight of the mast had submerged the buoyancy tanks and water was finding its way in between the joints.

He looked up at the clouds and prayed to Palmer believing in his boat building abilities. But then he remembered how Palmer had given up on God and realised he would have to relinquish the mast or the entire boat would go under leaving them flotsam upon the waves.

Eventually, as the stern totally submerged and the bow nosed upwards, the decision to ditch the mast was made for them. They too gradually slipped into the water. The boat sat a little higher but it would only be a matter of time before the buoyancy tanks filled entirely with water.

As Muir jolted down the last of the hull's tiers, he felt something in his pocket. Slipping his hand in, he pulled out the wax sealed booklet that Palmer had given him.

With only the bow of the boat above the waterline, they held each other in their arms. Cracking the wax casing against the hull, he was astonished to discover that it had kept the pages bone dry. It seemed madness to do this inches from the water but if he were ever to read *The Sympathy of Priests* it had be now.

With wet hands he turned the page. A droplet dragged through the text rendering the letters indiscernible. He read quickly, remembering when it had arrived for Palmer at Port Jackson.

The Priests spoke to him as if they knew of his current strife. In their words, they had seen him amid his bark's dread, his horrors brave.

They'd seen him rove beside the southern wave, anxious to learn through many a tedious day if Europe's freedom would flourish or decay. He pictured the priests in their cathedrals at Durham, Edinburgh and Exeter and thanked them for putting his struggle into print.

They compared Reverend Palmer to the priests of all religions, Archbishop Laud, Leighton and Biddles and wished to emulate his mind, to wrongs superior and heaven resigned.

Muir hung his head against the boat's side and looked at Jane. In his mind, he was thinking of his good friend Palmer, their journey together and their parting.

He regretted that he too should have considered freedom by degree, not as an absolute. Jane was becoming increasingly drowsy so he read from the next page.

'When peace, with all the virtues in the tain, over the wide world shall stretch her halcyon reign, and heaven born truth in simple beauty rise, such as the first descended from the skies.'

It seemed to stir her back into being. He read how the tyrant's league was in vain because for now the bounteous sire of man, through paths unseen, conducted the eternal plan.

They learned how the actions of Rome's pale despot, the Bourbon's slaughtering arm and Britain's minions were also in vain because all of man's truth and mercy to perform, rode in the whirlwind and directed the storm.

Muir also seemed energised by the priests' sympathies. They cited how rival priests were 'of Palmer's goodness, all agreed, from the sultry Tiber to the breezy Tweed.'

The Reverend's cause was being taken up by Germania, Iberia, Grecia, even Russia, till liberty of death be every nation's song. From the bleak North to Africa's sultry waste.

On the next page it mentioned Skirving and himself. Indeed, reading it aloud seemed to silence the waves around them as he shouted out:

'Ah, Muir! Thy cell they shunned, thy floating jail, no country's ties, nor Christians could avail...' The words woke Jane with intrigue. How had the priests known of his current woes?

'Though genius smiled upon thy natal hour, though science met thee in her classic bower, she who so oft allured thy generous youth with arduous toil to climb the steep of truth.'

Wonderful words about his life as it seemed to be coming to its end. What an epitaph, he thought. He read down, as if the poem held his fate in its last stanzas. But as he did so a wave clapped his face and threw water across the page.

Had Palmer given Muir the only copy? Feeling the slunk vellum shedding oil into the water, he suspected the worst. Surely, the priests would have another edition that would immortalise him and his fellow reformers.

Then Muir laughed that he was more concerned with his legacy than his actual survival. Who else needed to know but he and his dearest companion?

He looked around for the ship he'd seen earlier but the nearby rollers made the horizon tall and close so he curbed his disappointment by returning to the text, perhaps to read it for the last time.

He could decipher, 'delightful task, which oft as virtue pays, with sweet remembrance of those few short days.' And, through an unreadable few lines he picked up, 'yet more delightful task, should Heaven decree, the ruthless minion's fall, and Britain free! To hail the virtuous exiles on her shore, the apostate's envy, but his sport no more!'

Muir wanted to reread his epitaph but, now underwater, it had brayed across the page. Virtuous exiles. That is what they had become.

He longed to see any shore at this point in time but such wishful thinking wasn't wise and for the first time his head slipped under without much resistance. His body asked him to breathe again but he was resigned to the inevitable.

Until, that was, Jane grabbed him back out. And when he re-emerged the light was not the same. Was the salt water playing tricks with his eyes?

She held him up against the boat's side and suddenly they found themselves in shadows.

Strange, since he remembered the sky to be cloudless.

Opening his eyes, he saw a crucifix towering over them.

Was this the prelude to death?

He looked again.

It was the highest of a ship's yardarms.

As it approached, Muir searched for the name, dreading the thought that it might be HMS *Providence*.

With the bow heading straight towards them it was difficult to count whether it had two masts or four, nearly impossible to determine whether it was friend or foe. Muir held Jane as she had held him and they both waited for the ultimate of all verdicts.

XIV
34° 13' S
151° 30' E

The ship was practically upon them when Muir kissed Jane, having sighted Henderson on the bowsprit and the most valiant of names in their grasp, *The Otter*.

Emerging into a cabin, lit from a tiny porthole in a hue of green light, their hair intertwined like winter branches canopying a lane. Sitting up he tried not to wake her, but found it impossible for their legs were rooted together beneath the sheets.

He longed to engage in the sacred love of freedom but his mind fed on the mystery of Ebenezer's warped explanation for their delayed departure.

Had Governor Hunter really delayed *The Otter's* departure by twenty four hours? Had they really been forced to spend another night tied to their pontoon, knowing their friends were out in the ocean in just a rowing boat?

Had someone called in at Hunters' Hill to an abandoned house. Or had Kidlaw or those on the patrol boats raised the alarm.

Palmer may have delivered the governor's letter on the Saturday instead of the Sunday. Finding out the truth was a preoccupation. Ebenezer could have considered abandoning him. Had Francois directed him back on course? Yet, Ebenezer traded virtually nothing at Botany Bay. He must have been sent by President Washington to rescue him.

Eventually he aborted these newborn anxieties and amused himself in the delight of the present circumstances coupled with his letter to Governor Hunter.

Muir could still remember the words he wrote, thanking Hunter for his hospitality but bidding farewell on an invitation to practice law in the United States.

Had a colony governor ever been addressed by a convict in the manner a resident might address an hotelier? Had anyone ever before declined a compulsory jail sentence citing career ambitions? The cheek of it!

He imagined the governor at congregation, singing away, trying to hide the simple unavoidable fact that his authority had been so outrageously and yet so elegantly undermined, that the Scottish advocate had reduced the sentence of fourteen year's imprisonment to just over fourteen months!

But what of this brave new world. This was no time to be bound inside a cabin, day or night. That he couldn't decipher.

Lifting Jane up in his arms, he took her on deck. They were both struck by a majestic light coming from the waters and the smell of meat cooking in a clay stove.

It was indeed neither day nor night. The sails collapsed and filled from the swell more than the wind.

Mist locked the boat in a bubble of perhaps a few leagues.

Beyond that, HMS *Providence* could have been lurking ominously but at that moment they were too tired to contemplate such trials.

What was most spectacular was the dazzling magic under lighting them. For the ocean top was awash with phosphorescence.

Shoals tore through the waters as if on fire. Occasionally, a dolphin would dart passed leaving a trail of light, like a shooting star. It was as if nature's creatures were joining with them in their celebration of freedom.

Muir was convinced that the phosphorescence was sent by God but Ebenezer thought it just something in the water, lots of tiny creatures trapped in their own small worlds, very much like them.

They sent a bucket over the edge to examine the water.

'The naturalists call it Medusa,' said Ebenezer.

'But the mariners call them Flemish bonnets,' said Francois.

Whatever it was called, whatever its cause, nature or providence, they were undivided in chinking their wine filled goblets, their cups of kindness and letting their alcohol induced minds glory in the serendipity of the moment.

The green tinged sails, the green tinged everything. This wonderful light shining on nothing else but their world and the other free creatures in their sphere.

Francois then placed his clenched fist onto the palm of Muir's hand and unclasping it like God himself, released the globe of the world. Jane returned Francois' compass and delightedly Muir passed his globe to Jane.

But she missed the catch. The globe rolled down the deck. Everyone expected it to land in the ocean. After fifty yards though, it stopped under the foot of Alasdair Henderson.

After studying it, he handed it to Jane concluding that, 'our worlds are once again our own!' They all chinked their goblets, all except Henderson and Captain Ebenezer Dorr.

Crashing into their bunk, Muir soon succumbed to an entirely different world. A wine cellar. Margarot's or Watt's? The dream had not yet decided.

Robert Dundas was watching soldiers drop pikes on the ground whilst reading a letter from J.B.

Immune from detection, Muir peered over his shoulder.

Attached to the letter was Angus Cameron's plan of insurrection. Having provided this information, J.B wanted to end his espionage work requesting settlement of five guineas and his letters returned to avoid future judgement.

Dundas smiled.

Footsteps echoed from the stairway. Dundas covered his lamp and hid. Watt, now in person, perused the wine racks holding the labels close to his lamp searching for a 1764 French red.

As he walked deeper into the cellar, a clattering, a yelp, a thud and a smash of glass ended in his lamp going out and the wine trickling across the slabs, like blood.

The darkness was short lived for Dundas pulled his cloak away from his own lamp and accused Watt of plotting armed revolt, pointing out the sixteen pike heads.

'These are not mine.'

'They're in your cellar.'

'So are you. Master. It's J.B. Your diligent spy.'

'Robert Watt, I don't know you by any other name. Soldiers, arrest him.'

'I've written to you as Watt, also.'

'I know nothing of that business,' insisted Dundas.

Muir knew he was dreaming but was too intrigued to acknowledge the fact, finding himself next in the dungeons of Edinburgh Castle.

Perpetual dripping cursed their minds. Watt languished beside him in torn stockings and dirty linens, cut by the light from a sole arrow slit.

A newspaper was flung through the cell bars.

He requested that Muir read the news.

'You are to be hanged by the neck but not until you are dead. For you are to be taken down, your heart to be cut out and your bowels burned before your face, your head and limbs severed from your bodies and held up to public view, and your bodies shall remain at the disposal of His Majesty, and the Lord have mercy on your soul.'

Watt wrote a request for a pardon from His Majesty, and screamed with injustice at pleading forgiveness for something he hadn't done.

In Weymouth, Muir looked over the shoulder of King George III. A letter from Dundas detailed information from the spy, J.B, concerning himself and Palmer. But it had been dealt with a few months back so the King committed it to the flames.

What concerned him now was the fate of Robert Watt.

A government report stated he'd lost his money in the wine trade at the beginning of the war and was indiscreet enough to associate too closely with the radical reformers.

Five thousand insurgents armed with pikes, guns and grenades, were to seize the chief dignitaries of the City, the Public Offices and the Banks, and besiege in the Castle such soldiers as refused to go over to the rebels.

The same night risings were intended in London and Dublin. The King would be compelled to dismiss his Ministers and to dissolve parliament, and the new one would consist of such men in whom 'the people' could confide.

'Why hadn't J.B. identified this radical earlier,' the King said to himself?

Despite Watt's betrayal of Muir, in his dream Muir still called out, 'Robert Watt is J.B. He betrayed me but he served you and now you are to send him to the gallows.'

The words went unheard.

The jailers in Edinburgh Castle placed a red nightcap on Watt's head and wrapped him in an old coat. Muir and he concerned themselves with the stars, staring at the heavens whilst hundreds of onlookers stared at Watt.

Blindly, the hangman unbound him and conveyed him to the Tollbooth. Muir caught sight of the hangman's face beneath the hood. It was Dundas. Watt knelt and prayed with the Minister on his left hand side.

'The whole paths of the Lord our God are truth and mercy sure, to such as keep his covenant and testimonies pure. Now for thine own name's sake, O Lord, I humbly entreat to pardon mine iniquity, for it is very great.'

Muir wondered which injustice the Minister was begging pardons for, Watt's or the government's?

The condemned man then read the fourteenth chapter of John's Gospel: 'When I have gone away and have prepared a place, I shall come back to take you to myself, so that you may be where I am.'

Then Muir thought J.B and Robert Watt would be one.

The crowds listened to Watt.

'Have I been so long among you...and yet you do not know me?'

Some were as hooded as the hangman, obsessed and ashamed in equal measure by the approaching spectacle. They knew nothing of the truth but in Watt's reading of the gospel there were words that coded something of the government's betrayal.

'What I say to you, I do not say from myself. The father who dwells in me does the work.'

After praying some more Watt walked to the scaffold, embracing both Ministers. He ascended the platform by three steps but then came back down and prayed again.

'The rope will be placed around your neck and the platform will be dropped beneath you.'

Watt recognised Dundas' voice and replied, 'I brought the Society to its knees and this is how I'm repaid.'

Dundas led him onto the trapdoor, slipped the noose over his head and tightened the loop until it rested against his Adam's apple and vertebrae.

He then whispered, 'my father tells me these abuses are imaginary. The Scottish nation does not feel them to exist.'

Watt fell with a jolt and a bleak vertebral crack preceded the rope's creaking.

He hung like a steadied pendulum.

Watching the clock, thirty five minutes later the rope was lowered. Dundas pulled Watt's body to one side with a hooked staff and heaped it onto the planking. Before any rigor mortis set in, he prised the rope from his neck with crude incisors.

Now laid out on a black table before the expectant crowd, he lifted the larger of the two axes and passed it by the oil lamp's flame to show the crowds and to warm it in the belief that it would cut more decisively. Cries and shouts of horror burst forth as he held the axe high in the night sky.

Those whose sympathies had calcified, who could coldly watch, saw the first axing rip open the jugular, tendons, muscles and throat, pooling blood all over the table and Dundas.

The second axing broke through Watt's spine. Dundas pulled the head from the strips of skin and muscle that had evaded the blade.

To just Robert Watt's body, Dundas whispered, 'you asked me not to reveal my correspondence with you to anyone and that I have done. No one knows anything of that.'

The Minister found it strange and with blood still cascading, Dundas held Watt's head up.

'This is the head of a traitor!'

He made his way to the front of the stage and the Minister began... 'May the external blessings we have long enjoyed be transmitted unimpaired unto future generations. May our gracious Sovereign, long reign over a free and a happy people.'

*

Screeching roused Muir. They had slept for days. Robert Watt's spirit had instilled nightmares in Muir's mind and he was glad to realise that he had been beside Jane all that time.

Their cabin had become part burrow to their mutual affections and part bunker protecting them from the wilds of the elements as they followed a bearing to Cook's River, north of the Sea of Coral.

He recalled Gerrald's letter concerning Watt. He'd suspected that Dundas' need for Watt had disappeared when the Society floundered.

But he hadn't entirely discounted the possibility that Watt may have abandoned spying on the Society when he was won over by its ideals, taking it too far by engaging in the excesses of militancy.

Muir doubted Watt would have taken that route though. Although devious he was not a man of war, rather a man of letters. It came to Muir that Dundas had a secondary fatal occupation for Watt following his use as a spy.

To stem criticism in Parliament for being heavy handed against the corresponding societies, Dundas needed a means of showing parliamentarians what might have happened had he not been so aggressive against the reformers.

That 'might have been' was Robert Watt's plan of armed revolt against the state. Dundas could say that had he not been so harsh, a plethora of revolts would have materialised, not just Watt's.

Muir then remembered what he had hypothesised at his trial. He had wondered why some ruffians had not been procured who could at least give a manly testimony to the Society's 'atrocious' plans rather than relying on a servant girl and a hairdresser to prove a crime which required the cooperation of many thousands of bearded men.

Dundas had taken note of Muir's idea and put it into practice. After all, the supposed armed revolt was never demonstrated.

Muir then realised something else; by getting rid of Watt Dundas had also rid himself of someone who knew intimately his own dubious methods and the depths of his subterfuge.

The scaffold was the establishment's way of tying up loose ends and they didn't give a second thought to killing a man who had served them, who had perhaps single handedly, through collecting documents and providing reports, brought down the Society for the Friends of the People on the instructions and payments of the state.

With these thoughts heavy on his mind he remembered another thing that Gerrald had written. A prisoner recently incarcerated with him in the same cell at Newgate, having come down from Scotland, vouched that Dundas had even watched Watt's trial knowing fine well he was his diligent spy, J.B.

Given that Watt's supposed armed revolt was never demonstrated, Muir concluded that the government had overridden the legal principle of being innocent until proven guilty and replaced it with the horror of being assumed guilty without the opportunity of proving one's innocence.

The screeching hadn't quietened whilst he'd been thinking through these lines of reasoning. Pulling the sheets over their heads made little difference either so Muir went up on deck keen to find out where their night wanderings had brought them.

Red tropical birds were circling around the crow's nest where Ebenezer was studying the horizon through a telescope.

'A few more degrees south, Francois!'

Following Ebenezer's instruction, Francois pulled the tiller towards him and the ship off the wind.

Through the telescope was the glimpse of an island, though it was lost to the ship's motion only to be found again amongst a thick wall of sea spray.

'Reefs ahead!' shouted Ebenezer.

These islands were, however, more elusive to the monocle than the cartographer's charts for if *The Otter's* log and bearings were correct they were about to embark upon Mongo Lahy.

An hour later Jane was shaving Muir's face on deck whilst he was trying his hand at splicing a rope end. *The Otter* was closing in on the thick walls of sea spray that were rearing up on themselves to create standing waves.

Henderson had climbed the foremast to act as a second lookout and passed on intelligence to Ebenezer, although the captain didn't seem to listen to him at all.

Being wrecked in this wilderness spelled the dire end for all of them. For they were still miles from the island, they knew nothing of the islanders' culture and expected only the worst.

The white water was now thundering down just two hundred yards to their port and starboard sides, warning them away from the reefs that were beneath them on either side.

Confidence resided mostly in Ebenezer during this tight manoeuvre. He had insisted upon passing between the reefs not deviating around them for they were very long indeed.

He knew the hull's depth below the waterline, how far the keel and rudder extended to the nearest inch, and measured it against the colours of the sea, avoiding the turquoise in favour of the deep ocean blue and avoiding at all costs the coral coloured patches of reef lurking below.

The waters between the reefs and Mongo Lahy were as flat as a lake. All of nature's energies had been absorbed. Now a mile from the shore, they made continual depth soundings to drop anchor at the first convenient spot.

A little time passed before indigenous people began to come out in their double canoes.

Perhaps eighty men and women climbed aboard.

Colouring *The Otter's* decks with bananas, watermelons, oranges, yams, sweet potatoes, pineapples, coconuts, bread and sugar cane, they stayed aboard whilst the sun set.

Only armed with short knives, friendly in nature and enthralled by the hen coop, the natives encouraged *The Otter's* crew to their share in the nutritious bounty. Later, when trading had finished the crew were particularly happy to show the women their private cabins.

When night came, Ebenezer fired a cannon.

Muir shuddered at this fearing that it could alert a nearby British Naval ship to their position. Jane calmed his nerves.

The natives understood the signal, took to their canoes and went back to their island in vibrant moods having acquired, amongst other things, a cockerel and two hens.

Following a headcount it became apparent that *The Otter* had not only lost some of its animals but also a crew member. As Muir studied the canoes dwindling in the distant light he noted that one of the paddlers had white skin and was taking a rest to put his arms around the native woman next to him.

Rather embarrassed by his spying, Muir turned the monocle away when they began kissing. But intrigued, almost in the same breath he pointed it back to the canoe.

'Francois, you're right. It's Henderson.'

The Frenchman loaded the firebox with wood.

'He returned your favour, Thomas.'

'What do you mean?'

Ebenezer could be heard approaching.

'I'll tell you some other time but you owe your life to him as much as he owes you his. Now, no more on the subject. Ah! Captain Ebenezer Dorr, we've found calm seas at last, a good night's sleep is in store after dinner.'

Muir looked through the telescope and found Henderson looking back at *The Otter*, at another confinement he had avoided, first the death penalty, then the colony, then the rock and now the ship.

He wondered what part Henderson had played in his own escape and imagined the politics surrounding departure, redefining his opinion of those he considered his saviours. But the conclusion was as unsettled as the fast darkening and still juddering image through the telescope.

As Ebenezer and Francois took transits to detect anchor slip through the night, Jane sat her bum next to Muir's and passed him a brandy.

They talked into the darkness.

Flames from the firebox lit up their faces.

They thought about Henderson, that he might become the chief of his very own island. He could start afresh amongst a gentle people who knew nothing of his murderous past.

*

A fortnight later a fresh westerly blew *The Otter* towards another island. With a telescope tied round his neck it was Muir this time who climbed through the trapdoor at the base of the crow's nest, having firmly left his fear of heights by the Glasgow docks.

After inspecting the horizon for naval ships, Muir noticed in the foreground, native people paddling out towards them. He had to double check what he thought he'd just seen and that he wasn't hallucinating. For, six pigs were aboard the canoes. He tried to remember the last time he'd eaten bacon... probably breakfast at Professor Anderson's.

During the entertaining process of hoisting them up on deck one or two slipped their harnesses and plummeted snout first into the salty water. Those that managed to place their trotters on deck then defecated making it as slippery as a frozen lake.

Jane soon had five convicts holding the yearlings with their back ends pointing overboard and downwind so that their effluent could flow effortlessly into the sea. It did so, plentifully. The natives had no concept of exchange for when it came to bartering for the pigs they demanded nothing in return and had no concern for the culture of deal making.

To satisfy their own desire not to fall into indebtedness, Jane, Francois and Muir lay out a cloth and placed in it items they thought the native people would find useful. Within it they wrapped two axes, some knives, a pair of scissors, a box of nails and a borer.

Once again out of sight of land, Francois put the finishing touches to the pig pen. He'd constructed it next to the hen coop. The remaining chicken and cockerel looked with concern at the pigs feeding off the chicken carcass the crew had eaten the night before that up until yesterday had been its neighbour.

With most of the journey expected to be on the port tack, any more pig muck would just flow over the side. But as Francois tapped the last nail into place, he caught sight of land on the horizon across to starboard. He told Ebenezer and within minutes the pigs had settled expectant that they were about to be on dry land again.

Closing in on the island from the north west, it appeared to be dissected by a strait. Ebenezer suspected that it was Annamouka.

Muir, Jane and Francois were dispatched to the island where they found the natives very sweet natured. Their smiles never seemed to leave their lips. The women did not appear to possess the slightest degree of modesty and gave themselves to the first person that happened to pass by.

This did little to challenge Muir's fidelity, naturally pleasing Jane. He seemed more interested in the fine climate and how the crusty top layer of sand broke against his stride as he and Jane traversed the beach.

They then sat with some of the natives, studying their bows and arrows. In return they inspected Muir's unloaded pistol. He noticed that the flower garlanded woman next to him had a joint missing from her smallest finger. Firing arrow after arrow against a palm tree, her archery seemed unhindered. But as another native took his aim Jane noticed the exact same amputation.

Indeed, some of the elders had two joints missing. Setting their bows upright in the sands, they played out a brief drama in front of Jane, Muir and Francois, who now sat cross legged.

The fattest native seemed to be playing chief, ordering the others to do tasks and being bowed at intermittently. In the second act the chief walked around slowly as if he had aged and then putting his hand against his heart, pretended to collapse and die.

The rest of the natives, presumably the people of his kingdom, sobbed, lowered their heads, hugged each other and part buried their dead chief in the sand.

Muir and Francois wondered what this had to do with their amputations, but all was revealed in the denouement when the natives paired up and rubbed the arrow shafts against their amputations.

'It's an expression of mourning for the death of their chief.' Francois and Muir's eyes widened as they took in Jane's interpretation.

Walking back to the boat, Muir remembered Watling describing the natives of New South Wales removing the first joints of their little fingers and the front tooth to show their devotion to their leader.

As much as he liked the islanders, he wondered why even in the middle of the Pacific Ocean, the relationship between the governed and the governing, involved suffering.

Rowing back to *The Otter* they passed Ebenezer rowing the ship's tender with five convicts aboard. The boats passed close enough to tap oars, Francois' way of saying farewell.

'Inspired by Henderson?' Muir shouted between strokes.

All but Captain Dorr nodded.

In the same breath Muir turned to Francois.

'What was it Henderson did to save our lives? I suspect we'll never see him again but I think we should know.'

Francois let a few minutes pass to make sure Ebenezer was out of earshot.

'Governor Hunter held back *The Otter's* release by twenty four hours. It had nothing to do with your escape but Henderson and I were worried for you both. He only found out about your disappearance when he went to your house to bid farewell before his own departure and found you'd had the same idea. I had to tell him your plan. In hindsight it's a good job I did.'

'How did Henderson get a place on *The Otter*?' asked Muir

'He didn't. He smuggled himself aboard. During those last hours in Port Jackson, well my mind isn't made up for his motive but Ebenezer lost faith in your rescue.'

'I thought as much.'

'The captain supposed you wouldn't have survived the storm. Henderson thought Ebenezer was only after your silver in the first instance and believed he'd never had any intention of meeting you offshore. Aboard *The Otter*, Henderson put a knife to Ebenezer's throat.'

'Threatening to kill him...?'

'And take the ship without him if he didn't come and rescue you both. Henderson's not so daft. Ebenezer couldn't report him to the governor; he'd have been imprisoned for smuggling convicts out the colony. So, the law of the ship ruled briefly with Henderson as captain.'

'So what happened after that?' asked Jane.

'Still with a blade to Ebenezer's throat, he ordered me to untie the ship from the quayside. I happily did this though with a sorry face for my disguise. Now you understand why Henderson left the ship at the first opportunity? Ebenezer would've taken him out sooner or later. But as it happened, he was saved by the natives!'

The Frenchman smiled, reflecting a smile on Muir and Jane's lips.

They climbed aboard *The Otter* and watched their captain's return. Muir's assertion that Ebenezer Dorr came on the President of the United States' orders began to crumble in his mind, striking his ego on the way down.

Francois thought how they could lift the anchor and leave Ebenezer in Annamouka and he with all his seal skins intact.

It must have crossed Muir's mind, too.

But speaking of such actions was tantamount to treason and he had tasted that before. Besides, the crew might side with the captain and take their places as first and second mate, once they had been thrown overboard.

Offering their hands to Ebenezer and lifting him back aboard, Muir noticed a hole within the armpit of his naval jacket outlined in old blood. Whilst they hauled the boat up, Muir wondered how the captain came about acquiring the jacket and whether he had a corresponding wound.

*

After a few more weeks at sea, uncharted islands were spotted. They assumed they were in waters never perhaps sailed by Europeans.

Once Ebenezer had found a suitable anchorage, Muir, Francois, Jane and four other crewmen rowed ashore in the direction of a village marked by huts covered with palm leaves.

The natives went down to the shore where the rowing boat was likely to land. Francois insisted they left their oars low down to entice the natives to come towards them but the natives remained for a long time undecided and then approached with spears.

The crew were ready to fire at the slightest sign of aggression. Muir and Jane held out gifts in one hand and kept their other hands palm up as a sign of goodwill.

They showed them knives and bananas but the natives ushered them away, whilst Francois pointed to their village and took a few steps in that direction whereupon the natives started screaming and shouting.

Francois mistakenly, tried to calm them by raising his hands to show that he had no weapons but this was misunderstood as a desire to capture them. The natives ran off only turning around from time to time to see if they were being followed.

Aborting the expedition, they rowed back to the ship.

Halfway there though, from nowhere the natives dashed towards them in canoes.

It is probable they had never seen strangers and so were understandably afraid of the whiteness of their skin and the shape of their clothes.

Once aboard, Ebenezer let the anchor slip so *The Otter* would drift into seas the natives would find unbearable, preferring this deterrent than shot and powder.

He searched the charts over rum.

'I believe we've the right to attribute to ourselves the honour of discovering these islands.'

And in that conviction Francois declared, 'we shall name them Iles de la l'Outre, after our ship, *The Otter*,' to which Ebenezer added, 'and we shall distinguish them separately as Muir, Peron and Dorr Island.'

Muir thought of the United Irishmen, whose place names had been anglicised. He was not keen.

When the sun was at its highest in the sky, Ebenezer and Francois set the ship's chronometer at noon, local time. They could now compare it with their Greenwich chronometer which read eleven o'clock at night.

'Every hour of time difference between us and Greenwich is fifteen degrees around the earth, so we're one hundred and ninety five degrees east of London as there's thirteen hours difference. Thirteen lots of fifteen are one hundred and ninety five.'

Now with their islands' longitude, Francois worked out their latitude.

'Polaris, the star above the North Pole, is concealed to us in the southern hemisphere. The equator hides it from us. Instead, we use the angle between our horizon and our sighting of the sun now it's at its highest altitude in the sky.'

Ebenezer brought the weighty brass quadrant out on deck and took several readings of the angle between the sun and the horizon.

'If we were on the equator, the sun would be directly above us, at ninety degrees to our horizon. As we move south the angle between the horizon and the sun, at midday, becomes smaller. It tells us our latitude. It's called declination, the degree to which the sun declines from directly above to our northern side.'

Ebenezer scribbled down a basic equation, that factored in the time of year, fifth of April 1796, and using an old almanac he admitted stealing from a naval ship, he estimated that the islands lay ten degrees and fifty two minutes south of the equator.

Readings of the angle between the moon and the horizon were taken for good measure. In an attempt to be as accurate as possible, he also made a note of the *The Otter's* position relative to the islands, which he estimated were two leagues to the north.

Francois was impressed. Muir and Jane were a little baffled. Their interest was born out of how it consecrated their escape relative to Greenwich, not far from where George III would be tucking himself up in bed, they thought, given that there it was nearing midnight.

The idea of having an island named after him at a moment in time when he was supposed to be in Botany Bay made his escape from the British Government all the more satisfying. But he still resented the impact this could have on those it peopled.

He therefore, insisted that the island not be named after him, suggesting Jane's name instead.

'Jane Island doesn't sound right. No offence, Jane. Why not Muir Island?' asked Francois.

'What do I know of its inhabitants? I've never stepped foot on it. I'd be no better than George III laying claim to Scotland a place he's never visited.'

'Nonsense, I'm not asking you rule it!' said Ebenezer.

'But the people should name their country. Do as you please with your islands but I don't want my name attached to such…'

'What?'

'Imperialism.'

'Muir, you're too principled. Your island's the one we never even visited. It is most probably deserted.'

'Seriously, not in my name…'

'You're having the island whether you like it or not. Francois, get this man a drink.'

Muir necked the rum and into his mind came the moment the government would learn of his contributions to Pacific exploration. The gall they would feel was perhaps worth the momentary tarnishing of his principles.

Looking at the compass, he lifted two fingers directly at Greenwich and Edinburgh, at Lord Braxfield, Robert Dundas, Lapslie and all the other rogues who'd conspired against him. Greenwich Mean Time, he mused. Mean, it had certainly been.

'As long as you're sure there weren't any inhabitants on the smallest island.'

'I didn't see anyone. Did you Francois?'

'No. Not one native.'

'Did you see anyone, Jane?'

'Not a soul.'

'Well look, I will share it with Jane.'

Next to Francois' name, Muir wrote his own family name under the smallest, most easterly island that Ebenezer had plotted onto the chart.

When Muir heard that his sentence was transportation this part of the world had sewn fear into his heart. Now he knew it for what it was; an enchanting place in danger of being plagued by Britain's problems. He hoped his island didn't succumb to such blights and watching it out of the porthole, wished his distant kingdom the best of luck.

Ebenezer had other concerns in the weeks ahead.

The north easterly headwinds had forced them west of Hawaii on a starboard tack.

April had been a slow and most uncomfortable month.

In Botany Bay, Ebenezer had learned that Vermont and Kentucky had joined the union. Jane busied herself adding two more stars to their flag. But she struggled to find enough material for the additional stripes.

Muir looked at the chart. They were heading nearer to eastern Siberia than they were America. He now at least understood the principle of tacking either side of the wind direction to make progress but wondered whether, rather than stitching stars on flags, they should be stitching the seal skins together to combat the looming Arctic conditions.

Crossing the Tropic of Cancer, they passed to port of Midway Island. Fortunately, the wind backed north westerly, allowing them to reach across the wind on a bearing towards America. His anxieties diminished.

Intermittent knocking from above their aft cabin woke Muir and Jane the next day. Curious, he went up on deck.

A rope trailed in *The Otter's* wake.

Muir asked whether they were fishing. Francois laughed as Ebenezer counted each time a knot went over the transom.

'Concentrate Francois and tell me when...'

Francois looked at the chronometer they'd brought up from the chartroom.

'The minute is up...now.'

Ebenezer closed his eyes as he worked out their speed.

'Seven knots. Hmm... Not bad. If we keep this up we'll be in Boston for Independence Day.'

The idea made Muir forget his ridiculous suggestion that they were fishing and that Henderson had forced Ebenezer to search for him out in the ocean. Previously, it had always haunted his mind in the captain's company.

He looked at each sail to check that their leading edges were not fluttering and losing power. Ebenezer and Francois grinned at how political ambitions were making him a better sailor.

'Tomorrow, I'll show you how to read a chart properly.'

Muir saluted Ebenezer and about turned back to his cabin.

Back, to Jane.

Sunday had arrived. The ship was at a stand still, drawn only by ocean currents. The ship's bearing drifted through all the points of the compass. Progress was put on hold as if God had intended it to be that way, a day of rest owned by the Pacific heat. Ebenezer tried to use the rudder like a paddle waggling it to one side repeatedly to point the ship eastwards.

But it came to nothing.

Muir had gone down below to imagine his island in the darkness. He amused himself in his unintended likeness to George III. They could both lay claim to islands that were once foreign to them and a people of which they knew nothing.

He considered his regal style more responsible. He didn't send his subjects overseas to fight wars that did not concern them and the natives had been left to their own devices.

They didn't even know he was king.

He and Jane picked up the game of cards begun by Francois and Ebenezer weeks ago. It seemed increasingly unlikely that it would be played out by them.

Muir had Francois' hand. And thankfully, more of the court cards. Lovers ordering kings and queens around, sacrificing them to battle chance as they had the ordinary people for so long, brought with it much satisfaction. But this playfulness evaporated when Ebenezer unfolded a chart between them. Separated from Jane by the entire Pacific,

Muir went up on deck and had a look around at the real thing that far from separating them, bound them together.

The rope they'd used to measure the speed in knots a few days before, coiled down into the depths. Without another thought, Muir jumped into the ocean imagining his position on the chart.

Soon he was making sure he had hold of the rope.

Within minutes, Jane joined him to cool down.

Their dives disturbed the ship's perfect reflection.

Taking deep breaths they let their hands slip over each knot. Deeper still, they embraced making themselves each other's poles.

Twisting around the rope, they began a maelstrom of their own making that would have been just visible at the surface had anyone cared for their intimacy.

Slipping into the depths of their souls with no record of the seconds, everything but the knowledge of each other blurred into insignificance. Knot after knot they followed the rope down. Above, *The Otter* blotted out the sunlight as if hours had passed and sunset had come early.

They then let themselves sink beyond the rope until all that remained was what it felt like to hold and what it felt like to be held.

Colouring the darkness with only themselves, they burned through the last of their breath to reach the surface, exacerbating the corporeal until the sun slipped from out of the hull's shade making happy the skies, drawing air into their lungs and light into their eyes.

XV
51° 10' N
128° 30' W

With the first sight of land since leaving their now chartered islands, Muir looked towards a country that had an authority far greater than their own kingdoms.

He held out his pocket globe and identified North America. He knew Philadelphia and the President to be on the eastern side. Now looking at the western shore, the sea hemmed in a strip of sand beneath a thick forest that climbed until it met rock and finally snow covered peaks. Although daunting, it meant fresh water something they'd been short of for the last two weeks.

But the interior seemed impenetrable. Had anyone crossed it, he wondered. One would have to, he initially thought, to get to Philadelphia. Few had crossed the Pacific but venturing inland, no crew would be there to help him navigate the glaciers.

On his globe he looked southwards. The landmass thinned around Mexico, Acapulco, Darien and Cuba. But chanting interrupted his studies. For, in the choppy seas a long canoe appeared and disappeared in and out of the troughs.

Nine native Indians could be counted.

Ebenezer and Francois armed themselves.

Between the crashes of breaking waves, a war song could be heard rising and falling in intensity with each passing wave.

Now fifty yards from *The Otter*, all nine native Indians stood up and dropped their leather garments. Muir and Jane wondered whether they should do the same but thought it would be quite inconvenient and unrehearsed. Before any of them could respond, however, the canoe began heading back to shore as if the strange meeting had never taken place.

Some hours later they secured *The Otter* in a sheltered haven north of Nootka Sound. Having lowered the rowing boat over the side, Muir, Jane and Francois went ashore to collect wood and fresh water. They worried that Ebenezer might abandon them. But jobs had to be done. They sensed he was still not happy about taking Muir to the Port of Boston and despite their earlier rapport, Francois had no doubt that the captain wanted all the seal skins for himself.

Whilst Muir and Jane brought wood down to the shore, Francois climbed the headland and spotted smoke coming from a settlement further down the coast.

The rowing boat was laden with as much wood as it could reasonably carry. Noticing a tidal mark of stranded flotsam along the shore, an anxiety grew that their boat would be marooned and would have to be emptied to be relaunched, if indeed it could be before the flooding tide.

Muir looked up to the headland and spotted Francois filling up their casks from beneath a waterfall.

He called to tell him to hurry up. The ship fired its cannon in the same instant deafening out his request. Ebenezer had done this near the coast before to ward off potential enemies and Muir thought nothing of it. He called again to the Frenchman.

But when Francois returned he wasn't so relaxed.

The wet sand stuck to the boat's underside like mud.

Fortunately, a rogue wave sent white water up the shore and their troubles washed away as the boat careered into the surf.

Halfway between the shore and *The Otter*, Jane noticed that the ship was moving.

The anchor had either come unstuck or Ebenezer had plans.

It crossed Muir's mind that only the captain had seen them leave the ship. He could quite easily have told the rest of the crew on deck that they were down below sleeping.

Francois began to row frantically. Within a hundred yards of the ship, Muir tried to push his oar to match

Francois' pace, but it went in only after pushing something solid, deeper into the water.

As the boat span around on only Francois' efforts, Jane screamed. First boots bobbed to the surface. Then after Muir removed his oar, the legs of an officer.

Francois murmured 'Ebenezer Dorr' under his breath.

The pangs of guilt from having earlier accused Ebenezer of abandonment stuck in Francois' throat.

He helped Muir pull up the torso.

It was lighter than he'd expected. Then they learnt why. As they tried to identify whether their captain had been killed, they were met with further unknowns.

The corpse was headless.

Leaving it behind, they neared *The Otter*. Muir cursed himself for forgetting to leave armed. Jane took the other oar whilst Francois pulled out a pistol and crouched at the bow.

As they slid along the side from the transom to the anchor guard, Muir wondered whether the warning gun was Ebenezer's attempts to kill the attacker. Had he missed? Had he been slain?

Francois put his aim on a figure that had his hands on the anchor rope. No canoes could be detected but they could just as well be concealed on the starboard side.

Muir rowed silently re-enacting his stealth like departure from Botany Bay but just as Francois was about to pull the trigger, the figure appeared to be taking a transit off the land to see if the anchor had embedded.

'Francois!'

He pointed his pistol sky high and for good reason.

Francois had come within a whisker of shooting Ebenezer.

*

'You better be telling the truth, Francois. The headless corpse of a captain? You're not coming aboard until you bring me evidence.'

280

After being berated by Ebenezer, they went in search of the corpse to establish their innocence, traversing the water between the ship and the shore. Most of the crew were now on deck, some hoping the three would be unsuccessful with their own promotions in mind.

Francois had all but given up and lay down in the bottom of the boat. But just as he rested his head down, a premature knock sounded. He opened his eyes realising it wasn't his head against the deck and looked over the side.

A boot heel was tapping against the boat as it bobbed in the ripples. Francois held onto it with all his might, whilst Muir rowed the three of them back to *The Otter*.

Ebenezer looked overboard in disbelief. The reflection was everything he feared for in his altercation with Henderson. They hauled the corpse on deck and searched the clothes for any identification.

Nothing distinguished him as American, English, Spanish or French. They tied weights to the corpse and watched as it disappeared into the depths, a gesture they'd agreed upon to preserve the man's dignity.

As they sailed south, the wind eased and two canoes approached, not from the settlement but from the open sea. Ebenezer checked that he was armed and brought the ship into the wind.

After five minutes it came to a standstill. Each canoe was filled with eleven fat dumpy Indians. Like those they met earlier, these unfastened their blue cloths and stood completely naked.

The crew couldn't help but laugh but that was drowned out by the Indians' war song as they beat their paddles against the sides to keep time.

A short lived silence was broken by the shouts of 'can-zi-ca-gan!'

The crew of *The Otter* raised their hands and in return shouted, 'can-zi-ca-gan,' without the slightest idea what it meant.

The Indians tied their canoes alongside. Looking down into their vessels, Muir noted that they had fifteen foot fishing devices fitted with pieces of wood at the end shaped like rakes, about six inches across.

Their canoes were tree trunks with their innards carved out. They were teeming with herring. On the exterior, they were decorated with drawings of fish and birds in limestone that, Muir assumed, they hoped would attract their catch.

Jane had offered to shave Ebenezer's stubble to rebuild trust between them following the incident with the corpse. As she did so, a group of Indians became transfixed by the process. One stepped forward as curious as a cow and picked up the soapy black hair that had fallen down onto the deck.

The other Indians watched, intrigued as the blade swept away the soap and hair to reveal the sun deprived skin. Muir watched somewhat jealously. Henderson's holding of the blade against the captain's throat flashed through his mind like a desire.

As Ebenezer lifted his right arm to feel the closeness of the shave, Muir tried to identify whether he'd suffered the gunshot wound that was evident on his jacket.

He found no wound but couldn't be sure whether the faded blood stains were under the left or right jacket arm. He, therefore, didn't draw conclusions just yet.

No sooner had Ebenezer wiped away the soap and left, when one particular Indian jumped the queue and pointed to his hairy face.

The other Indians laughed. Unlike the bearded Indian their faces were painted red, black and white. Once, however, their compatriot's face had been lathered they seemed anxious as Jane trailed the blade across his neck, nonchalantly passing by his windpipe. Each had to restrain the other from intervening.

Francois then appeared from below deck having gone down to lock his cabin and hide any valuables. The headless corpse was still on his mind. As he came up, the shaved Indian paid Jane with five herring. The Frenchman was not entirely convinced by their bartering as each side did not understand the other's language.

Occasionally, he'd catch the Indians pulling faces at the crew and dancing, inadvertently revealing rifles and long polished blades beneath their bearskins. Francois had them down as mountebanks from the moment he returned on deck and pushed a pistol against Muir's side should he need it.

Looking overboard, he spotted another canoe approaching, aboard was just one Indian.

Now on deck, the others greeted him.

'Can-zi-ca-gan!'

They then chanted his name, 'Out-Cha-Chel', three times.

It was the chief, a middle aged man with long black hair. He frowned at the shaven Indian who lowered his head hiding the cuts around his neck.

As Francois finished tying up Out-Cha-Chel's canoe, he stepped back over the other two rafted canoes and caught his foot on something sharp beneath a cloth.

Tending to his foot, he moved the cloth to one side fully aware that he was being spied upon by someone on deck. As the Indian approached bearing a knife, Francois called out to Muir who turned the pistol on his assailant.

Meanwhile, Francois revealed from beneath the cloth a set of carpenter's tools, property of *The Otter*.

The disgraced Indian was taken up on deck and then punished by Francois by being pushed back overboard.

Ebenezer demanded that the Indians leave immediately by pointing out to sea with his right arm. Muir noticed the faded gunshot wound and realised that the wound couldn't have been suffered by Ebenezer. The captain must have 'acquired' the jacket off an injured captain.

Whilst Muir reassessed his view of Ebenezer, Out-Cha-Chel pointed to his settlement and then to the captain who surmised that he was inviting them ashore.

After some time, Ebenezer agreed but on condition that they kept a hostage aboard *The Otter*. Out-Cha-Chel gave

Ebenezer the Indian that had tried to steal the carpenter's tools but Ebenezer refused and picked an Indian that looked one rank down from Out-Cha-Chel.

As they untied their canoes, Muir, Jane and Francois freed the rowing boat. The chief hailed something at his people. The result was that the Indian who had thieved had to leave his canoe and swim ashore as further punishment.

This lifted Muir and Francois' expectations of the tribe.

Closing in on the shore Muir caught a whiff of salmon being smoked in one of the habitations. It conjured longings for Scotland, Hunters' Hill and his family meals together.

Muir then remembered what his father had said to him that the path God had chosen for him was of a world few Scots of his age would ever see. His father was right.

He checked his pistol but doubted its use given the sheer number of Indians and the time it took to reload. When he sensed it was shallow enough he jumped out at the bow and tied the rope up to the roots of a tree, where the sea had washed away the earth.

Jane had to usher Francois onto land as he was so preoccupied with *The Otter's* movements and had a heavy mind from the morning's events.

They walked towards the Indians' huts but the intensifying smell of salmon seemed infected by a stagnant stench. The hut walls were made of boards badly joined together, placed one over the other and fastened to the stakes with seaweed strings and animals' guts that had dried hard in the sun.

One of the women of the settlement beckoned them inside. In the centre of the hut, an open fire was roasting twelve salmon and several joints of meat, unlike anything they had seen before.

'Vacache! Vacache!'

Their hosts made them most welcome. Muir pointed to one of the many bearskins that the Indians were using for mattresses and then guessed the source of the meat joints. The children and women nodded, reassured that they had communicated an association with their guests.

Muir handed them treacle, biscuits and brandy that they had brought over from *The Otter*. The hut was dressed in mussel, oyster and scallop shells that occasionally shook in time with a knocking sound.

Muir walked outside. Five Indians were hollowing out a tree trunk that they had steadied next to the wall of the hut.

The Indians wore old coats down to their shins. Some had bonnets. Others wore top hats or had their hair done up in clubs. Clearly they had met white men before and by their dress had either pillaged from them or, Muir hoped, bartered with them.

They looked at Muir whose pistol was on show and pulled out their own muskets, detecting his fear by the whites of his eyes. But in the next instance that fear was cancelled for they showed that their gunpowder box was empty.

Their guns were reduced to clubs without any charge and Muir thought it prudent to withhold his own charge not wanting to risk being shot by his own powder.

Inside the hut, Francois was tucking into the forearm of a bear when the thief he had uncovered, entered. Lowering his arm, and the bear's, he reached for his pistol. But before he could show he meant business, the one time thief hugged him and pressed him close to his heart and the gun barrel.

With Jane, Francois followed the Indian to his hut. He insisted that Francois search his property for any goods stolen from *The Otter*. The Frenchman did his best to make him understand that he no longer suspected him of theft and was willing to wipe the slate clean. The Indian bowed and hearing something outside led them to the commotion.

Thankfully, Muir's unwillingness to barter with the canoe carving Indians was relieved by the arrival of Out-Cha-Chel who was keen to show off his numerous wives.

Francois arrived still devouring the bear arm and with Jane, met a perplexed Mr Muir. Out-Cha-Chel told them of his many battles through role play. Unfortunately, his wives were forced to adopt the roles of his soon to be defeated enemies.

With each blow the chief stopped his axe only a few inches from their heads, detaching strands of hair with each swing. On several occasions the women had to duck down to assure their continued existence.

Thankfully for them Out-Cha-Chel acquired a burning desire to take off all his clothes. But the wives were not out of the woods yet for a minute later he returned from his hut wearing buffalo armour, a helmet and a war mask. Calling out something to his wives, they followed his orders by jumping on him.

He flung them to the ground.

Francois, Jane and Muir looked at each other. Their eyes gravitated towards *The Otter*, still anchored off the headland. Clubbing together a brief applause as if they too were part of the role play, they watched the women pick themselves up as they began to take sidesteps towards the shore. Out-Cha-Chel, though, was having none of it and beckoned them to his hut.

Inside, he led them to a huge open chest. Lowering their heads they realised that it was decorated with human teeth. Desperately, they shook his hand and stepped towards the door but the chief shouted something. From out of the chest he lifted up the ends of two cloths, unravelling a pair of bulbous objects the size of pumpkins, that rotated round and round menacingly.

They hoped they were perhaps three or four lobsters bound together or a stuffed bear stomach but they were preparing themselves for the worst. As the layers of cloth unravelled a nose in each began to protrude more and more with each rotation. Tufts of hair then lapped out of each of the ends until two human heads banged against the edge of the chest, chipping a few of the inlaid teeth before rolling back into the chest, settling face up.

To the chief, they mirrored Jane and Muir's looks of trepidation. Out-Cha-Chel laughed above them, looking down on the four white heads like a God.

Francois stepped towards Muir and voiced that he feared it was quite possible the chief would put their heads next to these.

Jane answered for Muir, 'I think so too. But show no fear.'

Snapping out of his trance, Muir clapped and mimed a paddling motion. Out-Cha-Chel shook his head. Muir shook his head too, mimed a hammer and chisel, then moved his arm from vertical to horizontal to imitate the falling of a tree.

The chief looked as confused as Francois and Jane.

In the silence, the chipping of wood could be heard from outside. Between each knock, Muir raised his hand. The chief grinned a mouth of white teeth and black spaces. Muir then grabbed Out-Cha-Chel's sleeve and led him to the doorway.

Chipping away at the inside of the tree, Muir thought about using his pistol but there were too many Indians. He eyed Francois to the shore where their rowing boat was tied up and then, when no one was looking, cut his hand with the chisel.

The Indian in the bowler hat pulled out a gentleman's handkerchief and bound the wound. In the corner of Muir's eye, he could see that Francois had managed to slip away.

But the escape plan was further complicated when the Indian in the bowler indicated that he wanted to buy Jane from him to be his wife. Thankfully, Out-Cha-Chel had been distracted by one of his many wives, that, it turned out he had injured quite seriously.

As the man in the bowler hat wiped away Muir's blood from the tree's hollow, not wanting to tarnish the canoe with a bad omen for the future, Muir nodded to Jane that she should bolt for the shoreline and that he would follow.

Clambering into the rowing boat that was now in waist deep water, Jane pulled Muir in whilst Francois fixed his two pistols on the wading Indians, firing a warning shot above their heads.

They all froze but not Out-Cha-Chel who ran down after them. He had, perhaps, too much faith in his buffalo armour.

Muir and Jane rowed like buffoons jeopardising Francois' stability but managed to gain some composure when they realised that the chief was sinking in his armoury as he strode into the depths, much like Kidlaw had all those months before.

The next day they passed a solitary Indian in his canoe waving at them. In light of yesterday's events, they intended to sail by. Muir, though, sensed he had news for them and thought they should stop.

Taking his oar, Francois brought him against the hull and offered fresh water. They were after all nearly out of sight of land. The Indian bowed, took a gulp, returned the cask and pointed to the American flag on *The Otter*'s transom.

Ebenezer thought that it was the imbalance of stars and stripes on the American flag that the Indian was intrigued by but not long after he also began pointing further down the coast.

The Indian raised their fears that he'd sighted another ship with a different flag, so Ebenezer had him up on deck marking out how the flag he'd seen, had appeared.

With a wet hand, the Indian drew a plus sign and then walked to the transom holding a red stripe of the American flag in his hands. Ebenezer then pointed to the four squares around the plus sign and the Indian pointed to the white stripe.

They all patted him on the back and steadied the canoe whilst he stepped aboard. He'd perhaps saved Muir's life by alerting them to the fact that an English naval ship was down the coast.

Pacing the decks deep in thought, Ebenezer insisted that if they came close the British would want to search the ship. He was sure they wouldn't be able to outrun them and feared they'd blow them out of the water.

'If I'm caught, I'll be hanged,' accepted Muir.

'And if I'm caught I'll be charged with stowing away convicts. It may be time to part company. For both our sakes.'

With the ship pointing directly towards land, Ebenezer studied the chart and found they were destined for Nootka Sound.

*

Under the cover of darkness, they sailed into an estuary to provide shelter from the Pacific swell. When the crew had gone to sleep Muir went on deck deep in thought.

Studying the entire horizon he then took a second look at the landscape inland. Following the silhouette of hilltops he was almost certain a mast was protruding out of one peak.

Was it the English ship? Whilst he waited, he heard someone being sick below deck and cursed them for possibly drawing attention to their boat. His heart beat faster and he dashed below deck to alert Ebenezer.

Through the telescope, they took turns to study its side profile and the number of yardarms but they remained none the wiser to its nationality. A flag still waved from the transom but the low cloud prevented any moonlight from discerning its colours or markings.

They waited, making sure no light shone from them.

Some time later, Ebenezer watched the deck and rigging light up. A deckhand carrying an oil lamp traversed from the bow to the stern with another sailor.

'This looks promising.'

'They might be loading a cannonball. Their port side is pointing straight at us,' warned Muir.

'We're in range. Lift the anchor.'

Muir got to it whilst Ebenezer continued to watch the ship through his telescope. A few moments later, the tidal waters were no longer rushing past the transom but moving with them away from whom they suspected to be their enemy.

Muir began to release the sail ties. Through the telescope, the sailor with the oil lamp was now at the transom and in the process of untying the ship's flag from its mount.

289

As he and the other crewman folded away the flag, Ebenezer was able to see it fully lit up above the deck lamp.

Most of it seemed yellow although he couldn't be sure that wasn't just from the tint of the oil lamp.

When the two sailors brought the flag ends together, they revealed its red outer stripes running lengthways along the yellow belly hanging down.

'Muir, drop the anchor! They are Spaniards.'

'Not Brits?' Thank God, Muir thought.

Leaning over the cat head where he raised the anchor, he felt an overwhelming sense of relief.

'I can speak fluent Spanish from my days at university. It may finally be of some use.'

'Really. Well, we can trade then.'

Muir regretted what he'd just said.

'Trade? Right. But first we can sleep well. Goodnight.'

'What do you mean? They'll be gone in the morning. It's not time for bed just yet. We'll trade with them right now. Go wake Francois. Captain's orders.'

Close up, it appeared to be a Spanish gunboat. Ebenezer, Muir and Francois this time had their own lamp lit and held up high on a staff to make their intentions clear without any overtones of aggression.

They eventually made contact with the ship by its transom, reading along the arch board, *La Sutil*. Ebenezer rapped his knuckles hard against the captain's cabin hoping to wake him before asking Muir what Sutil meant.

'It means subtle, Ebenezer, something that you might want to take on board when you start bartering.'

Ebenezer didn't register Muir's point as the deck began to swarm with armed sailors. All three raised their hands in the air. The Spaniards checked the bottom of the rowing boat for weapons and on a hooked pole lifted up something drenched and sorry looking.

'We've two and a half thousand of these seal skins. That's just one of them. You want to trade with us?' asked

Ebenezer. They looked at him, utterly confused. 'Translate, Muir, I'll cut you in on the deal. With Francois' agreement, of course.'

A general shaking of heads prevailed once Muir had translated. Then in fluent Spanish, he declared, 'we're friends of Spain! I am Tomas Moro. We're English, French and American. One of us must be your friend!'

They were invited below deck to what was nothing more than a feverish den that stank of vomit, urine and rot.

Francois insisted upon going back out in the fresh air.

On deck Ebenezer relayed to the Spanish captain, via Muir, that it was clear his crew were terribly sick and he could offer some of his own crew as substitute.

Muir thought about it for a second and realised Ebenezer's intentions. Needing to get rid of the convicts, he had found a way of not only trading seal skins but also people.

Captain Tovar, himself was wheezing and sneezing with influenza and after Muir translated Ebenezer's offer, Tovar waved his arms as if he were drowning.

'I don't believe I need to translate that, Ebenezer. Sending the convicts aboard this ship will make them ill too.'

'They can stay on deck like we're now.'

'But they'll freeze trying to sleep out here,' Muir protested.

'Captain Tovar may be going south. It will only get warmer.'

For some time Muir and Captain Tovar talked in Spanish. Ebenezer became increasingly alienated until he demanded to be kept up to date. 'What's he saying?'

'Captain Broughton and his ship, HMS *Providence*, were seen last month at Nootka Sound. They're expected to return. Tovar intends to sail to Monterrey.'

'One way or another the convicts have to leave my ship and that includes you, Thomas. Talk with him some more. Did they search the *Sutil*?'

'Yes.'

'Well you've a ticket to America free of persecution from the Royal Navy. They won't search the same ship twice in so short a time.'

Muir thought about it but was worried about his health aboard the *Sutil*. He looked across at *The Otter* where Jane was sleeping and lowered his head. Some of the sailors below deck were on the verge of death and their illnesses looked contagious.

Thanking their hosts for the sangria and liqueur, Ebenezer persisted with Tovar trying to explain the wonders of seal skins pointing out that the material was used to make all manner of things from socks to hats.

Up on deck, Francois followed Muir as he inspected the *Sutil*.

'Thomas, my friend, as much as I'd be sad to see us part company, you should pursue a berth aboard the *Sutil*. Captain Tovar's confirmed what the Indian warned us against. What's more, Tovar plans to sail on to San Blas. Three months at most. Ebenezer's going to Boston via India and China. That could be three years.'

Muir held the globe in the lamplight, rotating it the distance of the Indian Ocean to the edges of Asia before spinning it back to the smaller more regional expanse of America and Mexico.

Francois picked up the lamp. 'I know what I'd do if I didn't have a contract for half the seal skins. I wouldn't be leaving the *Sutil* tonight.'

Up with the lark, studying the horizon for English patrol ships, Muir was sad to think that last night may have been the last that he would spend beside Jane.

He would try and barter a place for her but knew it would be difficult. Love could be a snare as much as a freedom he told himself. Again, he patrolled the horizon for HMS *Providence* until he was interrupted by water sloshing at the end of a paddle stroke.

Captain Tovar was rowing his way.

Muir helped him aboard and explained that he was a political exile from Scotland who had sought to reform the English parliament on the basis of freedom and universal equality.

Not knowing whether this would go down well with a Spaniard whose country was not known for pioneering political freedom, Muir tailored his politics towards religious freedom hoping that it might appeal to someone who valued the toleration of Catholicism.

He handed over a sketch of him in Scotland that he'd received with letters in Botany Bay. The portrait showed him in his wig and advocate's gown looking considerably plumper than now.

Tovar held the sketch before Muir, moving it back and forth until the advocate in the drawing was the same size as the navigator in front of him. His eyes glanced between the two, focusing and refocusing until he became tired.

Muir noticed that Jane had come up on deck and had sat herself down at the transom. He recalled the day she had put a pillow beneath his sleepy head when he had slept on deck for the first time.

She was still as delightful now as then and he couldn't see how he could be without her but he kept on telling himself that his affections towards her were holding him to *The Otter* and potentially, capture by the British. What did he value more, her company or his own life? He had to keep their relationship in perspective. But did they necessarily need to separate?

That was still an unknown.

Accepting the sketch's affinity to Muir, Tovar priced in his mind the berth aboard the *Sutil*, deciding to start at three hundred pesos. Muir knew he only had one hundred and fifty. He might be able to find another fifty amongst the crew so stated his highest offer of two hundred whilst pointing also to Jane.

He decided to keep the negotiations in Spanish to protect her from the sadness if they weren't both allowed to board.

Tovar looked to the transom, spotted Jane and laughed.

'I'm sorry, Tomas.'

He thought for a little while.

'Four hundred pesos for both of you. Or two hundred just for you. That is as low as I can go.'

Jane's imminent separation weighed down on Muir. He doubted there were four hundred pesos on the entire ship never mind amongst friends he could depend on.

Being irrational at this point could be fatal.

He was all too aware that when opportunities arose, they had to be taken. So, it would be today that he would go aboard the *Sutil*.

With, or without Jane.

The deal, though, was interrupted by a retching sound.

Jane then vomited into the crystal clear water. Tovar gave her his flask whilst Muir wiped her chin and hands clean.

She looked like she knew something deep inside but Muir mistook it for what he thought she sensed; their looming separation, missing the implications completely.

He was too preoccupied by his own life to consider the conception of another and yet confused that she was being sick when the swell was at its most settled.

Whilst she lay asleep back in their cabin, he packed up his trunk and hauled it up on deck. Remembering her sentence back at the chambers with Gathersby, he was confident her detection by HMS *Providence* would not result in hanging but a fine imposed on the captain and the demand that she be landed. He wished that could be the same for him and that they could stay together.

He set about preparing the rowing boat that Palmer had made him over a year ago and remembered the climax of the fraught voyage with her out of Botany Bay into the ocean; waking up to her determined rowing, slipping into the water with her as they waited for *The Otter*, it nearly ending there and then for them.

He recalled how she held his head from going under the surface. Without her, the crew may just have found the remains of Palmer's boat that day.

The jarrah wood had warped but as Palmer predicted, the boat had served its purpose by freeing two souls. Lifting out the replacement oars, he noticed her fine spun crimson blouse that Francois and Henderson had spotted from the crow's nest.

Weather stained and bleached, as he lifted it up it remained salt locked in the position in which it found itself drying, still celebratory of the moment it saved them.

He lifted it up to his nose to sense whether it smelt of her, or their experience, or Hunters' Hill back in Botany Bay. It still held its shape like a rosebud pressed between the pages of a book until eventually it began to soften.

Moving his head away he realised he was crying. His tears had softened the cloth once again, more salt to the wound but a reminder that he was human.

As his eyes regained a focus on the world he noticed to the north, dark waters and to his horror, the presence of a ship. The waters between were windless but the daily land breezes in this region would change all that very soon.

He knew he had to go that minute.

A ship of that size had to be HMS *Providence*.

XVI
48° 50' N
125° 13' W

The Otter led the *Sutil* by just over a nautical mile as they sailed in convoy away from HMS *Providence*. Passing a headland, they benefited from winds on the other side that eluded the British ship.

Below deck, he rummaged for the two hundred pesos that Captain Dorr said he'd slipped into his trunk for not taking him all the way to Boston. Emptying it, Jane's pillow bobbed across the wooden boards. His longing for her was not eased by its faint lavender scent. That said, she was still in convoy. He wondered whether there was still any chance of her boarding the *Sutil*.

As he searched, the creeping realisation that Ebenezer had cheated him, hardened from suspicion to fact. He'd have to spin some tale or he'd be back on *The Otter*.

A few shouts came from up on deck. Wondering what the commotion was, he went up to see *The Otter* approaching a stone jetty. It still had its sails half filled and the sight caused quite a stir amongst the Spanish crew who had seen nothing like it before.

As it slowed the *Sutil* caught up and from the bow Muir could see convicts being pushed onto the land. Francois seemed to be resisting the action but Ebenezer and his loyal crew overruled him.

One of the convicts had long hair. It was Jane. Out-Cha-Chel and the white men's heads flashed through Muir's mind. The wilderness was fraught with as much danger as capture by the British, he thought.

In Spanish, Muir pleaded with Tovar to pass by the jetty and pick her up but the Capitan repeated that the extra draught of the *Sutil's* keel meant he could not be sure that they could sail in such shallow waters.

Muir shouted up through the sails, past the crow's nest to God if he was willing to hear. But his concerns came to nothing. The Spaniards thought they had a lunatic aboard except for the helmsman at the wheel who seemed to understand.

When Tovar had gone below deck the helmsman rotated the wheel directing the ship towards the jetty. Muir hoped the captain hadn't noticed the change of course and prepared a rope to throw to Jane.

They sailed for a few minutes towards land but the occasional scraping of wood against rock from beneath the ship worried them and then after a particularly loud piercing sound, Tovar ran up on deck and within yards of the jetty pointed his pistol at the helmsman firing above his head to show that he meant business.

The explosion rang in Muir's ears. Jane by now was in the shadow of the ship trying to get to her feet despite her injuries.

Not knowing whether the pistol fire was aimed at them, some convicts had taken to the water to use the jetty as a shield. There was a moment of hesitation. Putting his life before Muir's union with Jane, the helmsman steered downwind and offshore until the wind crossed from the port side to starboard, gybing the sails in mid turn.

Tantalisingly close, Muir shouted out that he loved her in broken pathetic sobs. As she sat with her head in her hands she called back that she thought she might be pregnant.

Her sickness began to make sense. He'd remembered something his mother had once said, about when she was pregnant with him, the bouts of sickness early on. In Spanish, he explained to Tovar, what they had witnessed when bartering that morning. But it came to nothing.

Muir watched her whilst the Spaniards trimmed the sails on the new tack, until the convicts were the size of matchstick men and she was no longer discernible from the others.

Now just a figure on a jetty as she had been the first time he'd seen her aboard the *Surprise*, things had turned full circle two continents later on their voyage around the globe.

All too soon his memory of her was free falling helplessly into the past. This once life affirming person in his world was now a torment of loss.

A Spaniard patted him on the shoulder and brought him a tankard of beer. He swallowed it gulp by gulp. The dregs lapped towards his mouth until the tankard's glass base brought the jetty into view one last time, as if he were looking through a porthole that encircled a world he'd never see again with Jane at its centre.

Exhaling, as his breath funnelled down the tankard his view of her fogged over. Tovar took the tankard. It was his. He'd given it to Muir to lessen his impoverishment, to remind him of the advocate in the sketch.

Muir though, wanted Jane and their future not that of a stuffy advocate with an insincere partner like Elisabeth. He undressed fully intending to swim ashore but to the north west on a fresh land breeze and within a few nautical miles of the jetty, HMS *Providence* peered around the headland.

Tovar still had his doubts about Muir and wondered how this high ranking gentleman from Scotland had come to be persecuted by the British government for defending his mother country and the Christian state of Ireland.

But Muir had relayed parts of the petition his society had sent to parliament, which had softened Tovar and brought him closer to the Scot.

With no orders to the contrary, Tovar thought it right to provide Muir with a safer passage to America than he would have experienced aboard *The Otter*.

Muir looked across at the ship that had sailed him across the Pacific and thought of Ebenezer callously casting the convicts off into the untamed wilderness, as far as he could make out with none of their possessions.

Sailing further south, Tovar pointed out the Juan de Fuca Strait cutting east inland. As they crossed its mouth, HMS *Providence* fired its cannons and *The Otter* heaved to.

Tovar's *Sutil* continued three leagues offshore confident that their previous search would protect them from another. Muir reflected that he couldn't have left it any later. But he still longed for Jane.

Following the search, *The Otter* sailed up the strait contrary to their agreement to sail in convoy perhaps, Muir wondered, on the orders of HMS *Providence*.

As they found themselves in line with the strait, passing *The Otter*'s stern, Tovar decided to continue down the coast and so Muir parted with the ship he'd been on all those months.

He waved for several minutes. His farewell was not intended for Ebenezer but his dear friend Francois Pierre Peron whose companionship he'd miss for some time to come.

First meeting him by his tent in the woods, tripping on the guy rope into the embers and explaining to him the events of the French revolution, these were the only memories he could muster as they sailed their different ways.

He wondered how the sealskin trading would pan out and what other deceptions Captain Ebenezer Dorr had up his sleeve. If indeed they were his sleeves. Muir suspected they were those of a dead American captain's, from whom Ebenezer had pilfered. Perhaps the jacket's owner was the true captain of *The Otter*. He would never know.

Coughing and spluttering drowned out any sounds from the waters of the Pacific coast. He tried to spend as much time as possible on deck in the sea air to windward of the rest of the crew so his current woes would not be exacerbated, but it was at night that he feared the worst.

After two weeks at sea, having been slowed by an easterly storm that had blown them way out into the Pacific, they had crawled upwind towards land and it was the voice of an angel that declared they would now be calling into port.

*

Don Diego Borica was in Monterrey when they disembarked and Muir wasted no time, leaving the ship to follow the crowd up the main thoroughfare to make contact with the governor of California, a tolerant, amiable and enlightened individual according to Captain Tovar.

How changed his circumstances had become since trying to convince the governor of Botany Bay to allow him ownership of a rowing boat.

But this was no time to rest on his laurels and within minutes of introducing himself, the dog eared sketches of him in his gown were on display.

Borica swung his arms outwards and inflated his cheeks to suggest that the man in the sketch was much bigger than the lean man that stood before him.

Muir began his charm. 'I was arrested for championing the Irish state. They're Catholic like your people. Three million are denied rights. Their properties are exposed to sanctioned robberies. Their persons, to insult and persecution. I transmitted a solemn address to the assembly that sat in Edinburgh on their behalf. I read and published it and with all the energy of my abilities, defended its principles. For this, I was exiled.'

The governor was fascinated. 'We've many missionaries. You must see the fabulous Cathedral of San Carlos Borromeo. It was built just two years ago, in stone. The original burnt down. Our ancestors made that one out of wood!'

'Did I tell you we encountered huge storms on our way from Nootka? I've never bailed so much water in all my life. The invalided sailors were nearly drowning inside the ship.'

'Glad to have your feet on dry land?'

300

'Yes, yes. With no prospect of the horizon we lost all steerage and ended way off course. The sails flogged endlessly. Sheets of sea spray were our only encounters. Our sleeping quarters were drenched. I thought it the end of our days. Had it not happened we'd have been here weeks earlier.'

'You'll be glad that wasn't the case,' said Borica seriously.

'Why so?'

'HMS *Providence* has been in the bay.'

God had held him back from shore for his own benefit.

The real providence was Muir's as he had predicted.

'A drink Tomas Moro? I believe God wants me to look after you too.'

'Well... A drink would be splendid.'

Governor House was palatial in all but name. Stairways climbed up both walls of the lobby to the first floor. As they ascended one, the governor's wife passed down the other.

She listened to their exotic visitor, 'I have literally circumnavigated the globe, Senor Borica. A man of the gown has made his first début to the world as a navigator.'

The governor's wife was awestruck. The more he impressed this man and his wife, the more likely he would gain passage to Philadelphia, the President of the United States and his friends, Millar, Priestley and Tytler.

'What of this French Revolution, Senor Moro?'

'I tried to stop them killing Louis but I was too late.'

'Yet you're against the King of England because he is protestant?' asked Borica.

'He doesn't believe the people should play a part in the political process. He doesn't believe in the good life for his subjects.'

'Ah yes, the good life is very important. We've the good life in Alta California. I make sure of that.'

Muir woke up in a four poster bed without a Spanish sailor in sight, a novelty in recent weeks. Jane had been struggling through the wilderness in his sleep, a few months' pregnant but still coping.

Freshly squeezed orange juice, grapefruits, smoked salmon, honeys, and many things he hadn't the faintest chance of naming, lay on his bedside table. Jane, he doubted, would have these luxuries. He felt guilty eating them but couldn't let them go to waste.

A pen and some paper had been left for him. As he wrote the date on a letter intended for the President of the United States, he realised it was the fourth of July, 1796. Twenty years had passed since America had gained its independence from Britain.

Could Scotland follow suit, he wondered.

The church bells began to ring. It was Sunday. He quickly dressed and within minutes was following the crowds to the Cathedral of San Carlos Borromeo.

Despite an education in Latin he couldn't abide how the congregation were refused the bible in their own language. But with the governor and his wife by his side and all the eyes of Monterrey on him, compliance was key.

Even when it came to communion.

As a Protestant he didn't believe that the bread and wine was literally the flesh and blood of Jesus Christ. Consuming both was to bring judgement on him. He so bitterly regretted this given how God had kept him at sea to avoid the British naval ship in Monterrey Bay, but explaining that he was a Protestant could be fatal.

Any possibility of passage to Philadelphia required that he maintain the pretence that he was a Catholic. Thankfully, some of the deference that the priest paid to the governor washed onto Muir. For he was next in line.

Walking back to his seat, the governor could not see the insincerity of Muir's act and within minutes they were all content singing hymns again. No mentions of American independence were made. Muir had to celebrate this privately in his mind.

Back in his room he continued his letter stating that he was sure his trial, exile and the Parliamentary debates surrounding his plight were no doubt news to the President.

He stated also that, had he gone to the United States earlier he would have become known to the President, that from the perspective of the English Ministers, it was his legal right to choose to retire to any part of the world except Great Britain and that he was determined to depend alone upon his own exertions and the providence of God, regardless, he thought to himself, of that morning's divergence from his true faith.

In the next paragraph Muir explained how in a few days he would sail for St. Blas and remain there until the Viceroy of Mexico gave his permission to pass through the country.

Muir hesitated a little to think over what he was about to scroll, finished off the tray of fruits, felt re-energised and asserted that he would claim the protection of the President's name and hasten to Philadelphia to justify the alliance.

Pouring himself some of the governor's Evan Williams bourbon, he was given an idea that could only better his circumstances. He penned that he presumed to draw upon the President for what necessary expenses may attend his journey. Needless to observe that these bills would be joyfully reimbursed in Europe.

In an attempt to personalise the letter, he explained his association with Professor Millar, an advocate at the same bar as he, who has also sought the President's sanctuary.

Muir added that his own health was infirm and shaky. Partly, this was a result of the overly generous pouring of bourbon. He ended with the assertion that if he couldn't revisit his own country, free and emancipated, he would seek to spend the rest of his days in the United States and devote himself to the land of his asylum.

America.

He promised to write at every opportunity in the course of his travels and curiously signed off as his Excellency's servant, Thomas Muir, somewhat contrary to the freedoms enshrined by the United States. But he felt the kowtowing would pay off dividends.

A letter of celebration was written next to James Maitland, the Earl of Lauderdale, in which he anticipated the day he could indulge in his long passed freedoms. Lastly, with business out of the way he wrote to his mother and father to inform them that he intended to travel overland through Spanish America to General Washington where he believed he would receive the kindest reception.

He asked his parents to rejoice that he was again at liberty in the midst of a good, a kind and humane people and told them to write to him via and under the cover of General Washington.

Knowing that his letters would no doubt be read by Senor Borica and the Viceroy, he added that it was impossible for him to express sufficiently his gratitude to the Spanish nation and he had no doubt he would gain permission to pass through New Spain, the lands of the Viceroy, and on to Philadelphia.

High on the wave of letter writing, he passed on news of his improved circumstances to Stanhope and Charles Fox in England and Joseph Priestley, Tytler, and his old tutor, Millar, in America.

With the day of his departure now upon him, Senor Borica and his wife handed Muir two boxes filled with tubs of soup.

'You must find your freedoms, Tomas. The letters have gone to the Viceroy.'

*

From Asadero to San Blas, the coast soon succumbed to a thick overgrown interior. But before that lay a coastal track on which for the third time that morning, Muir had spotted a horse drawn coach. The winds were light and they were in no way sailing at a speed the horses were capable of cantering.

This set Muir's mind thinking that they were perhaps being tracked. Eventually, a sea breeze overturned the fickle easterly and the *Sutil* seemed to awaken.

Muir opened the last of the soups.

Spotting the coach again, it seemed to have accelerated to keep up with their seaward progress. Telling Tovar might lead him off course and scupper his own plans.

Keeping quiet could herald danger.

He went below deck to dispose of the cask.

When he returned, the coach had gone.

Tovar followed Muir up on deck.

'Tomas, are you sure you want to be dropped off in St. Blas. The last few weeks have shown that our association may be good for each other.'

'What are you suggesting?'

'Staying with us on our way to China.'

Muir had considered the possibility but he felt he had used up nearly all of his lives dodging the Royal Navy and longed to head inland out of their reach.

'Captain Tovar, you have your government on your side. I don't. You're free to roam. Indeed you are paid to roam the seas as a predator. I'm another government's prey. Thankfully, not yours.'

'Tomas, I only wanted to give you the option. I'll drop you off in St. Blas. But beware, Pedro de la Portilla and his gang roam the interior. They're vultures in the guise of men. They may track you on your journey to Mexico City. They've recently plagued our gracious government with uprisings.'

Muir took note and felt ungrateful but as with his departure from his dearest love, Jane, he had to put his own safety first and for that reason China was out of bounds.

Primed in Borica's enthusiasm the last few weeks had been memorable. He enjoyed looking back on the peculiarities of the voyage with Tovar like the time they'd chanced upon Jews keen to do business from their canoes, around Cape de la Luz.

They'd exchanged chamois, otter, wax, potatoes and fish for beaten copper and cloth as well as various trifles like large buttons of dilde metal, rings, plates, cups from Puebla, knives, guns and powder. Muir once again felt like a citizen in the world experiencing its riches. He longed for this to continue unimpaired.

At St. Blas, they lowered sail. The onshore wind against the ship's side was enough to push them onto a leeward pontoon. Tovar sensed more activity in the harbour compared to all the other times he'd called into port.

It was then that he and Muir spotted the mule drawn coach. The door opened and closed with the shifting breeze. When it eventually closed on the latch they noticed that it was painted with a red barbed cross on a white rectangle.

The flag of New Spain.

Government agents had been following them all day.

But Muir was not the immediate casualty. For, as soon as the boarding plank had been secured, Tovar was stripped of his captaincy and confined to the coach with his hands and feet bound.

'Where's the Protestant? Where's the Protestant?'

It was no time for Muir to protest. He gave himself up willingly. Before long, he had to explain to some very angry Catholics, amongst other things why he had taken communion with Governor Borica.

From the interrogation he learned by proxy, that Captain Tovar had received a court martial. It pained him to think that his own interests might lead to the death of an innocent well intentioned man.

All he could do was write to protest against Tovar's treatment. But he was in effect a second class citizen in New Spain and charged his petition with little hope of remedy.

Whilst on his way to the harbour he spotted a British frigate out at sea. Perhaps he shouldn't even deliver the letter. It would reveal that he was still in port. But he wanted so much to help Tovar whom he had let down. He decided upon

306

tearing the date, August the eighteenth, from the letter. Instead of delivering it in person he slipped it under the door. After one last glance at the approaching naval ship he began running inland again.

After a month in a town called Tepic, Muir returned from its heights to sea level to meet his government escort, a man called Fidalgo.

The additional letter he'd sent from Tepic to the Viceroy seemed to have undone the damage of impersonating a Catholic for when he met Fidalgo he was handed the reins of a mule, a luxury given that he'd expected to walk to Mexico City.

Recognising the first day's journey from his travels, Muir was more of a guide to Fidalgo as he was to him, pointing out the route between the mangrove swamps.

But as they passed Tepic and ventured to the interior, Fidalgo led and the full extent of their journey east began to dawn on him. Walking the distance would have been fatal, Muir realised, as the hinterlands dried to dust.

It was July, 1796. He had escaped from Botany Bay in the February of that year and spent nearly all of that time crossing an entire ocean and sailing down the Pacific coast.

The interior to him was as foreign as it was for sea birds. As he rode inland, motions from the ship made it feel as if he was still at sea. Illusory images began appearing through Fidalgo's sweat drenched shirt in front. Creatures and people possessed his guide's shoulders. The peaks of the Sierra Madre thinned the air.

The midday sun ebbed in and out of shade.

He looked up.

Not one cloud bleached the sky.

Vultures were circling, casting their shadows below, expectant that any second the mules would drop dead and become carcasses for the taking. From up there Muir and Fidalgo must have appeared the size of insects.

The Viceroy's hair was styled like the Edinburgh lawyers but he wore more imposing attire. His jacket was collared and hemmed in crimson and gold. Beneath the elongated right lapel an indigo and ivory stripe passed around his waist and neck.

The letters that Muir had written many months ago all lay on the government desk.

He could not determine whether they were of his own hand.

'I trust the originals have been posted?'

'They have…' answered the Viceroy.

'…to the addressees?'

'To the Spanish Prime Minister.'

'As well as the addressees?'

The Viceroy enjoyed the silence as much as it disappointed Muir. All of his thoughts over how his letters might be received now seemed inconsequential. He could be dead for all they knew.

'And has your Excellency had time to consider my passage through his lands?'

The Viceroy grinned.

'His Excellency was so enamoured by your address he has requested a meeting. You'll go to Cadiz or Corunna.'

'Spain, not the United States?'

'I don't believe a New Cadiz or a New Corunna exists. He definitely meant Spain via our territories.'

XVII
19° 20' N
097° 43' W

Twenty three days on a mule had left Muir with a sore backside. So, news he was to travel by official coach to Vera Cruz was met with a degree of enthusiasm. He now knew that they feared he would be harmful to Spain if protected by George Washington. As he considered his plan, he looked out of the coach window. To the south were two gigantic volcanoes.

Fidalgo leant back from his riding seat. 'The one on your right is La Malinche. The one to the east is Pico de Orizaba.'

'Are they still active?'

Fidalgo nodded. Muir remembered his thoughts on Arthur's Seat and Edinburgh Castle. Mere metaphors. They were extinct volcanoes. Unlike here, where they were alive, protruding a youthful energy through the landscape. It inspired a possibility. Whilst the Viceroy had plans to ship him to Spain, as a freeman in Vera Cruz he could still catch a ship to the nearest port of the United States and make his way to Philadelphia.

Tearing a page from his diary, he began writing a request for assistance to the French Directory in the Windward Isles.

He would deliver it at port.

No ships were destined for America in Vera Cruz. It would be Cuba, after all. Muir did, however, have chance to deliver the letter to the Windward Isles.

On the ship, he picked up a newspaper left on deck. He read that in Milan, Napoleon had granted the new Transpadane Republic full civil powers.

What was he doing sailing to Cuba, he thought. He should be working with those liberating enchained societies. He remembered this Napoleon from Gerrald's lectures as he and Francois fished that day in the estuary. The same man had saved the Directory from Royalist infiltration in Paris a few years ago.

Unfolding the paper to reveal half the front page, bold letters read, 'Spain allies with France'. Good news he initially thought given the recent letter he'd posted to Victor Hughes, the French agent.

Flipping the paper over changed that, though.

It read 'against Britain.'

The newly forged national alliances didn't take long to collude against him. At Customs he was shackled and sent straight to the governor of Cuba who declared that with England now hostile to Spain, he would be considered a prisoner of war and as such would be committed to a prison.

The freedoms of the last few months seemed fleeting. Transitory. The cries of madmen, the dealings of gangs, the dire needs of base men and women, the ferment of disease, beatings, wakeful nights and cell darkened days, all plagued Muir's mind over the next four months.

His only outlet was alcohol and the mirroring of the prisoner's behaviour so that he might blend in unnoticed. Occasionally he would lapse back home and imagine the constituency he'd once hoped of representing.

He laughed that such an ambition had been used against him at his trial and remembered their walk to Skirving's house through the night, sighting as they did what they thought was an owl looming above them on a branch.

Their hopes for the meetings, Palmer's enthusiasm to liaise with the English Corresponding Societies, his own wariness, their idealism, the long journey it had aggravated, it all seemed pointless given his current predicament.

A hymn from his childhood that he sung with his father in their local church would arrive into his mind from time to time. Privately, he would conjure animations of the other prisoners singing a language they had never learned until his sleep deprived mind lunged into uncontrollable imaginings.

The Scottish soil was foreign to him but he recognised those who traipsed over the heather with him, eastwards. Edinburgh castle was now in sight. Specks of red between the leaved branches told them the Hanoverians were close enough for combat. On his left, now crouched out of sight, were the tobacconist and watchmaker from the first meeting, on his right the churchwarden and Dr Martins.

Two men walked passed them towards the troops. He ordered them to get down. They carried on relentless. Through the leaves he could see Francis Martin-Shore, Braxfield and Dundas. He tried again to stop the two men from leaving themselves so vulnerable to attack. This time they turned to him. One was Gerrald, half transparent to the dark clouds behind, the other was Skirving. A musket ball pierced through him but he kept on pacing forward.

Looking into the blackness of the prison wall he re-established that, as far as he knew, Skirving was still alive. Each day he hoped for news from the French Consul in the Windward Isles but the disappointment and fading hope drove him interminably to alcohol, handed around the prison to quell dissent.

He remembered aboard *The Otter*, Jane revisiting Kidlaw's attack as if talking it through might lessen the damage. These memories appeared in his mind like fish breaking the ocean's surface. Rarely and unexpected. Inspired by Gerrald, he committed them to his diary. But this made them seem more like history than ever before, accentuating the loss.

The prison's sickening monotony was one day fortunately broken when he was moved to La Principia Fortress. Indecent behaviour, he could not remember, was alleged the reason.

All the move brought was new enemies, illnesses and dangers. He clasped the pocket globe. The landmasses still stood out from the oceans but it was too dark to read any of the place names. Robert Watt once again, visited him in his

imaginings as did recollections of days gone by with Henry
Erskine.

As Muir had been escorted out of Parliament Hall,
Erskine had tried to make contact. Passing the doorway to the
Advocates' library, Muir recalled the evening they'd spent
there acting out a play in front of the Dean and the Faculty. A
poem that Erskine had read out had entered his mind as it did
again in the prison.

'Extraordinary actions belong to the great, the soldier, the
patriot or premier of state, but we unconnected with party or
faction, spend our time and our breath on an ordinary action.'

Every one of the advocates had had affiliations with the
state, particularly those that had become judges, and even,
dare he say it, Henry Erskine even if he had subsequently
objected to the war with France.

He recalled a few more lines. 'Though peaceable folks,
yet we often petition, though not like our neighbour, slurred
up by sedition, so just are both houses, that when we're
refused, we petition again, nor think justice abused.'

*

On the third of December 1796, he found himself in a
military hospital. His piled up post was finally delivered. Four
weeks ago to the day, the French consul had drafted a letter to
him only for it to fester on the other side of the prison bars.

Dated the third of November, it explained how an envoy
would be sent in due course. Muir was furious. If he'd had
this hope in La Principia Fortress, the ordeal wouldn't have
been half as bad.

Had the French already arrived and given up hope of
finding him? He had to think positively. They would arrive
any day now and in due course he would arrive at his adopted
country.

He'd hoped for America but the next best place was
France.

Recalling his story to an English speaking fellow in the next bed, sanity appeared to be returning to his surrounds but he now found the anticipation of the arriving envoy to be the source of his wakefulness as he placed all his hopes upon the next day.

When he awoke, the patient who had slept in the bed next to him, had gone. He thought he could hear French being spoken on the other side of the wall and banged it frantically, calling out, 'Aide! Aide! Help! C'est Thomas Muir!'

Other prisoners laughed at the spectacle. So much so that they deafened out his attempts to interpret a response from the other side. The riotous crescendo warranted his removal by hospital staff.

Everyone was against him.

'I demand to see the French. They've come for me.'

Straight jacketed, his observations were treated as hallucinations and within hours he was being carried down to the port and along the gangplank of a ship that sat desperately low in the water.

He listened out to discern the crew's nationality hoping French words would bless his ears. Swinging his head around, he tried to make out the ship's flag but he was too close to see what hung at the transom. Through the ordeal, he did spot a ship on the opposite quay. A French tricolour waved at him.

The ship he was boarding could also be French, he thought. Perhaps they were ships from the Windward Isles sailing in convoy.

Thrown below deck still in the straight jacket and unable to steady his fall, he cracked his head against something solid and lost consciousness.

A gilded face was staring at Muir when he awoke. He thought it a dream until Fidalgo smacked him. As he came too, he was blinded by the sight of gold in unimaginable quantities.

Later that night he realised that as far as the British ships were concerned, these treasures were shining a light straight on him. If they didn't know of his stowage aboard he would almost certainly fall victim to their thirst for Spanish gold.

He'd never felt so powerless and vulnerable.

As he watched the waves the next day, he wrote in his diary that they were the same waves that had witnessed battles long ago. Those on the coasts of the Peloponnese, or more probably the trading wars against the Spanish. Absconding into history made the imminent threat less real as if in a sense the imminent catastrophe had already happened and the pain had passed.

Fidalgo spotted a slave ship. Their pestilence arrived on the breeze as they passed directly to windward. It was this cruelty that had been supported by the 'eminent' Henry Dundas.

After a month crossing the miles of Atlantic longitude, on his pocket globe Muir marked his journey, however inaccurately, past the Bermudas and the Azores. Now nine months since having separated from Jane, he calculated that she might now be giving birth to their child. His own world was consumed by a torrent of rain. Fidalgo spotted Cadiz and, to Muir's horror, an unfathomably large warship. What he feared would happen was unravelling in front of him.

Through Fidalgo's telescope, Muir passed each and every one of the seventy or so guns. That was until one smoked. Thus commenced the thundering cannonade. About to add another battle to the history books, the enemy raised its ensign.

Muir convulsed. A union jack slivered in the breeze.

Their ship, the *Ninfa* was still abnormally low in the water. The gold made it heavy on the rudder. They were in no condition to navigate the reefs dotted around Conil Bay. The British knew this and were purposely driving them that way.

Further ahead they watched their sister ship, the *Elena*, run aground. The winds three leagues from the coast had once again succumbed to showers.

They came broadside to HMS *Irresistible* and anchored.

Muir hoped the British would be careful not to sink them.

Doing so would lose them their Spanish treasure.

It was perhaps their only advantage.

Igniting the powder, they returned fire.

A lull followed whilst both sides recharged their guns.

In the second wave came the first hit.

The wet decks steamed as the sail store caught fire.

Muir thought it safer to be higher up.

Thinking every minute to be his last, he imagined Jane, their baby and the struggles they'd had with nature and the elements. At least there was something precious in one life starting as another was destined to expire.

But he wasn't going to give up easily. Clambering up a rope ladder, he found it aflame behind him. He didn't know whether to jump whilst he was still low enough to land safely or try and outrun the encroaching inferno.

This was the closest he'd been to British blood lust since the trial. It was relentless.

Fire floats drifted onto them with the hastening tides.

Amongst the plumes of smoke on deck, Muir heard Fidalgo ordering someone at the bow to release the anchor.

But Muir had concerns of his own. The rungs supporting his feet were snapping, braid after braid. Stepping onto the next and the next he found his trousers ablaze.

He dived over the yardarm into the belly of a sail. It was harnessing a water pool left by the downpour. No longer on fire, he took a moment to bequeath God the well being of his newborn child.

As scores of cannonballs hurtled between him and the skies he prayed also for himself but they fell short as a cannonball strike obliterated the crow's nest. The lookout crashed to the deck in various body parts. His arm slid down the sail and landed on Muir.

Still twitching.

As the pool bloodied, Muir realised his fate might be the same if he didn't find a way down. The quarterdeck netting was still intact and was the only place to crash land.

315

Thankfully, the crow's nest had landed on the yardarm of the mast aft of him and directly above the quarterdeck.

With the fire floats upon them, Muir assumed the anchor must have fouled. The decks were increasingly ablaze. He had to move fast. He shimmied along the snapped mast but progress was momentarily halted when to his astonishment a cannonball obliterated the deck below.

Looking down, flames whipped over the gunwale like the tentacles of some unholy sea monster. The smoke aggravated the crew like swarming bees. Those on fire jumped into the sea.

His landing net would soon be ash.

The leap of faith would have to be imminent.

He jumped.

Fell through the air.

Landed and bounced upwards.

On the second landing, the flames disintegrated the hemp, and he crashed onto the deck.

Darting below, he slid on what he later realised was spattered brain and found Fidalgo on the verge of death. He cradled him until his last breath and then quickly swapped their jackets before heading down to the lower deck.

Capture was inevitable, Muir thought and at least now he could acquire Fidalgo's identity.

This was no time to be Thomas Muir.

But just as he was rehearsing this plan an explosion consumed the cabin. Knife sized splinters ricocheted everywhere and his hearing deteriorated as if insects had filled his head.

Then, he lost consciousness.

Finding his bearings he realised that one side of him was entirely crippled. Only able to lift his left arm and leg, with half his face feeling on fire he was sure this was his coup de grace.

The hole in the hull gushed sea spray sporadically cooling his powder burn before evaporating, leaving his skin to sting atrociously.

Through one eye he looked out at the cruel world.

Whilst he'd been knocked out HMS *Irresistible* had come alongside. Hand to hand combat would commence for the others but not for him.

He thought to open his other eye but couldn't. He felt the damaged side of his face and found only his eye socket. Then rolling with the ship's heel he saw his eye looking back at him.

The unbelievable was demanding that it be believed.

He crawled towards his eyeball cursing the ship's tilt when suddenly it rolled out of his field of vision.

Something dug into his stomach as he tried to reach out.

It was a piece of facial bone. His, he assumed.

As he gave up on retrieving his eye, the surface below him pooled with blood. He looked and in it saw his mangled ear.

Resting his head in his blood he heard something roll towards his remaining ear. He tried to grab it but this time didn't need to. It came to a halt in the blood. He clenched his detached eye in his hand and lost consciousness again.

The crack of grappling irons hounded the *Ninfa* and informed Muir the British were now aboard. The pain was such that he now wished for his last friend, Death, to relieve him.

He retreated to times past, Anderson testing his propaganda machine, Tytler's abandoned home, Burns in the courtroom, boxing with Millar, setting up the Society with Palmer, standing up for the rights of the people with Skirving, suffering the consequences with Margarot.

He remembered the skeleton in Tytler's room, the zygomatic bone forming the prominence of the cheek, the mandible his lower jaw.

When he awoke, he had been piled amongst the dead that he sensed were soon to be thrown overboard. He felt neither alive nor dead but immersed in the dire constraints of excruciating pain, graced only by the fact that he might have a son or daughter now breathing in a free land.

Rumbles of footsteps made him more alert still but he sank the recognisable side of his face into the congealed entrails of a corpse and listened as best he could to the English being spoken around him.

The words horrified him. For they demanded that no bodies be thrown overboard until Thomas Muir be found. Amidst the bangs of boot steps, he felt his pulse being taken. Before he could reach for his dirk, his neck was twisted upwards.

'Muir?'

He opened his one remaining eye and saw a man he'd last seen walking from Parliament Hall. That man had taken time from his surgical training to support him at his trial. He couldn't quite believe it. Palmer's speculation concerning who was aboard HMS *Irresistible* in Southampton was absolutely correct.

'It's Martins. From the Society. And school. Don't try to speak.'

Then, Captain James Jervis approached.

Martins turned Muir's head back into the corpse.

'Our man in Cuba told us Muir is aboard this ship. Now find him. You're the only one who knows what he looks like now do your job and bring him to me alive or dead, I don't care which...'

'He could be aboard the *Elena*, Captain Jervis.'

'Our spy said the *Ninfa*.'

Muir remembered the British patient in the prison hospital and cursed himself for talking so carelessly.

Captain Jervis headed to the bottom deck.

When he was gone, Martins ushered two men over.

'Stretcher bearers, take this Spaniard to the field hospital on the next raft.'

'Thank you, Martins,' whispered Muir.

Martins followed the captain up to the next deck. Up the stairway, perhaps ten minutes later, Muir heard Martins again assuring Captain Jervis that he had checked all the decks apart from the one they were now on.

'Search the dead and the wounded. Every last one of them. Find him and I will share the bounty for his head.'

Muir fretted. Captain Jervis lifted a wounded man's head by the hair, to face Martins. The screams of mercy went unheard.

An hour past until he heard Martins again, still on the upper deck.

'Here he is.'

'Is he dead?'

'Yes.'

'We get more money that way. How do you know it's him?'

'I recognise his face. The colour of his eyes, the auburn hair and look, his diary. There, it says Thomas Muir.'

Muir remembered he'd left it in his lapel pocket when swapping jackets, a valuable mistake.

'Well done, Martins.'

Before Muir could contemplate his and Fidalgo's strange reversals of fate, he felt his broken body being tipped onto a stretcher and lifted upwards.

His bible remained on the ground. Muir pointed to it. Realising it was in English he thought it foolish and regretted the action. It was too late. One of the stretcher bearers had reached down to pick it up. Muir prayed that the bible would not be opened. He waited until finally he felt it placed by his side.

Carried out to blue skies, the rainfall had all but evaporated.

'You're a very lucky Spaniard, my friend.'

Muir listened to the English sailor before wheezing an almost inaudible 'grazias.'

'He means to say thank you. Don't you Senor?'

'Ce, senor.' The pain was excruciating.

'By his papers, the ship's surgeon says he is called Fidalgo.'

The Spaniards in the hospital treated their diplomatic escort with the utmost respect. While forceps were used to extract loose fragments of bone, wood and shot, a conversation ensued between the Spanish nurse and doctor.

'The British captain does not believe they have the man they are after. The man they call Muir.'

'He will probably be dead, doctor.'

'It's of little consequence. They've offered the Spanish their ship in return for handing over the Englishman. Dead or alive.'

Muir wheezed in distress.

'What do you think, Fidalgo?' asked the doctor. 'You escorted him, after all. Is he a man who could survive the Spanish and the English? Enemies made allies by a man called Muir. When you are better you may be asked to identify him.'

'I remember him to be a very weak man. He couldn't swim. He will have succumbed to his injuries. He probably drowned or is buried amongst the dead.' Muir's reply was exhausting.

'Let him rest, doctor.' The nurse continued, 'Fidalgo is probably sick of the name, Thomas Muir, after all the trouble he has caused.'

'You're right, don't try to speak. Your welfare is our only concern at the moment not that villain's fate.'

He was turned on to his side so they could attend to where was once his ear. Through the curtains he spotted a bureaucrat comparing a sketch of him with the bed bound.

His time was up.

Closing his remaining eye he slipped into memories of home, his parents, Glasgow and Jane but they were destroyed with the excruciating ointments and piercing stitches.

A curtain rail skidded across.

His treatment ceased.

An enduring pause ensued.

'Señora, I will not delay Fidalgo's treatment any more for your head hunting. You were right, nurse, I shouldn't have asked so many questions. He has suffered enough. I can tell you now he looks nothing like that fat lawyer in the sketch you have there.'

Muir clung to the bible his parents had given him, the only possession he had left. It had to be kept closed.

English words could be his downfall.

He waited for the curtain to be drawn across again.

Eventually, they left.

In his mind, he imagined releasing Anderson's balloon from the window with a message that he was inside the hospital, hoping that a French passer-by would find it and alert the Directory.

When he awoke he conceded that it hadn't happened and was panicked by the silhouette of a figure passing from patient to patient.

He pushed the undamaged side of his face into the pillow.

'Muir. It's Martins.'

Muir tilted his head and opened his remaining eye.

'I've informed the French Directory. They'll be here within days. They will stop negotiations between Spain and Britain for you. Jervis found amongst other things a crucifix tattooed on Fidalgo's back and suspected a Scottish protestant would not adhere to such imagery.'

'Goodbye, Martins. Thank you again.'

Muir's health deteriorated with the hope of French intervention. He wondered whether Martin's visit was just a hopeful dream. Further surgical attempts to stop the bleed were successful until they became aggravated by sleeplessness. He knew the stitches they'd inserted around his jaw would eventually fail, even if they were strong enough to stop him from speaking.

Beneath his pillow, the bible was encrusted in blood. Each morning he wanted to separate the pages so that he would not lose the stories it entailed but that was impermissible and it became increasingly encased in the blood of his own story's end.

Neither the English nor the Spanish surgeon came that day. He urinated through the mattress, picturing in his mind the yellow pool further down from the bloody one directly below his head.

The wound had become grotesquely inflamed.

He hadn't the energy to move. Speaking was impossible with his jawbone and nerve endings still exposed.

Night sweats came again.

And then daylight. Or at least that was what he initially thought. For, on closer examination he realised it was, in fact, unnatural light from the doorway. Oil lanterns swinging hectically sending shadows across the walls.

Words spoken in French. The inspections of patients. Definitely a dream he would soon forget when he awoke. If he awoke. God was being kind to him, soothing him with premonitions of his desires, before finally ripping him from what had become this tangled sphere of life.

'I'm Thomas Muir,' shouted the prisoners, each of them repeating the phrase as the lamplight lit up their hopeful faces.

The diplomats had to rip the clutching hands from their cuffs.

Everyone but he wanted to be Thomas Muir. But then a dawn breeze from the open window shook him from this thought.

He felt the bible with his fingers beneath the pillow. It was wet again. The taste of blood trickled down between his nose and mouth. Dreams were incapable of recreating these sensations, he thought.

His rescue was real.

'I am Thomas Muir,' he wanted to say. He tried to speak as the Frenchmen passed but the stitches tormented him. Trying to lift his head, he found the recognisable side of his face bound to the pillow by dried blood.

He hoped the blood flowing between his nose and mouth, would flow onto the pillow. With all his energy he tried to break the bloody seal but his face remained in darkness.

God wanted him more.

The Frenchmen looked at Muir's broken jaw, his bandaged hollowed eye socket and his missing ear.

With pity they bowed their heads in prayer.

The patients continued to shout the claims that they were Muir.

Sick of the insane chanting, the diplomats got up to leave after crossing their chests and looking up to God.

Then Muir breathed, 'Mur', the closest his injuries allowed him to return to his self. The stitches then broke free but he couldn't contend with the pain. The diplomats looked at the hospital notes and addressed him as Fidalgo before the curtains were drawn and they stepped away.

In the pain and frustration Muir flung his bible onto the floor.

It tumbled under the curtain.

The footsteps stopped.

The diplomats handed the bible back.

Muir shook his head towards the bible's spine.

'He wants me to read to him.'

The other diplomat hurried his colleague.

'We haven't got time. We have to check the other ward.'

'Just one page, that's the least a dying man can expect.'

'We must find Thomas Muir.'

Disobeying his superior, the diplomat turned the first bloody leaf.

' Monsieur. Look!'

'To Thomas Muir, from your afflicted parents.'

The words absorbed the lamplight like life itself.

XVIII
44° 50' N
000° 31' W

Knowledge of being in Bordeaux came to Muir by way of an article in the Gazette Nationale.

The celebrated Scot, Thomas Muir, having escaped from a thousand dangers, is on the point of arriving in Paris. His transportation belongs to the history of revolutions. His courage in the face of adversity must serve as an example to the converts of philosophy and the happy issue of all his misfortunes must encourage all the martyrs of liberty.

The Scots have never forgotten their ancient independence and the massacre of their ancestors. Perhaps our revolution was the cause of the revolutionary movements that appeared in Scotland in 1792, in which Thomas Muir played one of the premier roles. An enlightened thinker and impassioned orator, he left his mark on parliamentary reform.

The uprising in Scotland gave great hopes to our revolutionary government. When the old committee of public safety learnt of their deportation, it sent out several frigates to rescue them but they did not succeed.

Muir was surprised to learn of the rescue attempt. Considering what might have happened had it been successful, he noticed Talleyrand standing on the lawns outside, swatting flies that came close. Sitting up, he found himself a little disappointed that they'd considered him, not a reformer but a revolutionary.

Next to the article was his pocket globe.

An ink line marked his circumnavigation.

He dressed and looked into the mirror. A leather mask had been made to cover his disfigurement. He walked outside to meet Talleyrand who, out of exile, was now the French Foreign Secretary.

'Muir! We meet again. They had plans to send you to Madrid! I stopped the negotiations between Britain and Spain on the grounds that you were an honorary French citizen. I didn't mention I'd once been exiled from France and lived in Suffolk! Are you ready to be entertained?'

Muir brushed a fly away from his face whilst a coach passed by the gatehouse. Talleyrand then remembered something.

'Ah, Monsieur Muir, you will recognise my driver.'

The coachman took off his top hat. It was Mr Vear.

His gunshot wound seemed to have paid off.

'Monsieur de Vere, you took my advice.'

'Could say that. Hop in, Mr Muir.'

As they drove into Bordeaux's Grand Place, hundreds of supporters lined the streets.

Once Muir was a man of immense oratory, now each word brought great pains but at least he was able to speak a little.

'The Patriots...' The crowds calmed down as Muir began.

Talleyrand waved at the encroaching swarm of flies.

'...The Patriots of Scotland...'

Muir felt a fly rummage between his flesh and the mask.

'... Of Ireland...'

He tried to pincer the fly through the leather.

'... And England...'

It was now crawling up to his eye socket.

'... Will soon break their chains!'

The crowds cheered. To Muir it was persecution, both to speak and to have a fly feeding on his flesh. Without any vanity, he ripped off the leather mask and showed the crowds the true nature of his suffering.

The cheering stopped. Draws of breath, looks of ill placed shame and the occasional sob left Muir crying from just his right eye. Talleyrand pounded his hands together and the crowds once again cheered for their guest.

In his invalid chair, Muir was escorted to the Hall of the Societe de la Grande Quille. In the first shop window, he noticed his old face. He read the poem and biography.

No mask or disfigurement was portrayed.

Both his eyes in the sketch looked at him whilst only one of his looked back at the sketch, a contradiction he reflected upon. Every shop on the way had his portrait alongside the poem.

'An apostle of philanthropy.' He liked that.

As they carried him up the steps to the town hall, Mr Vear gestured to refit the mask. Muir refused. He remembered the use of excrement and urine to make the Parisian leather.

At the banquet Mr Vear and Talleyrand sat either side of Muir, who asked the coachman whether he had seen much of England since they last parted company.

'Seen your old chum, Wordsworth?'

Muir thought his dig at Mr Vear worth the pain of talking.

'Those days ended when you left me with Talleyrand.'

'But you've been on diplomatic missions to Britain?'

'Oh yes, London and the south.'

'How's it?'

'Six hundred sailors a month are deserting the Royal Navy. Despite the sentence of hanging if you're caught.'

'Because...'

'Because they've not been paid for two years, Mr Muir. Last time I sailed out the Thames, May time it was, British naval mutineers controlled the traffic. Saw with my very own eyes, Pitt's effigy hanging from the yardarms. Was also a mutiny, around that time, at Spithead.'

'Think you made the right choice working for the French?'

De Vere carved up his serving of swan.

'I'd say. Royal standards been replaced by the red flags of revolution. A President of the Floating Republic's been elected!'

'Really?' Muir was intrigued.

'In the North, your friend Dundas is introducing the Militia Act.'

'When?'

'Next month. July... So far they've relied on volunteer forces. They're clever like that, the establishment. It's cheaper so they don't have to raise taxes for it, excludes the poor also as they can't afford the musket, bayonet and uniform. Less chance of rebellion that way. That's how the minds of the powerful work.'

He was about to respond to Mr Vear when Talleyrand tapped his wine glass with a spoon and helped Muir to his feet.

Once the cutlery had settled, everyone faced him.

'Citizens, I am not accustomed to speak the French language in public. But were I endowed with all the facility of speech it is possible to possess, I should not be able to express the sensations I now feel. I'm transported with joy to find myself at this moment amongst you. But when I compare my present situation with my brethren and countrymen who sigh in dungeons or languish in exile, I experience sentiments of the most profound melancholy. The same spirit that animates you animates them also. They're worthy of your esteem, for they aspire after liberty. We shall one day be free like you and then by our sincere affection we'll prove to you that we are your brethren!'

The band played once the applause had subsided.

Soon after, Talleyrand prepared to leave.

'Will I see you in Paris, soon?' asked Muir.

'Of course.' He looked to see if anyone was watching and handed Muir a wad of Francs. 'For the journey north. Farewell'.

*

Inhalations turned acrid as they passed into Paris. Muir remembered where he was from his previous mission and recognised the Rue Mouffetard.

'Not that way. Take a different route! Any street but the Mouffetard.'

The orders yielded nothing. The coachman persisted without detour and slowed into the traffic. The others in the coach turned away as he removed the leather mask so that he could vomit.

After several convulsions he looked up to find a man staring at him. He was about to give him a piece of his mind for dwelling on his wounds when he realised that the man too was afflicted facially. He had smallpox scarring. Muir then realised who was before him. It was Citizen Joubert.

'You do not know who is before you, do you?'

Muir's question stole from Joubert, his affinity to care for one as scarred as himself.

'Not the man you left at Le Havre but someone who has circumnavigated the globe. You knew me when I lacked experience. We waited for your countrymen to decide my fate. That day, at the checkpoint. All those years ago, when bodies hung from trees. You taught me to say citizen to avoid attack. And now I'm your nation's hero. Once you joked I was this nation's foe man! I recognise you from your afflictions Citizen Joubert yet mine mask you from this timely reunion.'

'Citizen Muir?'

He threw Joubert the pocket globe.

'Free your horses. Get out of Paris. Go and discover the world!'

'It is Citizen Muir? Non?'

'Perhaps.'

'It is!'

'Adieu…'

'I remember now. Yes...'

Muir raised the coach window fading out Joubert, before wiping from his disfigurement, sick that was beginning to burn the raw exposed flesh. Slipping his detached eye into the case of the now wandering globe, he knew the journey of a lifetime was over.

In many ways, but not all, he had made it back. Work still had to be done but that concerned lands that required no globe to navigate, lands he wanted to return to the displaced Scots.

Minutes later, he clambered up a seemingly insurmountable set of steps. Talleyrand was at the top trying to descend, his club foot hindering him on every ledge.

'We must return Scotland to the Scottish people.'

'Come on in, my valiant comrade.'

Bottles of port waited for them. Talleyrand made sure a straw came with the glass to help his friend. Muir placed it on the desk and lowered his head to take a sip.

The alcohol seemed to lessen the pains of speech.

'Did you hear what I said?'

'Muir, it is high treason to send money into France so I have afforded you a pension from the French state.'

Muir tried to steer the conversation back onto Scotland.

'If the government lands in Scotland, all that is furnished to me will be paid there with interest.'

Talleyrand lowered his head. 'That's very generous but our French forces are stretched dealing with the Royalist coup. It has made the Directory cynical and despondent to the ideals we had in ninety three.'

Though thankful for Talleyrand getting him out of Spain, being rescued by an aristocrat of the old regime left many questions unresolved in his mind and he sensed in his friend's apathy, old tendencies reforming.

'Are you not the French Foreign Secretary?'

Talleyrand nodded proudly though fully aware of what reasoning lay ahead.

'Then why are you engaging with homeland issues when you could be addressing countries like Scotland? Paris does not require the French Navy! We've a once in a lifetime opportunity to free Scotland from Pitt's policies. You told me yourself you detest the man. As I seem to recall, you gave him your apartment in Saint-Thierry for his vacation. Ten years later at Downing Street, he barely spoke to you.'

Talleyrand hid his malice towards Pitt under a veil, leaving Muir to guess what he was thinking.

'I cannot let personal dislikes influence national policies.'

'Please, Talleyrand!'

The Foreign Secretary's despondence was finally fractured when a man entered the room.

'Molet here will act as your personal translator.'

'My French is fine thank you. Have you heard from Angus Cameron of Blair Atholl, James Kennedy of Paisley and the other United Scotsmen?'

Molet seemed confused by Muir's question and uttered a few comments. As he spoke, his London English sent shivers down Muir's spine. This was no English speaking Frenchman but a French speaking Englishman. Or so he feared.

Talleyrand then remembered something.

'Tomas, we've a special treat. Tomorrow, you will have your portrait painted by the great classical artist, David.'

Disappointed, Muir lowered his head remembering Anderson's paste cameo of classical distinction, lost to the bottom of a bureau drawer.

He finished his glass of port.

After a few seconds the glass appeared to be filling back up. Talleyrand and Molet thought this some strange party trick until a pitter patter flooded the desk.

'Molet! Call my doctor!'

Talleyrand used the face mask like a tourniquet, encasing the source of the bleed.

'Take it easy, Tomas. You're opening old wounds. Relax. Put your head upright.'

The tan leather began to spot red. Trails of blood continued to descend, reluctantly now, like raindrops down a windowpane. He lost consciousness.

Wolf Tone was by Muir's side when he awoke in a hospital bed. Although his injuries could be traced back to supporting the United Irishmen, Muir was still glad to see his old friend.

'You didn't miss much in America.'

'You made it?' asked Muir wearily.

'I was an emissary to the Americans. But it's from France that we will save our homelands. We might learn from America's war of independence, but we must fight our own.'

'Our own?' Muir sensed solely Irish interests in Wolf that aggravated him when he reflected on his own sacrifices.

'We must fight Pitt with the French not the Americans, I mean. And that's only if Napoleon brushes up on his knowledge of Ireland. He still thinks the population is only two million!'

'Have you met him, this Napoleon?'

'Briefly. How are you feeling?' Wolf asked.

'The drink starts off the bleeding.'

'Tom Paine's a bad influence.'

'He drinks like a fish. Cognac, too,' Muir said, remembering their days at the Palais Royale.

'You can when you've no children,' Wolf mused.

Jane trickled into Muir's mind. Their fatherless child would now perhaps be taking its first steps, learning its first words.

Wolf noted Muir's distance.

'I read that, with the French you attempted to retake Ireland from the British.'

'Yes. The Expédition d'Irlande! Fourteen thousand French troops we had with us, under General Hoche.'

'You arrived at Bantry Bay?' asked Muir.

'Arrived is taking it a bit far. We outsmarted the Royal Navy but the winter storms stopped us landing. England had its luckiest escape since the armada. As it appears, have you.'

'What have they done to my wounds?' asked Muir, looking at his face through a nearby looking glass.

'They've inserted sponge tents. So, the doctor informed me. Don't touch them. Rest... Ireland would have been a different country had the weather been on our side. As it is, sources in Cork tell me, just last month the British interrogated a group of United Irishmen for the names of other members.'

Wolf's throat dried up as he spoke.

'They knelt them in front of coffins, with guns to the backs of their heads, demanding names. Not one of them informed.'

Muir shuddered at the poor men's fates and touched his wounds as if somehow it connected with their suffering.

Later he asked, 'why are there no sponges here, Wolf? Did the doctor say anything about this?'

'The surgeon thought it best to expose as much of the bone as possible. Bleeding is recommended to counter the inflammation and symptomatic fever. So he said. A few more weeks and you'll be free to go.'

*

The Indian summer in Paris was not doing wonders for Muir's wounds. He longed for the winter to ward off infection.

Convalescing on the balcony with Molet, much joy was to be had from the view of the Palais Royale's quadrant gardens. He reminisced about his days here when on bail, with Paine. Then, it crossed his mind that the hotel staff had thoughtfully given him the same room he had stayed in half a decade ago.

Finishing his soup, he noticed someone approaching.

'Don't worry. I'm not a spy!'

It was Paine.

'I spotted you from the Directory terrace when you were looking out on the street.'

'Noticing me wouldn't be difficult. I've been ordered to seek peace with myself and rest,' Muir lamented.

'Talleyrand said as much. He also told me, though on condition that I didn't tell you, that...'

'We are to reclaim Scotland?'

'No, that Austria has made peace with France. We also signed the peace treaty with Portugal in August.'

'So?'

'So Britain's alone in its fight with revolutionary France and now we can put all our resources into taking England.'

Muir reattached the leather mask ready for battle.

'Hang on though. The British are seeking peace on very favourable terms so liberation is not written in stone.'

'Peace? After what they've done. Hypocrites,' snapped Muir.

'They're accepting practically all of France's territorial gains.'

'Peace will not last. We have to act now,' shouted Muir, 'look at these letters, dozens of them have arrived these last few weeks. The Scottish people are ready. They're waiting for the bells of Saint Giles' to ring telling them it is time to rise. Once they have the signal other churches will ring their bells until all of Scotland is awakened to liberty. When I was locked up in Edinburgh I learned of a little known tunnel into the castle. We could use it to gain access and control...'

'Hang on, hang on, you're thinking about the detail when we don't even know whether it's going to happen.'

'I never thought I'd be more radical than the great Thomas Paine!'

'I'm just telling you so you don't become deluded. You have to be realistic. You want your country back. I understand, even if it now requires liberating by invasion.'

'It has been five years since we last met. So much has changed in myself and in the world,' reflected Muir. 'Why should I now jettison peaceful means you might ask? Well, I have exhausted those methods and the British government haven't shown peaceful means towards me. Everything we hold great about the Glorious Revolution wouldn't have happened had William not invaded and liberated England. This is the next logical step in the cause of the people and the progress of freedom.'

Paine smiled. He'd critiqued that historic event many times.

'Muir, I'm the last person you need to convince of your change of approach. You've exhausted every other means to strive for goodness.'

Alone, Muir looked down through the gardens again. Scotland had to be reclaimed for those who had been cleared, he thought. People like Alexander Lockie needed at least the option of returning to their homelands.

A breeze knocked the first leaves of autumn onto the pristine lawns. He picked up his untouched glass of red wine and noticed what he thought was the last fly of summer drowning in the darkness. He would have liked to have met Alexander but not doing so in Botany Bay was a sure sign the man had escaped successfully.

It was time to dress his wounds in wet linen. This, Muir would do until there were no more leaves on the trees or warmth in the air, until winter provided a bandage for his wounds.

*

A blast of artillery fire awoke the blackened hotel room. December had crept up on him and parting the curtains, the glow of virgin snow illuminated the interior.

A second explosion echoed around the quadrant. Branch tops of snow fell as birds took to the skies whilst soldiers paraded through the gardens blackening the white ground.

Half dressed, Muir ran across the corridor onto the street side to watch them march through the crowds towards the Luxembourg Palace.

Still barefoot, he headed onto the snow laden balcony where others chanted 'Napoleon', holding onto the freezing balustrade to keep his balance.

Now fully dressed, down in the street and in pursuit of the celebrations, he poked his head between shoulders in front to gain vantage of the man he'd heard so much about.

'When the happiness of the French people is based on the best organic laws, the whole of Europe will be free.'

For such a short man, Napoleon's voice travelled far beyond the gold epaulettes broadening his shoulders.

No one uttered a word, except Talleyrand who, brushing past Muir, was heard to say, 'there lies the future.'

Once introduced by Talleyrand, Napoleon celebrated the fact that Muir was the first non-Frenchman to be made a citizen of the Republic. The leader's adamantine stare drove Muir to break eye contact but it was an honour to be with someone who had achieved so much.

'Are we to liberate Scotland then?' asked Muir.

'We've liberated half of Europe. Why not England, Scotland and Ireland, too? But Captain John Jervis smashed the Spanish fleet at Cape St. Vincent back in February. Had he not, we'd have twice the ships we presently have to attack England.'

'The very same man searched for me aboard the *Ninfa*.'

'I've been told. But he failed. Perhaps you are a good omen, Citizen Muir. They've made peace proposals...'

'You cannot accept.'

'We cannot compromise freedom as you know fine well.'

In Napoleon's company, Muir felt like the exiled Thucydides or Pericles, the champions of Athenian democracy. He told Napoleon that the approaching battle with Britain would be their Peloponnesian War.

Talleyrand's warning at the Luxembourg Palace influenced his judgement but if there was ever a time to inspire those who might act, it was this meeting with Bonaparte.

'The Scottish people are ready,' claimed Muir. 'The bells of Saint Giles will ring out. Mail coaches will be prevented from leaving major cities. They're the signs that the Scottish people should rise. Will the Directory support us?'

'I signed the Austria treaty without consulting Paris. Talleyrand usually appeases the Directory when it's needed. They know they wouldn't be here if it wasn't for me!'

'I read about your battle with the Royalists in Paris.'

'I have promoted Thomas Paine to leader of the English Directory. Wolf Tone will lead the Irish. Do you want to lead the Scottish Directory?'

'Of course!' celebrated Muir.

'Are you well enough?'

'I have never felt better!'

'You will not be alone.'

Colonel Norman Macleod entered the room and waited at the door. 'Good evening, Mr Muir. It seems we've come a long way from the Berean Meeting House. It has been seven eventful years.'

Muir remembered their first meeting and how curious it was having the MP for Inverness in his company with the great Napoleon.

'Things have come full circle, or certainly I have,' said Muir.

'Once I was a member of the British parliament and now I am a director of The Provisional Government of the Scottish Republic! Lord Daer has been working for the United Scotsmen. Do you forgive him for his objections to your Irish Address?'

'Has he helped Scotland since?'

'He helps the United Scotsmen meet every couple of months in secrecy. The government has just made them illegal. He might be an aristocrat but he at least uses that for the people's benefit. They won't arrest him because of his family connections. Our country's tired of its government.'

'And the Militia Act they introduced, they're tired of that?'

'Yes, and the troops they use to silence protests.'

'Then, there's no better time than now.'

Macleod turned to Napoleon.

'Commander Bonaparte, Scots are staging mock funerals to move coffin loads of pikes from place to place.'

'Fifteen thousand men in Perthshire are ready to rise... and fifty thousand highlanders... and there's huge unrest in the navy. The United Englishmen can use diversionary tactics whilst a main force lands in Scotland. To win over British naval crews we could offer them the value of their ships as a way of recovering the wages they haven't been paid. It'll also reduce the opposing fleet.'

Napoleon considered Muir's plans seriously.

Later, the Irish contingent entered the war office, led by Napper Tandy and Wolf Tone. They sat on Muir's blind side.

Wolf looked a little uncomfortable before he began to speak.

'Commander Napoleon, we think the sole focus of invasion should be Ireland.'

Muir scraped his chair around so he could face Wolf.

'What about Scotland?' asked Muir and Macleod.

'We think Scotland should be used...'

Muir interrupted. 'Used?'

The pain from an abscess infuriated him.

'Used,' Wolf continued, 'to smuggle troops to Ireland via the Forth estuary and the Union Canal.'

'The Union Canal? Are you mad? I don't want to hear the word 'union' ever again. You want to use Scotland? Have you forgotten what I did for you in Edinburgh? I gave you a platform when you had no one! I spoke for your cause in the hope that one day you'd speak for mine! I trusted you Wolf to support me this day. Do you realise it was because I supported you that I was arrested? I've been pursued around the globe by the Royal Navy. I've suffered transportation, floggings, imprisonment. I've lost an eye, an ear, half my face!'

Napoleon interrupted. 'And yet you have not, how do you say, lost face, at all. You are more respected than ever, Monsieur Muir.'

'I fought for you, Wolf. I fought for Ireland and now you want to use my country.'

'Scotland is too stable to revolt,' Wolf said, 'the Volunteer Corps have had the effect of banishing sedition and uniting the classes in a common patriotism. That's what we think, in the cold light of day. Yes, without getting personal about it, we want to use Scotland.'

Blood trickled down Muir's neck and inside his shirt until it made contact with the cotton and bellowed for all to see. Paine got him back into his seat and settled his composure whilst Commander Bonaparte looked on with both admiration and concern.

'You want to use Scotland?' Muir murmured.

Paine then took to the floor. 'Commander Bonaparte, please excuse our differences. An invasion will be successful if we define clearly what we mean by it. I propose the building of thousands of small boats with cannons at the bow designed to make widespread landings over Scotland, England and Ireland. Lets not forget the Highland regiment refused to fire on the United Irishmen. There are widespread alliances amongst the people we must support.'

Napoleon interrupted. 'I intend to assess all our coastal ports and ships in the months ahead. But you cannot underestimate the force of the Royal Navy. Your thinking, Mr Paine, is welcome. Invasion will have to be in the darkness of winter. If it isn't, the British will have superiority over their waters. We will meet in a month's time. Agreed? Citizen Muir?'

XIX
48° 48' N
002° 20' E

Paine and Muir walked up the stairs to Commander Bonaparte's office. Several months had passed.

The huge doors to his office were closed.

'Wolf's right. He's gone to Egypt. The Directory want him out of Paris.'

'The time's passed for Scotland,' admitted Muir.

'You know the Directory have agreed to another invasion of Ireland?'

Muir stopped mid step. 'What?'

Paine walked along the corridor to the open doors of the Foreign Office. Talleyrand was in bed robes, hobbling to his desk. Napoleon stood looking out of the window with the countenance more of a logician than a military commander.

Muir walked up to Paine. Neither of them had yet been seen by either Napoleon or Talleyrand. Inch thick wads of banknotes were being counted out and dropped into Napoleon's case.

'One hundred thousand francs should do it?'

The Frenchmen shook hands.

Muir looked away ashamed that corruption was rife in this so called government of the people.

'I don't think we were supposed to see that, Paine.'

'You know Talleyrand made it to Philadelphia and President Washington wouldn't receive him. A letter of complaint had arrived beforehand from Governor Morris. Warned Talleyrand was immoral.'

Muir laughed, 'Talleyrand said he disliked the Americans because they were obsessed with money and profit.'

'It looks like he'd of got on with them very well if he'd been allowed in the country.'

*

As Napoleon walked out, he greeted Paine and Muir. 'My dear friends, it appears the Directory have used Talleyrand to control me. I normally use him to control them. Not this time.'

The three of them walked downstairs. Napoleon's speech seemed low and hollow, his manner cold.

'I assessed the channel ports but the Directory thought a British invasion too risky, and they want me out of Paris.'

'Don't let them kick you out like this!' asserted Muir.

'Wolf Tone will conquer Ireland. All is not lost. And my friends, when Egypt is ours, I'll take over British India for you both. That at present, is the best I can do for you. Good day citizens!'

As Napoleon walked out Muir noticed how he stooped and looked at least ten years older than he really was, just twenty eight, fatigued by one campaign only to start another.

'Farewell! Vive la Republique!'

Muir and Paine knew that they were not just saying goodbye to Napoleon but to each other as well.

The next few days would see to that.

Packing his few possessions from the hotel room, Muir looked out at the gardens, where he'd first learned of Napoleon's arrival. The trees hung devoid of leaves. Seventeenth century neo-classical pillars, once regal now civilised, once promising but now desolate, stood like pawns on an abandoned chessboard.

Hearing that a member of the French Assembly was supplying information to a relative in the British Treasury and learning that Molet had disappeared to London without notice, he knew his days in Paris were numbered. He wondered whether he could risk returning to Scotland to see his family and homeland.

With these thoughts heavy on his person, a room maid waited some time for his attention. Aware of his departure they had remembered to hand Muir the jacket he'd left drying by the hotel fire half a decade ago.

Although slightly mothballed and still smelling faintly of the cognac that Paine had spat out, Muir was glad to have something else his parents had bought for him on qualifying at the bar, along with the bible.

As he hurried out of the hotel, he placed his hands in the pockets and found a note. Scribbled on it were details of the hideout Paine had recommended all those years before.

The New Year celebrations of 1799 provided a smokescreen to leave the capital. Mr Vear drove him thirty miles north to Chantilly, a quiet enough place to meet the United Scotsmen.

Behind the mask, he recalled who knew about the safe house. Angus Cameron and the United Scotsmen had been told in writing and Talleyrand, in person, so his post could be redirected, and of course, Mr Vear.

Through the blizzard Muir could just make out the derelict château de Chantilly, one of the many gravestones to old Europe dotted across the continent.

They diverted from Chantilly's high street through a copse of poplars caped in snow to a tiny cottage where a local widow waited to walk him from the carriage to the front door.

Passing a few trees close against the cottage, Muir thought they were English oaks. He entered the front room. From wall to wall, it was cramped by a grand piano without even space for it to be played whilst seated.

The widow explained that it had been saved from the château. Striking a note, it lingered long after he returned his hands to his pockets as if searching for somewhere else to be.

The room had white washed walls, an open fire and a bed. The widow handed him a face mask made of muslin that had been stained auburn to match his hair. Post had arrived reassuring him that none could have been left behind at the Palais Royale.

Feeling dried salt on his hands, the brown envelope at the top of the pile reminded him of the convict ship's decks. He browsed down to the signature. It was Reverend Palmer's.

He was so pleased to know that his friend was still alive and coming to the end of his sentence. Muir thought that had he stayed in Botany Bay his own sentence wouldn't even be halfway through. Clearly, Governor Hunter's petition to the King had come to nothing.

Palmer wrote how his comrade in Dundee, George Mealmaker, had recently arrived at Botany Bay after a charge of sedition and a sentence of fourteen years.

Muir hoped he too would follow his lead and attempt escape but as he read on, beside the fire that the widow had lit, he became enthralled by Palmer's own tale. A drip of blood fell onto the paper as he turned the page. In time, a black corona of ink ran around the globule but he kept reading regardless of its implications.

According to Palmer, privateers had captured a Spanish galleon mid Pacific and had brought it to Botany Bay, the nearest admiralty port. He proudly boasted how he had only gone and purchased the ship.

As Muir once again stemmed the flow of blood from his face, he imagined Palmer abandoning the ship he had tried to build from scratch. Concerns for his friend surfaced, however. Similar dealings with Spanish vessels had caused his current woes and he worried that this would also be the case for Palmer.

Folding up the letter, he noticed on the back that his friend had transcribed a poem called *Fears of Solitude*. Recounting his exchange with the young poet in Cambridge of seven years past, he wrote how his poetry had been of great encouragement to him. Like the bard, who called himself Coleridge, he intended to have England once again as his own.

It would not just be the land of Mr Pitt's.

Palmer intended to sail the Spanish ship back to England once his sentence had expired. Muir feared that he did not know the two countries were at war. It did not bode well.

That said, his friend's entrepreneurship spurred Muir into writing his memoir again. Papers he'd written in Paris, on his exile and odyssey now filled two cases.

Sure that they'd make three thousand pounds with a London bookseller, he planned a two volume work. In the notes was a letter passed on by Talleyrand, from Francois Pierre Peron, he'd not had chance to read yet.

The Frenchman had been searching for him. He and Captain Ebenezer Dorr had ended up in a court case and Francois was in need of witnesses to vouch his side of the sealskin contract.

Ebenezer had tried to hand him over to the natives on several occasions. As it turned out, the sailors Francois regrouped as witnesses managed to convince the jury who found against the captain.

Muir remembered his game of cards with Jane.

Francois really did have the court cards and took home not half but the entire value of the seal skins. A happy tale if ever there was one. Muir looked into the fire. His mind set alight with fond memories of his old friend and their voyage together. He was pleased Francois' most recent dealings with advocates had been more fruitful than that day aboard the fishing boat with himself and Gerrald.

Whilst he slept in the chair by the fire, the oak branch tapped against the window as the winds gathered apace. Waking from the pain of the abscess and ulcerating bone, for a moment he thought he was going to die.

Melting snow from down the chimney spat on the fire coals. Spilt ink had dried over his manuscript. What little he'd written of his life was lost to darkness.

The pages of Palmer's letter were on the hearth. Gathering them up, he noticed an afterword he'd not yet read. Following the poem and Palmer's signature, he'd scribbled a note. Skirving had died of dysentery less than a week after Gerrald. The sorrow he felt for him, his wife and their family demanded that he went properly to bed.

Since autumn, he'd stopped dressing his wounds in wet linen. He preferred elm bark water instead. As it dried to form a natural bandage, he crept under the blankets but jabbing pains struck his underside. As the tiredness took hold he lost all sense of these torments.

During the night, a blizzard swept snow up against the cottage window delaying dawn's arrival, whilst the oak branches swung like spars in a sea storm.

XX
49° 11' N
002° 28' E

In the morning, he was awoken by banging. The rhythm had a human character. He tried to put on his mask but feared that his visitor would be long gone by the time it was properly fastened. Opening the door, he shouted to the figure disappearing between the poplars.

The postman showed no interest in his affliction. In return for his post, Muir handed over the bible that he had packaged up with the intention of sending it to his parents at Hunters' Hill.

Alone again, the wind cut through him. With a newspaper under his arm, he glimpsed at the snow that had packed against the wall. It continued the pitch of the roof down to the ground, giving it the form, Muir thought, of one of the pyramids he imagined Napoleon was now conquering.

But that was another world to his. He stepped back inside and shut the door. A letter from Angus Cameron was amongst the bundle. He recalled the letter he'd copied to him in the autumn. It was a revised plan to liberate Scotland. The original was sent to Talleyrand.

Before him, the enthusiastic response he'd so hoped for was absent. Cameron wrote little of liberation. Instead, he described recent news that the traitor to Muir's family, that jackdaw Lapslie, had been placed on the government pensions list for testifying against him. The dishonesty had been quite an investment.

Looking at the redundant piano, he remembered the day Lapslie left him to make his own way to court after staying at his parents' house. His bloodied bible would be all that his parents would have now to remind them of their son.

Perhaps they would rest it on the music stand.

No synthesis of souls would take place.

No air of well being would emanate from the room.

A gnawing silence would dominate as if the lands had never been populated by those able to believe in a cause for the people.

Sickened, Muir felt unable to read on but latterly, was glad he did, for Cameron reported that Lapslie's manse had been burned down after he tried to enforce the Militia Act.

The people had spoken and hopefully found warmth from the blaze. But the tale invoked in Muir a concern for his family property, Hunters' Hill. The people would do it no harm but that could not be said for the British state. Writing to his parents, he warned them to protect it as best they could.

Convinced he would freeze without the fire going, he put the letter down and searched the rooms for wood. He hoped it was stored inside and not out. Suddenly, whilst he searched a glass pane smashed. The fierce winds had snapped one of the branches.

Braving the blizzard, Muir dragged it from out of the window frame and into the cottage via the front door.

It was too wet to burn so he continued his search.

He was on the verge of smashing up the furniture when resigned to failure he sat down on the bed and felt the painful prods that had tormented his rest through the night. Looking beneath the mattress he found the space stocked full of logs.

Once the fire was going, he propped his case on the windowsill and insulated the edges with clothing. Returning to the letter, this time with a large glass of wine, as he sat down he noticed Wolf Tone's name and tried to put it into context.

But there was another knock at the door.

A young boy full of cold and curious about the snapped branch, handed him breakfast on a tray. Muir bid farewell and shut the door. He was more interested in the Irishman's fate than catching a potentially fatal ailment.

Angus relayed how after being delayed by bad weather Wolf Tone had eventually led the French in an attempt to regain Ireland. But at Lough Swilly they were out gunned by

British men-of-war and taken to Dublin Castle where he was found guilty of treason.

Refused a firing squad, he awaited the more gruesome death of hanging. Defiant to the end though, Wolf cut his throat to end it all quickly. Tragically, it had the opposite effect.

He ended up taking a week to die from his injuries.

Muir thought that had Governor Hunter been successful in commuting him to Ireland this would surely have been his fate too.

The news was all the more depressing for what Angus next wrote. Thirteen of the twenty regiments stationed in Ireland on the eve of the rebellion were Scottish. His own countrymen had fought against the independence of Ireland and Scotland.

Muir's sadness was not lifted by Angus' last note. It was a reminder to celebrate Burns' night. His good friend, Robert, had now been dead two and a half years.

Recalling how he helped at Portpatrick, Muir was interrupted by another knock at the door. The French boy had brought a saw. Trying to take it from him, the boy held fast and began cutting through the branch.

Muir left him to it and began a letter to Angus Cameron. Looking at the date of the newspaper and writing 'the twenty fifth of January, 1799,' at the head of the letter, he realised Burns' night was that evening. Some had celebrated his death in July but he preferred to celebrate his birth and life, caring little for the day people died but much for the lives people lived.

Angus had reminded him how *Scots Wha Hae* had been inspired by what Muir had said at his trial and was also banned as seditious. He knew that it was he that Burns was referring to, by Wallace's name.

That pride lessened the pain of realising that the failed Irish rebellion would mark the end of French involvement in Scottish radicalism, at least in his lifetime.

As the French boy gave up sawing the oak, Muir instructed him to fetch his mother over to celebrate. As the boy disappeared across the way, Muir thought of his own mother's loss.

*

Unable to recite Burns for the pains in his face, he wrote down what he knew for the boy to read whilst the widow kept the fire fed. Occasionally, he would translate words as best he could in the margins.

With Burns' soul very much alive, Muir watched his French hosts champion the honest man, though ever so poor, as the king of men. Together they celebrated how although a prince could make a belted knight, an honest man was above his might for the pith of sense and pride of worth were higher rank than all that.

They laughed at rank being but the guinea's stamp, of silk being for fools, of Lords being but dolts laughed at by men of independent minds.

Then, Muir joined them to pray that sense and worth over all the earth would come. That man to man, the world over would, brothers be.

Muir smiled reflecting that the first words his French friends had spoken from his language were those of the song's title; *'A Man's A Man For All That'*.

The French had put Muir to bed like how he remembered as a child, after braised rabbit for dinner, perhaps.

Later though he awoke to a bang.

Snow plumed into the room.

He eventually got up.

Where Burns had mused he'd acted, he thought as he stoked the fire. That was a fair assessment. The wind had blown the case off the windowsill. He forced the elements out jamming it back in place with what the boy had left of the branch.

The ordeal had drained him beyond tired and as he clambered back into bed he noticed the pillow wet with blood.

He hoped Angus Cameron would arrive in the morning.

But in his dreams he remembered Jane and wondered where she was, recalling the last time he saw her being sick that morning aboard *The Otter* and suffering from her injuries on the jetty.

He wondered again whether she had actually been pregnant. Amidst the wakeful hours, her journey walked through his mind across an entire continent, to his door, to show him a miniature of himself, their toddler boy he hoped.

Ecstatic to possibilities, his possessed mind tried to get up to answer the calls but his body lay catatonic. Then, he seemed boundless leaving his worldly carrier, searching for her amongst the ships crossing the Atlantic, the horse drawn carts heading towards Paris, the roadside taverns on the way to Chantilly and the dim lit pathway to his very own door.

But he found her nowhere except in the recesses of experience, those fractured outlets to infinitude where in one, that day mid Pacific, in the depths of darkness known only to them, their lives had been unified inseparably for the rest of time.

Toppling to the ground the branch drew him back to reality. But this time he was too weak to act. The case fell from the sill again and an icy breeze hit him hard.

Sitting upright he watched how the snowflakes lay on the stone slabs melting the closer they came to the weakened fire. Rolling over to sleep with his eye fast against the pillow and his wounds uppermost, the cold seemed to slow the bleed.

Palmer's claim about Priestley discovering oxygen flashed through his thoughts but the intrigue was replaced again by concerns about the loss of blood. He hadn't dressed his wounds in elm bark water that evening. He had lost the will to do so.

Occasionally, a crystal of snow would land on his flesh. He thought of the night he was shackled out on deck beside the ailing Reverend. Their roles, despite the difference of years, had now reversed. Muir now felt older, certainly more world wearied.

Trying to turn onto his other side he found the blanket heavy with snow. It felt to him that he was underground, buried by the seasons and the mounting disappointment of future times not for him.

Two centuries' worth perhaps and a mind might again travel his tale and fathom his life. With this thought, he tried to stop the pages of memoir blotting in the snow.

But he gave up, it was of no use.

Godwin had tried to write Caleb's life from the end backwards but that was fiction. This was real. Endings invariably merge into beginnings he remembered thinking as the concluding notes of Mozart's last piano sonata resounded around Hunters' Hill.

Perhaps he should try and write the beginning of the memoir now fully aware of the end but leaning over towards the hearth, he felt defeated and doubted Angus would arrive at the break of day, suspecting it more likely assassins at his door than his fellow countrymen.

The fire grew fainter.

Through the early hours the room grew colder. An imago of his parents watering the tree of liberty at Hunters' Hill configured itself in a shadow from the fallen oak branch.

In a few months, it would be in blossom but the figures weren't looking forward to summer as they felt their son's blood interleaved on every page of the bible he'd returned.

Thanks to them it had liberated him to the French all because of a name they had given him at birth that they'd taken the care to inscribe in a gift that would influence his destiny. Perhaps, he hoped, despite their loss it would be some consolation.

He longed to play the piano now quilted under the snow, to master Mozart's last sonata by the winter's end.

But that would be for someone else to do now.

All he could muster was imagining the ruination of the instrument when the snows thawed. Then, the thought was replaced by a warming recollection of his mother seated in the bay window, watching him play the piano as a child from the far side of the room, uniting them back down through the years of their lives.

Thuds from the other side of the door led to the turning of a key. The door jolted at Tytler's. The skeleton raced through his mind whilst three figures cast themselves against the wall. The fire shadowed branches were playing tricks on him and so he would them. For whoever it was, Angus, his assassin or his true love, they were all too late. All were now fossilised in a past the present would forget.

Cries of a youngster cut through the cold but went unheard. He ceased from mental fight and that moment that had brought meaning to every waking moment finally arrived.

That moment when thoughts lasted a lifetime.

A man who had dedicated his life to the cause of the people had left the world alone. Two weeks from now *Le Moniteur* would arrive with his obituary inside, dead at thirty three, two years younger than Mozart, having slipped away in the early hours after Burns' Night. To be buried in an unmarked grave, his sentiments would reverberate across Europe and beyond, like the composer's.

Mast high hopes had been made but his life, that great work of glory, was over. Now awake in his sleep and asleep in his wake, he could lull to his deserved rest until his wave lapped up on heaven's shore.

Lightning Source UK Ltd.
Milton Keynes UK
UKOW030749140912

199008UK00003B/4/P